Table of Contents

Preface

This book was written backward. We began writing a book to report on a research project we designed to describe the field of congregational social work. As we wrote our findings, however, the manuscript grew into a much broader description of this field as we reflected backward on (1) what we have learned from our own professional experiences; (2) our understanding of the culture of congregations developed from living more than six decades grounded in congregational life; (3) what our students have taught us as they have practiced social work in congregational settings; and (4) what we have most recently learned in our field research.[1]

Congregational social work has been around since the beginning of the social work profession, but very little ink has been used to describe or define it. We define congregational social work as providing social work services in and through a religious congregation, whether the employer is the congregation itself or a social service or denominational agency working in collaboration with congregations. Over a three-year period, with a generous grant from the Louisville Institute, we interviewed a convenience sample of 51 congregational social workers to develop a full-orbed description of congregational social work.

As we studied the stories these congregational social workers[2] told us about their work, we came to understand that congregational social work is a field of practice as diverse as the social work profession itself. The congregational social workers we interviewed serve people in poverty and people who are not. They work with young children and pregnant women; they work with older adults and families grieving the death of a member; and they work with individuals and families in all the stages between birth and death. They provide crisis intervention and counseling and prevention services; they lead support and educational groups; they train members in service; and they organize and lead community development programs in their congregations' neighborhoods and on the other side of the world. As congregational leaders, their work has taken them into the fields of health and mental health, child and family services, aging services, economic and social development, criminal justice, community development, and education. Moreover, we discovered that many of these social workers lead worship and Christian education, preach and teach Bible studies, and weave congregations into communities of support and care.

Their stories caused us to reflect on the 40 years of each of our own professional lives in which we have both worked in and consulted with congregations, religiously affiliated organizations, denominational agencies, and Christian schools of social work. As we learned about the work of these social workers, we developed new frames for seeing our own experiences. We had expected simply to tell their stories, and did not expect to have our understanding so dramatically altered as we studied the stories of 51 social workers finding their way into this field of practice and how they grew and changed as they served. As we listened, we felt the tug of connection to our own stories that surprised us.

We also began to reflect back onto other research we have conducted with congregations, on our experiences as denominational employees, as consultants with congregations, as well as teaching and supervising congregational social workers. We backed into writing a much broader book than we set out to write, based on our own experiences as well as our research.

Through the stories of these social workers as well as our own, this book will attempt to define how social work in the setting of a congregation is both like other settings where social workers serve as well as how congregations are unique settings for doing social work. We have shared our experiences with you, our understanding of what those experiences have taught us about working with congregations, and the meaning we have found in Christian scriptures for understanding our work. This book is a mix of reporting what *is*, that is, what we learned as the actual realities of social work practice from several of our research projects, with our own opinions of what *ought to be*, or our own distillation of what we have formed into principles for practice.

We interviewed social workers in a wide range of congregations from different traditions and worldviews. The social workers in these diverse settings have defined their practice in very different ways and probably would differ with one another—and with us—on any number of issues. We will try to express their voices as well as our own—and to be clear when those voices differ. We do not agree with how all these social workers have squared their work with best professional practices and the ethics of the profession, and no doubt, they would disagree with one another. You may disagree with us as well. We encourage you to read this book critically. We hope that you will use our work to craft a vision for what congregational social work can be in your faith tradition and community.

We set out to define this field across religions, hoping to interview social workers in not only Christian congregations but also those in other traditions as well. One social worker in a synagogue volunteered for the project. We have included what we learned from her. The remainder of the sample consisted of social workers in Christian congregations. As we steeped ourselves in their stories, we realized that it was enough of a challenge to describe congregational social work from a Christian perspective, one where our own professional experiences have occurred. We found it important to ground our work in our understanding of the culture of Christian congregations and our knowledge of Christian history and texts. We trust others to determine far better than we can what we have done and said that is adaptable in other religious contexts.

We are grateful for the lives of C. Anne Davis, Alan Keith-Lucas, and David Sherwood. We were privileged to work with each of them, and to learn from them. They were our colleagues as well as courageous pioneers in defining social work from a Christian worldview. Their work provided the foundations for our understanding of the relationship of social work and Christian faith, and for our understanding of social work practice in a congregational setting. We continue to use their work to teach our students about the ethical integration of Christian faith and social work practice, and about the church as a context for social work practice. Anne and Keith have preceded us into the next life, and were no doubt welcomed as good and faithful servants; we miss them. David Sherwood continues to be our faithful friend, and we are grateful for the care and encouragement he gave us in reading and editing the manuscript.

We are grateful for our dear friends and colleagues Ellen Netting, Helen Harris, and Michael Kelly, who carefully read the manuscript from their differing perspectives, giving us the gift of their encouragement, insight, and critique.

Class after class of our students read drafts of early chapters as course readings and gave us their thoughts. We are particularly grateful to our graduate assistants: Laurel Cluthe, Adreanne Dugger, Jessica Fancher, Bethany Molinar, and Emily Mosher. They have helped with interviews, emails, telephone calls, setting up spreadsheets and maintaining data bases, doing literature reviews, helping create presentations, and indexing. Their collective work has been invaluable to us.

Terry Wolfer took on the arduous task of editing the final manuscript. Terry has been a dear friend for decades and a frequent research partner in several of the research studies described in the book. Several years ago, we enjoyed teaching a course in congregational social at Baylor University, partnered with Terry and a class he was teaching concurrently at University of South Carolina. Teaching and conducting research with Terry have been important contributions to this book, in addition to how we have benefited from his editing. Virtually every page is better because of his wise counsel and engagement with our ideas. At the same time, we sometimes stubbornly ignored his advice, so we bear responsibility for what we have written.

We are grateful to the Louisville Institute that provided us with financial support we needed for the research project that challenged us to write this book.

We are most profoundly grateful to the 51 social workers who shared their professional lives with us, and to the students who have taught us as they learned social work practice in congregational field placements.

Finally, our families have supported and encouraged us. I (Diana) want to thank David Garland, who has been my husband for 44 years and a frequent co-author. David is a New Testament scholar and dean of the George W. Truett Theological Seminary at Baylor. I have benefited immeasurably from his deep biblical knowledge and insight, and I am grateful for how our lives and callings are woven together. We understand firsthand the meaning of the multiple roles that characterize congregational social work that Gaynor and I will describe later in this book—we are colleagues in the workplace, co-authors, consultants together in congregations, friends, co-parents and co-grandparents, and spouses who love one another deeply. Moreover, David is compassionate about the focus that writing a book requires and patient with the more-than-occasional crankiness writing evokes in me.

I (Gaynor) want to thank all of the people in my life (some may call them clients) who have been very patient and taught me, through person to person, person to family, and person to community interactions how to be a social work practitioner with a dual identity as a minister in the context of congregational social work. I am grateful to dear friends and colleagues, in social work and out, who have walked the paths of learning and experience with me. I am grateful for congregations and denominational agencies that have given me freedom to do social work in a congregational and agency context. Most of all, I am grateful to God, for parents who modeled for me what Christian service to, and with, others means.

Despite this wonderful host of friends and family, mentors, colleagues, and editors, responsibilities for the limitations and errors in our thought remain with us. We offer this book to you as a beginning effort. So much more needs to be done. But the time has come to share our thoughts and experiences with you, in the eager hope that you will respond and build upon our work and replace it with greater insight and best practices for congregational social work.

Diana Garland
Gaynor Yancey
January 2014

Chapter 1
Church Social Work

Beth[3] began her social work career in 2003 as a part-time minister with college students at First Baptist Church. She had just completed a dual master's degree program—a Master of Divinity (MDiv) and a Master of Social Work (MSW). Over the months as Beth worked with students and contributed to the leadership of the congregation, the senior pastor began to catch a vision of the value Beth could bring if she were full time. He contacted and negotiated a partnership with an agency that engages in community ministry through congregations, with the long-term plan that the congregation would gradually add Beth's full salary to their budget and the agency would phase out their involvement in the congregation. Together, the congregation and the agency were able to employ Beth full time, and Beth became the congregation's Associate Pastor. She had responsibilities for the congregation's community ministry, benevolence (emergency assistance) ministry, and tutoring ministry in a nearby school. She saw herself as a "minister whose skill set is social work." Beth incorporated her work into the weekly worship of her congregation. She loved preaching and someday wanted to be a senior pastor. In 2012, her dream was fulfilled when a large downtown Baptist congregation in another state called her as their pastor.

Carl began his work in 1990 as a Baptist missionary in an inner city neighborhood. He started a new congregation in an impoverished neighborhood, which he has continued to pastor for more than 20 years. Carl had completed a dual MSW and theology program, and then a Doctor of Ministry degree. He sees himself as a pastor primarily, although his social work education is invaluable to him. Many of his congregants have chronic mental illness; some are homeless. A day treatment facility for persons with mental illness is located across the street from his church building, and some of the clients have found a home in Carl's congregation. The congregation is ethnically diverse, also reflecting the surrounding community. Carl directs numerous children's programs and other activities that serve the community. Mission teams from Baptist churches in other states have learned about Carl's congregation. They use his congregation as a mission trip destination, creating a significant challenge for Carl. Their frequent attitude of coming to "help those in need" marginalizes the leadership that Carl has nurtured in his congregants. Therefore, Carl works to equip his congregation to minister to the mission teams, aiming to make the relationship between the visitors and his congregation mutual.

Glenda has been in social work practice since 1975, when she received her MSW degree. She is a social work professor in a large state university and also has a small private practice. Since 2003, she has provided contractual services in her Catholic parish. She is listed on the parish web site as a professional counselor for crisis counseling and referral. She provides couples wanting to marry in the parish with premarital assessments, which she forwards to the parish priest, including any concerns she has about the challenges these couples face. She also pursued training as a spiritual director, and she serves congregants in that role as well. She feels very much called to the work she is doing and sees no distinction between her role as a social worker and her role as leader and spiritual director in the parish.

Lois has been the Director of Senior Adult Ministries for a large Presbyterian church since 2003. She received her MSSW in 1989 and is a state-licensed clinical social worker and a certified mediator. Previously, she had worked for a geriatric wellness center. That experience served her well for her current responsibilities of helping older adults and their families as they navigate together the inevitable transitions that come with aging. She sees her role as empowering senior adults and their families by providing them with information about resources that are available to them. She has created a ministry called "pastor aides." Pastor aides are senior adults from the congregation who make regular visits to shut-ins in their homes and in nursing homes. Lois works closely with the pastor aides as well as family members, social agencies, hospitals, and the church to build a community of care for seniors and their families. She has also established an intergenerational day camp at one of the residential care facilities sponsored by the church. She loves facilitating children and older adults interacting and caring for one another.

Lynne has been Minister of Community Ministries in a large downtown Baptist church for more than 25 years, a position she took after graduating with her MSW in 1988. Lynne has provided leadership and vision for developing and expanding community ministries to include a variety of programs. Early on, Lynne directed all the work, but as it has expanded, the now 13 programs all have their own directors; Lynne supervises them all. Some of those programs include:

> *AIDS Ministry*: provides confidential ongoing, social, physical, and spiritual support to persons who are HIV positive, persons with AIDS and their loved ones.
>
> *The Caring Center*: provides food, clothing, household items, furniture and financial assistance to those in need; they serve 10,000 people annually, distributing more than 77 tons of food. More than 50 congregational members give their time to be the staff of The Caring Center.
>
> *The Children's Learning Center*: a licensed childcare center that provides high quality, affordable care for more than 90 children, with a special focus on serving children in at-risk situations. Scholarships provided by church members support those children whose families could not otherwise afford the care.
>
> *The Counseling Program*: provides not only individual and family counseling services but also support groups such as Grief Share and Narcotics Anonymous.
>
> *The International Ministry*: includes both international Bible fellowship classes and English as a Second Language and conversational English classes.
>
> *The Nehemiah Project*: provides multiple services as a Christian community development project in an impoverished community, including after school programming, a mentoring program for mothers, a kids club, summer day camp programming, GED classes, a job readiness program, and housing renovation.
>
> *The Prison Ministry*: offers regular programming for persons who are incarcerated in a women's prison, a men's prison, a youth correctional facility, and the county jail.
>
> *The S.T.E.P. (Strategies to Elevate People) Program*: mobilizes churches in the city to work toward the elimination of poverty; Lynne's church is one of 28 participating churches and provides space for the S.T.E.P. Foundation office.
>
> *The Teachers Supply Store*: provides school supplies for teachers in the public school system. Teachers may come to "shop" for donated supplies one afternoon each week of the school year.

All of these programs are housed within a building across the street from the congregation. Although the programs operate somewhat independently, they are very much a part of the congregation, with hundreds of people serving and leading in the programs at any given time. For Lynne, ministry and social work are "one and the same." She says that she lives "in a social worker's paradise," with the financial and people resources to do what she feels called to do, which is to care for persons who are marginalized and in poverty.

◆◆◆◆◆◆◆

These five social workers, along with two you will meet later in this chapter, illustrate some of the diversity of responsibilities and types of social work practice in congregations. Some congregational social workers are part-time; some are full-time. Some are pastors. Others provide clinical services or support services that mirror clinical social work in other social service settings. Still others lead in community development and equipping congregants to serve through community ministries. Some began their careers in other fields of social work practice and then moved to a congregational context; others came to the profession of social work because they wanted to serve in a congregational setting and have spent their whole careers as congregational leaders. Some see themselves professionally as ministers who use social work skills; others identify themselves as social workers, even though their title may include the words minister or pastor. Still others have blended the identities of religious leader and social worker.

Agency Settings for Church Social Work

Congregational social work is not limited to Christian congregations; there are Jewish congregational social workers, including rabbis, and other congregational social workers who serve in other religious traditions as well, such as Imams in Muslim mosques and priests in Buddhist temples. Congregational social work in Christian congregations overlaps a much broader field of practice called *church social work*.

"Church social work" refers to the work of professional social workers in any organization whose mission is to put into action the teachings of Jesus, including but not limited to congregations (Garland, 1992). In short, it is social work that takes place in Christian settings. In turn, church social work is only one subset of social work practice in religious settings that include congregations and organizations reflecting other religious traditions (see Figures—Chapter 1—presently located after Appendices).

The Church is the society of all Christians who have been made children of God by God's grace, in whatever tradition or place or era. We use the accepted convention of capitalizing the word "Church" when it refers to the society of all Christians who identify themselves as the children of God by God's grace, whatever tradition or time. The definition of Church is thus theological. When we are referring to a subgroup of that universal Church, we use the lower case "church." This subgroup may be a congregation in a particular place or it may be a group of congregations and/or other Christian organizations, such as a denomination (e.g., Presbyterian Church, USA) or fellowship (e.g., Cooperative Baptist Fellowship). The definition of church is thus sociological, in that it is an identifiable set of persons and organizations.

The society of Christians over 2000 years includes not only the local gatherings of Christians in congregations but also a variety of other organizations. Church social work includes social workers in Episcopal family and children's service agencies, Catholic adoption services, and Baptist advocacy organizations working to influence state and federal policy on issues that affect vulnerable populations. It includes organizations like International Justice Mission and Compassion International that have Christian missions but are not affiliated with any one denomination or congregation. Church social work also includes community service organizations that are sponsored by congregations with different denominational and nondenominational identities that work together to serve their neighborhood. Often, church social workers in Christian organizations work with congregations and so are engaged in congregational social work as part of their responsibilities; both Beth and Carl were denominational employees working in a congregational setting.

Jesus taught that the most important aim in life is twofold, to love God with all of our being and to love our neighbors just as we love ourselves (Luke 10:25-36). A central tenet of Jesus' teaching is that the way to know God is to care for the most vulnerable and powerless in society (Mark 9:33-37). Jesus said that his followers ultimately will be judged by the extent to which they cared for the needs of persons who are poor and oppressed;

"Just as you did it to one of the least of these who are members of my family, you did it to me" (Matthew 25:31-46). From its beginnings as recorded in the Bible, therefore, the church has cared for people who are poor[4] and abandoned in society, providing them with meals and financial support, and including them in a community of care (Acts 2:44-45). Christians and their communities of faith and the organizations they founded have been pursuing this mission ever since, including contributing to the birth of the social work profession (Johnson, 2012; Poe, 2012; Pryce, 2012; Scales & Kelley, 2012).

Denominations and Denominational Agencies as Church Social Work Settings

Over the centuries, since the life and death of Jesus and his first followers, differences in theology, beliefs, and religious practices have led to divisions within the Church, including those that resulted in early distinctions among Roman Catholic, Orthodox Catholic, Oriental Orthodoxy, Assyrian Church of the East, and the Anglican Communion traditions. Martin Luther's revolt in the 16th century against the medieval Roman Catholic Church sparked the creation of Protestant (i.e., "protest") denominations (Ozment, 1992). These distinctions were imported by their followers when they immigrated to the United States, from colonial America to the present. Moreover, denominations continued to divide, resulting in, for example, 31 Pentecostal denominations, 21 Baptist, 14 Methodist, and 9 Presbyterian denominations—all in the United States. Even smaller denominations generate multiple entities in the United States with, for examples,12 Mennonite and 6 Quaker bodies (Chaves, 2004). These U.S. expressions of Christianity will be the primary focus of this book.

Church social work—Professional social work in any organization whose organizational mission is to put into action the teachings of Jesus (including congregations)

Congregational social work—Professional social work that takes place in the setting of a congregation

Denominations pursued the founding of new congregations that shared their theology and religious traditions, both locally and through mission efforts around the world. Congregations, by joining their resources in denominations, have formed or supported organizations with specialized missions, whether it was the care of orphans, the building of universities and seminaries, or founding inner city community service centers. They also have supported publishing houses to provide religious study materials, including family life education materials and resources to guide the development and programming of community service programs. Social workers have been among the professionals who led and served in these organizations, and who wrote the educational resources used in congregations.

Protestant denominations typically control their agencies by appointing some or all of the members of their governing boards. Agencies

One Agency Story: Buckner Orphans Home

One agency illustrates how agencies as settings for church social work develop and evolve, often because a congregational pastor sees and feels a divine calling to respond to human need. In the mid-19th Century, R. C. Buckner, a prominent Baptist leader and pastor in Texas, was deeply concerned about children orphaned by war and by the physical hardships and diseases of the time. He convened the Deacon's Convention and urged them to develop an orphanage. Buckner Orphan's Home opened in 1879. The home provided residential care for children, including both orphans and those with a parent who could not provide for them in an era before social programs provided financial support to families living in poverty (T. Laine Scales, 2012) . It was a time of legally enforced racial segregation in Texas, and so the Buckner home served only White children. By 1900, however, Buckner also mustered support to establish an orphanage for Black children, in collaboration with a prominent Black Baptist leader, A. R. Griggs (Bullock, 1993).

In 1961, the name of the agency became Buckner Baptist Benevolences, and the agency began to serve children from all races equally in all of its programs (Bullock, 1993). The name reflected the agency's ties to Baptists, although Buckner also garnered support for his orphans' home from Methodists, Jews, Presbyterians, Lutherans, and Catholics (Cranfill & Walker, 1915; T. Laine Scales, 2011).

often have governance documents that specify that a majority or all of the governing board be members appointed or elected by a denominational entity, such as a Presbytery (Presbyterians) or Synod (Lutherans), Conference Board (United Methodists), or convention of "messengers" from congregations (Baptists). Roman Catholic agencies, such as the St. Vincent de Paul Society, are variously controlled by the dioceses, religious orders or volunteer societies of the church (Joseph & Conrad, 2010).

Despite the distinguishing characteristic of their Christian missions, denominational agencies often resemble other organizations in society that serve similar functions. For example, denominational publishing houses may resemble secular publishing houses in the way they organize their work, the staff they employ, the similarities of their stated mission, and the professional networks in which they are embedded. Similarly, denominational agencies that provide social services have similarities with other private and public social service agencies. They employ similar professionals to conduct the work of the agency—social workers, psychologists, and accountants. They may have to respond to the same public regulations and professional accreditation requirements. They may be similar in size, organizational structures, and even funding streams. A social worker who has worked in a public child welfare agency who then joins the staff of a Presbyterian child welfare agency may not experience a great deal of difference in their professional responsibilities and challenges—with the obvious exception of the stated mission of the organization. Or, there may be significant new opportunities and challenges—working with Christian volunteers, providing reports of the work to congregational groups, and translating professional knowledge and expertise into educational resources for families that integrate Christian knowledge and values (Baker, 2006; Bielefeld & Cleveland, 2013; Garland, 1992, 1994a, 1998, 2009; Schneider, 1999).

The Post-Denominational Church as a Setting for Church Social Work

In an era dubbed "post-denominational" in America, denominational identity is far less significant today than it was a century ago for individual Christians and for congregations. New congregations may form without denominational ties, and existing congregations may downplay or drop their historic denominational affiliation (Miller, 1998). One in five Protestant churches in the United States is now independent of any denomination, and 20% of Protestants now attend those independent churches, an increase from 14% in 1989 (Chaves, 2011a).

The trend away from organizing by denominations is heightened by the phenomenon of the growth of mega-churches of 2000 or more attenders. Although there are still many small churches, most Americans now attend large congregations. The top 10% of American congregations in size have half of the congregants and resources

Although two-thirds of these Protestant mega-churches are affiliated with a denomination, many downplay those connections; only 37% see themselves as openly identified with a denomination (Chaves, 2011a, Kindle location 696; Thumma, 2007). Instead, these congregations create their own networks with other congregations or start other congregations with whom they affiliate. Most (90%) of America's largest churches have two or more sites (Bird, 2007).

Large congregations often do for themselves what congregations have historically done collaboratively through a denominational agency. Almost half of these large congregations create their own educational resources and are creating their own mission and service organizations rather than supporting financially those of a denomination. They send their own mission personnel to serve internationally, publish their own curriculum resources for religious education, and choose to affiliate with para-church organizations or form their own mission-driven organizations (Thumma, 2007). For example, Lynne's congregation invited other congregations to join them in forming the S.T.E.P. (Strategies to Elevate People) program in their city. Because these congregations can afford to have multiple employees, they appear more likely to be settings where social workers are employed as leaders in social service programs, like Lois and Lynne, unless they are serving, like Carl and Beth, as the congregational pastor. The single most significant factor in the extent to which a congregation is engaged in addressing human need in its local neighborhoods and around the world is simply how large it is (Chaves, 2006; Grossman, 2009; Thumma, 2007).

As a consequence of these shifts from denominational loyalty to multi-site congregations and networks of congregations, financial support for many denominations has waned, and many have had to sharply curtail the support they provide to affiliated social service and mission organizations (e.g., Peck, 2011). The consequences of these shifts for denominational agencies have been less documented than the research on congregations themselves. It appears, however, that those organizations that historically relied on denominations for the majority of their budgets must find alternative income streams to survive. As a consequence, they may seek tighter ties directly with supporting congregations rather than relating to a mediating denominational agency, further undermining the denomination's role as mediator between agencies and congregations. For example, Beth's pastor partnered directly with a Christian agency to hire Beth to lead their congregation's development of community ministry rather than with the denomination with which that agency had historically identified. For social workers employed in these agencies, the ability to work directly with congregations becomes ever more important.

Para-church Organizations as Church Social Work Settings

Para-church organizations are Christian in their mission but operate autonomously from any congregational or denominational oversight, with their own governing boards. In the United States, they organize as nonprofit charities with government tax exemptions as defined by the Internal Revenue Service (Section 501c3). Although para-church organizations have long histories, with the waning of denominational identities, they are becoming much more prominent in church social work.

Para-church organizations relate to congregations who are their vital partners for financial and volunteer support in providing specialized services as diverse as building houses for families who are homeless or living in substandard housing, tutoring children, providing livestock to families doing subsistence farming, and publishing Christian resource materials. A sample of these organizations include clergy associations in local communities, Compassion International, Habitat for Humanity, Heifer International, International Justice Mission, Inter-Varsity Christian Fellowship, Kids Hope USA, Christian schools and universities, Sojourners, Navigators, Samaritan's Purse, World Vision—and we could go on for pages. Moreover, just as congregations can change over time from being affiliated with a denomination to being autonomous, so can, and do, organizations change over time.

Para-church organizations are Christian in their mission but operate autonomously from any congregational or denominational oversight, with their own governing boards.

All of these organizations, even those who are evangelical by tradition, spend more of their resources on social and humanitarian services than they do on evangelism (Ammerman, 2005). They also employ social workers who may have as part, or all, of their responsibility to work with one or more congregations.

The Story Continues to Unfold: Buckner International

In the past three decades, "Buckner Baptist Benevolences," described above as an agency governed by Texas Baptists, has become "Buckner International," stating that its mission is to "transform the lives of vulnerable children, enrich the lives of senior adults, and build strong families through Christ-centered values" through a multitude of programs and services around the world, including foster care adoption, community transformation centers, humanitarian aid, medical clinics and retirement centers. It operates with a budget of more than $100 million annually and assets of more than $400 million (Buckner Baptist Benevolences, 2010). The Baptist General Convention of Texas continues to elect 25% of Buckner's governing board but provides less than 1% of the operating budget (Albert Reyes, personal communication, January 14, 2014). Although the agency's mission is overtly Christian, it hires staff without consideration of their religious affiliations and practices (Aracely Perez, personal communication, February 15, 2013).

Religiously Affiliated Organizations (RAOs)

Although there are organizational differences among denominational agencies, para-church agencies, and agencies governed by a congregation or religious order, all of these together are identified as "religiously-affiliated organizations" (Garland, 2009). The term "religiously affiliated" is broader than Christian, including organizations that identify with non-Christian (e.g., Muslim, Jewish, First Nations, Hindu, Buddhist) religious beliefs and practices. Therefore, "church social work" occurs in the subset of religiously affiliated organizations and congregations that identify with Christianity. This distinction is important, given the centrality of religious beliefs and practices to organizational mission and, sometimes, to organizational realities such as funding and accountability, hiring practices, and nature of the services provided.

A religiously affiliated organization identifies with a congregation, multiple congregations, a religious order, denomination or some other religious organization. It often expresses its religious identity in its name and funding stream. For some organizations, the name may appear to be the only sign that a Christian congregation or denomination founded the organization. Others, however, may continue to pursue a mission and espouse values described in religious language. The policies of religiously affiliated organizations often reflect, at least to some extent, the organization's religious mission, such as hiring preferences for persons who are members of a religious group and including members of supporting congregations on governing boards.

For a subset of Christian organizations, at least one of the goals of service is *evangelism*. That is, one, if not the only, objective of providing services is to invite service recipients to embrace Christian beliefs and values. These programs may evaluate themselves, at least in part, by the number of recipients who become Christians (Garland, 2009). Social work often uses the term "proselytizing" to describe this social service objective, often with concern that this objective conflicts with the core social work value of clients' right to self-determination. In other words, the ability of clients to determine their own religious beliefs and practices may be compromised by perceived pressure to embrace the agency's religious beliefs and practices in order to receive needed services or as gratitude for those services. We will discuss this issue at greater length in Chapter 6, when we discuss the mission of congregations, which for many includes evangelism.

We use the term "religiously affiliated" to describe these agencies rather than "faith-based," the term used by the federal government in its "faith-based initiative" which was first approved and started by the Clinton administration in response to the Charitable Choice section of the 1996 welfare reform act—Personal Responsibility and Work Opportunity Reconciliation Act (PRWORA) (Governor's Advisory Task Force on Faith-Based Community Service Groups, 1996; Sherman, 2000; Streeter, 2000). "Faith-based" is often a confusing term, especially when it is used in relationship to organizations. The term "faith-based" reflects a Christian worldview and is not sensitive to the world views of other religious groups (Jeavons, 2004; Rogers, Yancey, & Singletary, 2005). For example, the term "faith-based" does not adequately reflect the work of Jewish congregations because their service is "deed based," meaning that the deed itself is a reflection of the divine (Robert Wineburg, personal communication, September 28, 2002).

Although there are organizational differences among denominational agencies, para-church agencies, and agencies governed by a congregation or religious order, all of these are together identified as "religiously-affiliated organizations."

Moreover, the term "faith-based" has often been used to include services provided by congregations as well as by religiously affiliated agencies like Buckner or Compassion International. Social work in a congregational context is very different from social work in a social service agency, however. This book will use the terms "religiously affiliated organization" and "congregation" rather than the term "faith-based" to describe settings for church social work.

Despite our preference and use of the term "religiously affiliated," "faith-based" is the language used in much of the literature and so will occur throughout this book when it is the term used by others. A burgeoning research literature is exploring the services provided and the impact of faith-based organizations, finding that they provide a narrower range of services than other service providers and, when compared to nonreligious services, are either equivalent or superior in their outcomes (Bielefeld & Cleveland, 2013). That conclusion does not suggest that religiously affiliated or faith-based services have the resources or mission to supplant public and nonsectarian service programs that have a broader social welfare mandate. It does suggest, however, that the profession of social work will continue to explore its role in this service sector.

Public and Non-religious Agencies and Congregational Social Work

Finally, other organizations may employ social workers to relate to congregations and so do "congregational social work," even though the organization itself is not religiously affiliated. Congregations partner with nonprofit organizations like the Sierra Club or the Red Cross as they do with para-church organizations (Ammerman, 2005). The Children's Defense Fund, a nonprofit advocacy organization for children, publishes a "Children's Sabbath" curriculum annually for Christian, Muslim, and Jewish congregations that include worship and study guides designed for each religious tradition. Federal and state governments have "offices of faith-based initiatives" where social workers seek to engage congregations in addressing human needs. Additionally, public child welfare agencies increasingly recognize that congregations can be vital partners in identifying and supporting foster and adoptive parents for children.

The illustration shows that church social work takes place in all these religious settings—congregations, religiously affiliated organizations, and public and non-religious agencies that relate to congregations. In turn, social work takes place in non-Christian congregations and organizations, forming a much broader category of social work practice that we have named "religious settings for social work practice."

1. Religious settings for social work practice.

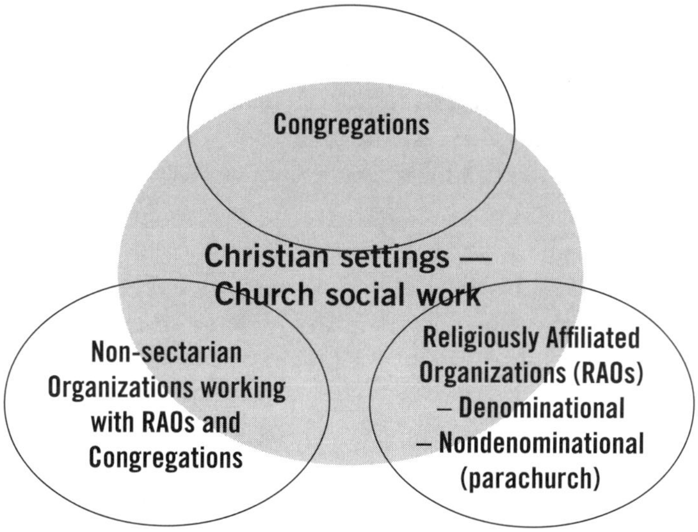

Congregations Helping in Love and Dedication (CHILD)

In Texas, the initiative Congregations Helping in Love and Dedication (CHILD) is a collaboration of congregations and the state's Child Protective Services agency that is legislated by Texas law. The goal of CHILD is to recruit and license as foster parents at least two families from each participating congregation and for the congregation to provide support for those families. Each region of the state has a "faith-based recruiter" who is a state employee, trained to relate to congregations (Texas Adoption Resource Exchange).

Congregational Social Work in an Agency Setting

The social workers employed by the CHILD program in Texas are doing congregational social work, even though they are government employees. Many social workers employed in religiously affiliated agencies and, increasingly, in other non-sectarian (i.e., non-religiously-affiliated) organizations, work with congregations, including, for example, (1) providing training for congregational members who want to minister with persons in need, (2) relating to board members who are appointed by congregations that support the agency, (3) recruiting foster and adoptive homes, (4) seeking mentors and tutors for at-risk children, (5) providing resources for congregations such as parenting or marriage courses, (6) helping congregations understand social problems such as hunger and poverty from a Christian perspective, and (7) providing consultation to congregational leaders in the development or expansion of congregational ministries.

We introduced Beth and Carl at the beginning of this chapter. Religiously affiliated agencies employed both of them to work with a single congregation. Other social workers have responsibilities for relating to multiple congregations from their location in the agency. Social workers employed by Texas' Child Protective Services connect to as many congregations in their region as they can manage to generate a response to the needs of children needing foster care or adoption.

Jeffrey and Melinda are two social workers we interviewed who illustrate agency-based congregational social work.

Jeffrey has directed a regional counseling service for the Catholic diocese in a large urban area since 1991. He supervises the social work staff, and the center manages more than a thousand counseling cases annually. Many cases involve family violence—women who have been abused, the men who abused them, and their children who have witnessed family violence. It is Jeffrey's responsibility to ensure that the agency's social workers deliver services that reflect a Catholic perspective. If a parish priest in their region has counseled with a parishioner more than a couple of times on an issue other than spiritual direction, then they refer the parishioner to the agency. The agency staff also provides marriage preparation courses in the parishes. They provide training and consultation for the parish priests and other parish leaders on topics such as how to deal with difficult people. Essentially, the counseling service is the social services for the congregations they serve.

Melinda, a Seventh Day Adventist, is a Consulting Therapist with a Christian counseling center that provides licensed counseling and social work services within the community. She sees about 15 clients weekly in a general private practice with a focus on family and marriage counseling as well as work with children. In addition, she is employed part-time as the Director of Case Management for Sister to Sister Reentry Ministries, a female prisoner re-entry program supported by volunteers and financial support from 16 congregations. Melinda meets with each client when the client has been released from prison or jail and connects her to community resources. Sometimes, Melinda provides transportation for the women to appointments, to find jobs, housing, and/or benefits as they re-enter their communities. Melinda worked with a female chaplain from the local jail to create this program. They now serve approximately 30 women at a time with mentoring, case management and accountability groups. Melinda supervises an assistant case manager who is an ex-offender and one of her successful clients. The program obtained a federal grant that provides some of the financial support for the program.

◆◆◆◆◆◆◆

Melinda and Jeffrey are employed by agencies for responsibilities that require them to understand and be competent to provide leadership and service in and through congregations, which was true of the five social workers we introduced earlier in this chapter. They are doing congregational social work even though a congregation is not their employer.

Virtually all church social workers do at least some congregational social work, in whatever kind of Christian nonprofit organization they are employed, relating to and providing consultation or leadership to congregations and their members. The profession of social work emphasizes that social work takes place in an organizational context, and that context shapes and give purpose to the work done. Congregations provide a unique shape to social work practice. The NASW *Code of Ethics* states that one of the core values of the profession is the "importance of human relationships," which results in an ethical principle that calls social workers to "strengthen relationships among people in a purposeful effort to promote, restore, maintain, and enhance the wellbeing of individuals, families, social groups, organizations, and communities." A whole section of the *Code of Ethics* is devoted to social workers' ethical responsibilities to their practice settings (National Association of Social Workers, 2008), which, for church social workers, is the congregation.

Social workers who are employed in the field of physical health need to understand the organizational context and culture of hospitals, medical clinics, nursing homes and rehabilitation services. School social workers need to understand how schools operate and the culture and issues of the field of education. So, too, regardless of what organization pays their salaries—government agency, private agency, or the congregation itself—social workers employed to provide leadership and service in and through congregations need to understand their organizational context. In the next chapter—and indeed, in the rest of this book—we will look at congregations as organizational contexts for social workers.

Chapter 2
Congregations as Context for Social Work

Some of us remember preschool Sunday school and Vacation Bible School leaders teaching us what a church is, using their hands as a model: "Put your hands together, lacing your fingers together pointing down to your feet, with your first fingers pointing up to the sky, and make your thumbs touch each other. You have made a church!" They went on into the sing-song little rhyme: "Here is the church, here is the steeple." They turned their hands over, now with fingers pointing heavenward, and we copied the action and said the rhyme together exuberantly: "Open the doors, and here are the people," and as we wiggled our finger-people, upright, the church now unfolded. This interactive exercise was meant to teach us that churches—congregations—are not buildings or places, but rather, the people themselves who gather to worship and live their faith in service together.

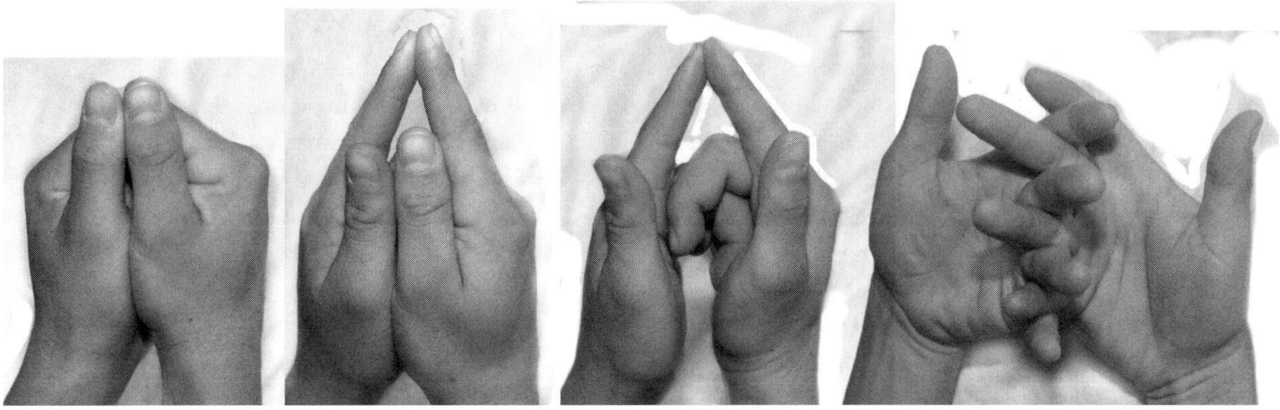

Defining Terms

Theologically, the Church is built on the foundations of Judaism; the Jews considered the synagogue to be not a building but a gathering (Burkhart, 1982). Jesus referred to his followers as "my church" (Matthew 16:18). Denominations, such as the Presbyterian Church (USA), may also refer to themselves as a "church." The concept of church, or the followers of Christ across time and place, takes expression locally as a congregation.

Congregation

Sociologists agree with Sunday School teachers, defining a congregation as *the people who come together regularly and voluntarily for worship at a particular location* (e.g., Ammerman, 1997, 2005; Chaves, 2004; Warner, 1994; Wind & Lewis, 1994). A congregation is the be-steepled gathering of wiggling people we symbolized with our preschool hands. People in a congregation may or may not know everyone else in the congregation, and the boundaries of who is in the congregation and who is not are very fluid, so the term "aggregate" is a more accurate term than "group." And the location may or may not involve a church building.

Although congregations are aggregates of people that come together voluntarily, all congregations, including the smallest, may function like organizations and businesses with budgets, buildings to maintain, and employees. They do strategic planning, have governing boards, establish membership rolls, hold business meetings, and apply for status with the government as nonprofit organizations. Even immigrants from religions that do not form "congregations" in other parts of the world organize themselves as congregation-like groups in the United States as an adaptation to the American cultural context (Ammerman, 2002; Warner, 1994). American Muslims, for instance, formed districts, while American Buddhists formed themselves into the Buddhist Churches of America (Ammerman, 2005). This dual nature of a congregation—both community and organization—creates complexity for leaders. Membership is voluntary; members can participate in the life of the congregation or not, as they choose. It is only in rare and extreme circumstances that American congregations excommunicate—exclude—members. In contrast, staff members are employees that can be hired—and dismissed—at the will of the governing body.

A congregation is the people who come together regularly and voluntarily for worship at a particular location.

Our society treats congregations as organizations rather than communities. This creates some ambiguity in understanding this context for social work practice. Government policies and practices see congregations as only a special case of the larger domain of nonprofit organizations and so other entities, like the social work profession, may also see them primarily as organizations. For example, one of the few characteristics of all American congregations, regardless of religion, is that they follow the rules established by the Internal Revenue Service for all 501c3 organizations (Stout & Cormode, 1998).

Most American congregations are small; 71% of congregations have fewer than 100 regularly participating adults. Only 10% of American congregations have more than 350 regular participants. Most Americans who participate in congregational life go to large congregations, however, and the trend is toward larger churches (Chaves, 2011a, 2011b; Chaves & Anderson, 2008). That requires some thought to understand—most congregations are small, but most people go to large congregations. Obviously, size is critical to capacity in providing social services, or what many congregations call "community ministry" (Dudley, 1991, 1996).

Most congregations are small, but most people go to large congregations.

The larger the congregation, the more likely it will be to have community ministry programs and services (Chaves, 2004). Although it would seem that social workers would more likely be found in large congregations, there are also social workers, like Carl, who serve as pastors of smaller congregations, sometimes in inner cities and other resource-challenged areas, where the knowledge and skills of social work are particularly valuable in the pastoral role. Still other congregations may employ social workers in more generalized roles because they value what the social worker can bring to congregational leadership. For example, Beth was hired to be an Associate Pastor and Lois as Director of Senior Adult Ministries in their respective congregations. In short, our interviews indicate that social workers may be found in congregations of all sizes, although their work may look more like social service agency work when they are located in large congregations, like Lynne's administration of multiple social service programs.

Congregant

We use the term "congregant" to refer to the people in the congregation other than the paid or nonpaid congregational leaders, i.e., the congregational staff. "Congregants" are persons, who, when asked, would say, "This is my congregation," regardless of membership status or frequency of attendance. "Congregant" is a self identification, not an organizational status. We use the term "congregants" rather than members because membership in a congregation has different meanings in different traditions. For example, in traditions where children are not baptized until they are deemed old enough to make their own decision about whether or not to embrace Christian faith, they are not considered "members" until baptized, even though they may have been attending the congregation with their parents for years and rightly consider the congregation "my church." In others, children become members when baptized shortly after birth. Some congregations have long processes of preparation before an individual is accepted as a member. In others, persons can make a decision to join, announce that decision at the first service they attend, and become members immediately. Some persons attend a congregation's activities and worship services multiple times each week; others may only go on high holy days, like Christmas and Easter. Other congregants who have relocated to another city or state and so cannot attend at all may still be considered "members," though they may not have actually been in attendance for years.

Due to the external focus of many congregations through their outreach programs to the people in their neighborhoods, the term "congregant" may also refer to those who participate in the social service programs of the congregation, even though they do not attend worship services. There may actually be two aggregates of people in a congregation—the congregation of Sunday and the congregation of the weekday. The "weekday congregation" may be children who spend all day each day in the congregation's child care program, teenagers who use the congregation's gym and participate in activity clubs, and senior adults who come for a hot lunch, Bible study, and time with friends. Hearing a child tell another child who attends an after-school program offered by a congregation, "This is my church," indicates the importance of the congregation to the child who may never attend Sunday worship and Christian education. A family who is homeless except for the car they live in may declare that this is their congregation because the congregation has provided them with financial assistance, food, and care.

Neighborhood participants may have experienced alienation and painful rifts in their histories with other congregations. Because of a particular congregation's work to build community and develop relationships with neighbors, however, they may ask congregational staff to conduct a wedding service, a funeral service, or to visit them or members of their families if they are in the hospital or are sick at home. They may begin to identify themselves as belonging to the congregation through these initial contacts, even though they may or may not become regular worship attendees..

Service and Ministry

The terms "service" and "ministry" are synonyms and are often used interchangeably in the literature, or as elements of terms such as "Christian social ministries" (e.g., Wind & Lewis, 1994) and "ministry outreach" (e.g., Dudley & Roozen, 2001). It is helpful to give these terms different connotations for understanding social work practice in congregations, however.

"Service" connotes identifying and addressing a human need. Service programs are often preceded by community needs assessment, with the implicit expectation that the organization conducting the needs assessment has some responsibility for addressing identified needs. Public social service agencies often conduct needs assessments and have a public mandate to address the needs of the community. Service is the term used by the helping professions in all kinds of settings, public and nonsectarian as well as religious.

"Ministry" connotes that the service is done in response to the Christian mission to love others as an expression of devotion to Jesus. Ministry is motivated primarily by a desire to care for others as a way of loving God and not by a public mandate to meet needs. In many traditions, there is a sense of being called by God to address the needs of others. Therefore, we often use the terms "ministry" and "social ministry" as well as "service" when we talk about the social services activities of congregations, to emphasize the importance of the underlying motivations for engaging in service activity. Not all ministry is service, nor all service necessarily ministry.

"Ministry" connotes that the service is done in response to the Christian mission to love others as an expression of devotion to Jesus.

In the average congregation[5] with social ministry programs, about 10 individuals volunteer their time to serve, making congregations a significant source of people resources for community organizations (Chaves, 1999a). Moreover, 6% of congregations have a staff person who devotes at least quarter time to social ministries (Chaves, 2003), and at least some of these congregational staff members are social workers.

Serving as a staff member to lead the social ministries of a large congregation may seem to be the logical place to find social workers in leadership—like Glenda, Lois, and Lynne. But social workers also serve in other roles, such as pastor and associate pastor—like Carl and Beth. Finally, agency-based social workers may serve congregations of all sizes as consultants or on specific projects—like Melinda and Jeffrey.

Congregational Social Work as a Field of Practice—A History

Congregations have been settings for social work practice since the beginning of the profession in the late 19th century. Specht and Courtney (1994) have suggested that the profession's very name, "social work," is derived from the religious terminology of "good works" (1994, p. 21). As we have traced the development of congregations as a field for social work practice, we have identified three entities beyond congregations and denominations that have shaped this field—social work education; African American institutions; and a professional organization, the North American Association of Christians in Social Work (NACSW).[6]

Congregations have been settings for social work practice since the beginning of the profession.

Education for Church Social Work

Christian organizations founded "training schools" and "deaconess homes" that contributed to the development of the nascent social work profession. From 1870 through the early Twentieth Century, more than 140 such institutions opened in the United States, representing Catholics, a diversity of Protestant denominations and some that were interdenominational (Keller, 2001). Women's religious organizations, often auxiliary to their denominations and therefore autonomous, founded and supported these schools as independent, freestanding schools that included both social work and religious education in their curriculum. Women were prohibited from attending established church institutions like denominational seminaries and colleges, so these schools trained women to address the needs of immigrants pouring into the cities and of impoverished rural communities (Keller, 2001).

As these training schools developed, social work was attempting to define itself as a profession, seeking the prestige and power from which other professions benefited. It was a blow in 1915 when Abraham Flexner informed the National Conference on Charities and Corrections that social work did not have the exclusive knowledge and skill base to call itself a profession. This lack of knowledge base was just one of several shortcomings Flexner noted. As a consequence, social work leaders doubled their efforts to achieve professional status; they did so by adopting the developing social sciences as their knowledge and theory base.

Social work leaders also sought to professionalize by adopting a process of academic accreditation in 1932, limiting social work education to institutions of higher education with graduate education rigorous in the social sciences (Kayser, 2007). The Association of Training Schools for Professional Social Workers had established itself in 1919; it would later take on the name the American Association of Schools of Social Work (AASW) and, still later, it became the Council on Social Work Education (CSWE). Baccalaureate social work accreditation did not develop for another 40 years, until 1973 (Council on Social Work Education, 2014). As a consequence of the 1932 accrediting standards, the freestanding training schools were faced with having to affiliate with institutions of higher education if they wanted to seek accredited status.

Higher education had adopted Freudian and positivist scientific theories, however, which left little room for religion and its institutions. Moreover, some social work leaders opposed accrediting any school operated under religious auspices because they saw religion and the social sciences as incompatible. Schools faced the inescapable dilemma of either giving up their religious mission and identity to provide social work education or of keeping their religious mission and giving up social work education (Kayser, 2007). In this untenable situation, the training schools founded by women's religious organizations faced uncertain futures and dwindling enrollments. Several relinquished their independent status and affiliated with a university and its social sciences in order to acquire the professional recognition for their graduates that accreditation provided (Kayser, 2007). By doing so, they gave up their autonomous female leadership and their religious mission. Their original educational purpose—to prepare women for religious service and leadership—seemed endangered or even lost.

By the 1950s, the profession, and social work education in particular, had become almost entirely secular, despite the fact that there were Protestant, Catholic, and

Jewish social work agencies that employed social workers. Prominent social work educators railed against the Christian beliefs and practices that had motivated many to choose social work, first as volunteers and then as a profession (e.g., Bisno, 1952). For a social work student to self-identify as Christian, and particularly to seek to integrate faith with social work practice, could have meant rejection from social work school (Keith-Lucas, Kuhlmann, & Ressler, 1994).

As a consequence, and also contributing to the bias against religion by social work leaders who wanted the prestige and societal clout of professional status, denominational and other religiously affiliated agencies often hired staff members who were not professionally educated but identified with their religious groups and gave them the title "social worker." They chose religious leaders rather than social workers as heads of their organizations. Given the dilemma of having to choose between social work professionals or leaders who identified with their mission, they chose those with the mission identity. For example, in 1973, a Baptist children's home hired me (Diana), a Baptist pastor's wife with my BA degree in sociology—not social work—as a "social worker." My job was to supervise house parents and provide counseling services to children in residential care and to their families; I had no professional preparation in social work. The president of the child and family services organizations was a former Baptist pastor, also with no social work education.

Judaism and its social services did not seem to incur the same distrust from the social work profession. American Christian social services were tied closely to congregations, whereas American Jewish social services were relatively independent of synagogues (Marty, 1980). A second reason that the Judaism-social work relationship seemed to be more positive was that Judaism has no equivalent compelling value to make converts, whereas Christianity does, as expressed in the Great Commission (Matt. 28:19-20). Therefore, Judaism did not raise the same questions about the role of social work in proselytizing, the attempt to convert others to join the faith group (Popple & Leighninger, 2008).

This history of the relationship between social work education and religious institutions has not been well documented. Therefore, the examples below are illustrative but are by no means a comprehensive review of the development of social work in Christian higher education.

Methodists

The Methodist Church played a critical role in shaping the social work profession. Lucy Rider served as a professor of chemistry at McKendree College in Illinois from 1879-1881 and then became "field secretary" for the Illinois State Sunday School Association. In 1885, she married Josiah Meyer, a Chicago businessman who, with Rider, shared a strong commitment to the Methodist church and its ministry. Shortly after their marriage, they opened the Chicago Training School for City, Home, and Foreign Missions, where they served until 1917. During their tenure, Lucy Rider Meyer organized the women students into the first house of deaconesses in the United States; these women students lived together and served the urban poor while cultivating the inner spiritual life of those called to the role of deaconess. The Chicago Training School curriculum included biblical and theological studies, medicine, mission work, social and family relations, and evangelistic visitation. In order to be able to communicate with the immigrants they served, the women students also learned the first languages of the immigrants they served. Rider tried to include everything in the curriculum that she believed would help in the establishment of the Kingdom of Heaven on earth. She believed that social conditions would improve as the reign of God on earth increased through their service (Warner, 2013).

More than 40 service organizations grew out of the Chicago Training School, such as hospitals, retirement homes, and orphanages; it was the school with which Jane Addams and Hull House were most closely affiliated. The deaconesses ministered with immigrants living in the slums of Chicago through friendly visiting, nursing, employment, counseling, groups for mothers, English classes, advocacy for social reforms, industrial schools, and children's Sunday Schools (Warner, 2013). They responded to both the physical and spiritual needs of immigrant families:

> Josiah Shelley Meyer tells of an immigrant family whose wife had fallen very ill and the husband could not work and take care of her. A neighboring church reported the need and a M.E. [Methodist Episcopal] Deaconess went to the family, sending the husband to work and nursing the wife eventually back to health after also putting the dilapidated house in order and providing food and other supplies. After one week the wife was growing much better. Before the M.E. Deaconess departed, the man asked who she was and why had she done this. She assured him that he owed her nothing and tried to explain her "ideals of Christian service." To which he replied, "'Well, long ago I read in a book about some apostles. You make me think of them.' As she was leaving he called after her and asked if she attended a church. She said she did and told him where. When she arrived at the church the next Sunday morning the man was there in the vestibule, waiting for her." The M.E. Deaconess, while providing for the physical needs of the suffering she encountered, also offered an evangelistic witness of love and compassion for the spiritual well being of persons (Warner, 2013).

By the time Lucy Rider Meyer retired in 1917, the Chicago Training School had educated 5,000 deaconesses and was considered the largest training school of its kind in the country (Encyclopaedia Britannica, 2013). It faced hard times in the 1930s, however, presumably at least in part in the face of the social work profession's move toward accreditation of only institutions of higher education. In 1934, it merged with Garret Biblical Institute, later to become the Garrett-Evangelical Theological Seminary, and expanded the vision of that institution to include the education of women for church leadership (Garrett-Evangelical Theological Seminary, 2013b). Lucy Rider Meyer and the Deaconess Movement contributed to the reshaping of the Wesleyan tradition in work with the immigrant communities of Chicago (L. Warner, 2013). Today, Garrett-Evangelical offers degrees for both women and men in theology, Christian education, pastoral care and counseling, music ministry, spiritual formation, and evangelism—but not in social work (Garrett-Evangelical Theological Seminary, 2013a).

In 1892, just a few years after the founding of the Chicago Training School, the Woman's Missionary Council (WMC), affiliated with the Methodist Episcopal Church, founded the Scarritt Bible and Training School in Kansas City, Missouri. Scarritt's mission was to train women as missionaries and as ordained deaconesses; the school did not admit men until 1923, when it moved to Nashville, Tennessee and became Scarritt College for Christian Workers. Scarritt offered degrees in social work, Christian education, and religious education (Van West, 2009).

While the students and graduates of the Chicago Training School worked with urban immigrants, Scarritt also engaged in "rural work" in isolated communities and migrant camps; Scarritt graduates established and managed settlement houses, hospitals, schools, and orphanages in the United States and throughout the world (L. E. Myers, 2006). Myers documents the life of one such woman, Willena Henry, who attended the Training School from 1906-1909 and then served in logging camps and sawmill villages, where her work included placing orphans in adoptive homes; organizing a night school for working men; leading Sunday school classes, youth programs, and women's missionary societies; and teaching cooking classes. Henry later worked with immigrants employed in coal mines in Oklahoma, where she managed a community center and directed social services for women and children and a night school for men (Myers, 2006).

Scarritt College became Scarritt Graduate School in 1981, offering a degree in Christian education, but not in social work; when faced with having to choose to keep its Christian mission or to pursue the accreditation of its social work program, it apparently chose its Christian mission. Only a few years later, in 1988, Scarritt closed (Scarritt-Bennett Center, 2014).

Roman Catholic Church

In the Roman Catholic Church, priests have often been in short supply and have been assigned primarily to pastor congregations, leaving community ministries to women who, like many of their Protestant counterparts, were otherwise denied leadership opportunities in congregations. In fact, during the time that the training schools were developing, some priests taught that women's groups, not the clergy, ought to have responsibility for works of charity. Oates quotes an article entitled "Who shall take care of our sick?" published in *Catholic World* in 1868: "'This duty has devolved especially upon the female sex, because it is better gifted than the male for the ministry of compassion'" (Oates, 1995, p. 165).

There was much for Catholic women to do; during the time that the social work profession was developing, the Catholic Church was largely an immigrant church. Its members came to the United States fleeing poverty and famine in Europe and Asia. As Catholics, these immigrants looked to their church for help in their new world (Joseph & Conrad, 2010). Catholic women joined sisterhoods that were dedicated to serving vulnerable children and persons in poverty. Religious orders could freely launch ministries, but they had to be endorsed by the church to have official status (Oates, 1995). Initially, Catholic women learned social work by following the examples of their supervisors. Loyola University in Chicago, founded in 1914, initially the School of Sociology, was the first Catholic university to admit women and offer courses in social work.

Fordham opened its School of Sociology, later the School of Social Work, in 1916 under the leadership of Terence Shelay, a Jesuit priest. He had earlier founded the Laymen's League for Retreats and Social Studies in 1911 as a means of creating an "elite body of apostolic laymen whose combination of piety and social concern could help the Church penetrate and transform society" (McShane, 1992, p. 578). The League focused on applying Catholic principles to the social and economic problems of the day. But the attempt to combine religious education for justice and professional social work education fizzled as the university leaders believed that it had to become more professional and less pious in order to achieve social work accreditation (McShane, 1992). Choosing to pursue accreditation and professionalism meant moving away from the church and religious service, because the two were seen in opposition.

Baptists[7]

The Woman's Missionary Union (WMU) founded The Woman's Missionary Union Training School (WMUTS) in Louisville, Kentucky, in 1907. The WMU, an independent organization auxiliary to the Southern Baptist Convention, was the women's society for Baptists that paralleled women's organizations in other denominations (e.g., the Methodist Episcopal WMC), all with the expressed purpose of supporting women in missions and ministry (Scales, 2000).

The year WMUTS was founded, 1907, is the same year Walter Rauschenbusch published *Christianity and the Social Crisis*. Rauschenbusch was a Baptist pastor and a leading figure in the Social Gospel movement; his theology resonated with that of Lucy Rider Meyer. Rauschenbusch had come to believe that the calling of the church was to spread the Kingdom of God by addressing the evil embedded in social institutions that bring about oppression and poverty. He explained that the Kingdom of God "is not a matter of getting individuals to heaven, but of transforming the life on earth into the harmony of heaven" (Rauschenbusch, 1907, p. 65). It was in the midst of this theological foment and recognition of the role of social and political systems in the growing social injustices of the Industrial Revolution that WMUTS took shape. In 1952, its name changed to the Carver School of Missions and Social Work, in honor of W.O. Carver, a beloved (male) professor. At that point, it became co-educational. It admitted its first two African American students in 1955, as a result of a long-time partnership between the WMU and the National Baptist women's mission group for African American women (Brice & Scales, 2013).

In 1957, after years of facing economic hardship and the same challenges accreditation created for other schools, the WMU gave its school to its denomination, The Southern Baptist Convention, which in turn merged the school with The Southern Baptist Theological Seminary, a recognized institution of higher education, with the stated goal of seeking accreditation. The school was subsumed in the seminary's School of Religious Education. Students could take some coursework in social work and then transfer and complete their social work degrees through an agreement with the accredited University of Louisville (UL) nearby.

WMUTS first principal, Maud Reynolds McLure

THE COURIER-JOURNAL, LOUISVILLE, THURSDAY MORNING

NEW BAPTIST WOMEN'S TRAINING SCHOOL DEDICATED WITH APPROPRIATE EXERCISES

A New Era—The Accreditation of Social Work for the Church

One of the last graduates of the freestanding Carver School , C. Anne Davis, joined the faculty of the School of Religious Education of The Southern Baptist Theological Seminary. She was determined to pursue the development of an accredited social work program that would prepare Christian leaders. Davis successfully advocated with the new seminary president, Roy Lee Honeycutt, to develop a Master of Social Work degree by hiring the additional five faculty members required as a minimum for CSWE accreditation. The CSWE accredited the Carver School of Church Social Work of The Southern Baptist Theological Seminary in 1985, the only seminary it ever accredited.[8] Originally, the school's faculty had planned to integrate theological content and courses into the social work program, but the CSWE ruled that it was not authorized to accredit theological coursework. In order to achieve accreditation, therefore, the Carver School faculty revised the program, removing the theology courses from the social work degree itself but requiring all students to complete a year-long Certificate of Theological Studies as a prerequisite to enrollment in the Master of Social Work program.

The Carver School thrived for more than a decade. It, too, closed in 1996, a casualty of denominational leadership shifts, including a new seminary president, with more conservative theological positions. The new seminary and denominational leadership held the position that women should not be permitted to serve in church leadership positions, a position that the faculty and its female dean would not support. When the faculty and dean objected, the seminary leadership closed the school and sold its assets (Garland, 1999c).

As a consequence of the closure of the Carver School, Baylor University, another Baptist institution independent of the Southern Baptist Convention, added a graduate social work degree program to its undergraduate degree, created a School of Social Work, and continued the work of preparing both women and men as professionals for the church and other settings for social work practice. Other Baptist schools, including Campbellsville University (Kentucky) and Union University (Tennessee), as well as a Free Methodist school, Roberts Wesleyan University (New York), developed social work educational programs with a focus on the church as a direct result of the closure of Carver and the dispersion of its faculty to these institutions.

By the late 1990s, other denominations were also opening graduate—and undergraduate—social work education programs and obtaining CSWE accreditation, and even public university social work programs began offering courses in church and congregational social work (e.g., University of South Carolina). CSWE described 186 social work programs as "Religion-Affiliated Social Work Programs" (Council on Social Work Education, 2012). During this same decade, the federal government was devolving its social welfare policies and programs. For the first time in history, grant funding was made available through the 1996 Personal Responsibility and Work Opportunities Reconciliation Act (PRWORA) to congregations providing social services. The PRWORA legitimized the relationship between religiously affiliated social service organizations and government. In 2001, President G.W. Bush officially implemented the White House Office of Faith-based and Community Initiatives that was earlier approved in the PRWORA, under President Bill Clinton (Chaves, 1999c; Farnsely, 2004; Farris, Nathan, & Wright, 2004; NEWS, 2002). In the midst of these significant changes in how social services were being funded, social work education and research began to rediscover—perhaps acknowledge for the first time publicly—the church as a field of social work practice. Although progress is being made with accreditation of social work degree programs in religion-affiliated schools, the categories of congregational social work or church social work are not yet listed as fields of practice or within the categories for field placements (Council on Social Work Education, 2012).

African American Social Workers for the Church—A History Apart

Social work as a profession was developing at the same time, and intersecting with, the development of African American communities during the years following emancipation from slavery in 1863 through the era of legalized discrimination that lasted through the 1950s. African Americans broadened the functions of the church, making it the most powerful institution of racial self-help during an era in which the larger society remained segregated and oppressive. The Black church became one of the few public gathering places for African Americans. Largely through the fundraising efforts of women, the Black church developed a host of social welfare services and established schools, colleges, orphanages, and homes for older adults (Higginbotham, 1993). Settlement houses were started specifically to meet the needs of African Americans from the South who had become known as Negro migrants as they moved into urban areas in search of employment.

A sense of spiritual calling, mission, and duty "to struggle for the freedom and uplift of Black people" motivated this work among poor African Americans, both in and beyond the church (Martin & Martin, 2002, p. 95). Women joined clubs that provided opportunities for African American women and girls to learn how to do social work, such as the Women's Loyal Union of New York, the Woman's Era Club of Boston, the Ida B. Wells Club in Chicago, and the Neighborhood Union in Atlanta. "Lifting as we climb" was the motto of the national organization of women's clubs (Bent-Goodley, 2001; Hine, 1993). They had learned how to organize and lead themselves in women's church societies (Brice, 2012; Higginbotham, 1993).

Nannie Helen Burroughs
photo courtesy Library of Congress

W. E. B. Du Bois was a well-known educational figure in social work among African Americans (Martin & Martin, 2002). Du Bois and his associate, Alexander Crummel, taught that God had called African American social workers to this work, that they had a spiritual mission, and that they were paying back a debt they owed to their ancestors and to God. They taught that the Black church had a responsibility beyond saving souls; it was to be an instrument of social, economic, and political uplift in order to strengthen families and stabilize the African American community (Martin & Martin, 2002). This "race work" and "uplift work" of the church thus became the profession of social work for African Americans (Martin & Martin, 2002, p. 133), anchored in religious institutions and congregations.

African American women started their own schools to educate girls and women, focusing initially on reading, writing, and arithmetic. In 1909, social worker Nannie Helen Burroughs founded the National Training School for Women and Girls in Washington, DC; Burroughs was a leader in the National Baptist Convention, the leading denomination for Black Baptist churches. The school trained African American women for vocational ministry and missions (Allen, 1987; Smith, 2008).

In Raleigh, North Carolina, the Bishop Tuttle School was established by the Episcopal Church as a National Center for the Training of Women Church Workers in 1925 in response to the need expressed by the bishops for educating African American women:

> Bishops have asked for women who will carry Church teaching and social service into parochial schools and into parish visiting, who can lead in club work, and will understand domestic science and hygiene. In the North and South, in rural school and city parish, are children to be taught, mothers to be guided, the sick and unfortunate to be reached. Sunday Schools are in need of better teachers, and communities are waiting for some plan of wholesome recreation, the uplift of new ideas, and the leadership of a strong personality (Hoke, 2009, p. 23).

The Tuttle School's two-year curriculum included religious studies and social work; the school defined social work as "applied Christianity" (Hoke, 2009, p. 23). Many poor rural Black congregations could not afford a priest; these women stepped into the leadership gap, even though, as women, they could not be ordained to the priesthood (Kayser, 2007). Like the Baptist's WMU Training School and other religious schools of social work, the Bishop Tuttle School operated a settlement house and community center, preparing graduates to lead both public and "church-based" social services.

Like the Chicago, Scarritt, and Carver Schools, the Bishop Tuttle School faced a crisis with the development of social work accreditation; it, too, was freestanding and so not eligible for accreditation, resulting in dwindling enrollments. The school was also struggling with opposition from the denomination, apparently because graduates were becoming less content with the subservient roles ascribed to them by male White leaders. The Tuttle School chose in 1938 to give up social work education and become only a religious training program, but enrollments continued to drop until it closed in 1941 (Kayser, 2007).

The North American Association of Christians in Social Work (NACSW)

It was in this social work professional and academic climate of indifference and even hostility toward Christian religion and its organizations that Christian evangelical social workers organized the Evangelical Social Work Conference (ESWC) in 1954. Perhaps of all Christians, evangelicals raised the most suspicion for leaders in a profession wary of any hint of social workers engaging in evangelism. The focus of the ESWC was two-fold. First, it sought to provide support for evangelical social workers through fellowship, conferences, and publications, encouraging them to continue to work within the profession of social work. Second, it promoted professional standards among "evangelical agencies and workers" (Keith-Lucas et al., 1994). Over the years, the membership of the organization, as well as its name and focus, broadened to embrace Christians from across the diversity of Protestant and Catholic traditions, becoming the North American Association of Christians in Social Work (NACSW).[9]

Although NACSW focuses broadly on the integration of Christian faith with professional social work, it has provided an outlet for 60 years for both practitioners and academics to publish on the topic of church social work, and more narrowly, congregational social work. NACSW published Garland's *Church Social Work*, the first book on the topic of church social work, in 1992. NACSW's professional journal, *Social Work & Christianity,* published articles on church social work and congregational social work when few other publication outlets for the field existed.

In some ways, the suspicion of and exclusion by the social work profession of Christian organizations and institutions paralleled the exclusion of women from church ministry education and the exclusion of African Americans from White institutions of higher education. NACSW has provided a professional home for Christians in a profession suspicious of their faith just as the Training Schools had earlier been founded to provide an educational opportunity for women who were not welcome in church educational programs, and as the Black church provided training programs for African Americans in an era of segregated higher education. In its own way, NACSW provided a critical and needed link connecting professional social work with Christian institutions, preserving the possibility that church social work could become a recognized field of social work practice.

The Literature of Congregational Social Work

Abbott (1995) has studied how some areas of practice that were included in the emerging social work profession at the end of the 19th century disappeared from the literature over subsequent decades Practice contexts such as "manual training," home economics, probation, and kindergarten, were lost to other emerging professions. Boundaries defining social work emerged from this competition with other professions. Although Abbott does not address congregational social work, it is one of the fields that seems to have disappeared—almost—from the literature, as competitive professional education emerged in denominational seminaries, dominated by men, for the fields of Christian education, pastoral care and counseling, and missiology. Coupled with the dominance in social work of scientific theories that ignored religion, it is of little surprise that the professional literature, largely controlled by academics, became silent on the practice of social work in congregations and other religious settings.

Johnson's *The Social Work of the Churches: A Handbook of Information* (1930) is the earliest work on congregational social services that we can identify. He described congregational social services that took place under the auspices of the Federated Council of the Churches of Christ in America during that time. His description included social services provision; churches cooperating with community social service agencies; religious groups focusing on issues of social welfare and social justice; and research defining effective strategies of service.

The National Conference of Catholic Charities launched a series of monographs entitled *Certain Aspects of Case Work Practice in Catholic Social Work* in 1942 that focused on casework practice in Catholic social service agencies.

The first publications on congregational social work we can find in the mainstream social work literature are two articles published in 1962 (Ferm, 1962; Taggart, 1962). Alice Taggart described her work as a "parish assistant" in a Unitarian congregation in New York, and Martin Ferm used the term "parish social work" to describe the role of a social worker on the staff of a Lutheran congregation.

Taggart's work consisted of counseling services, consultation with groups in the congregation, and services to the neighborhood. She described the informality of her work, which took place through home, hospital, and retirement home visits, as well as through encounters with congregants as they participated in church activities. She noted that social work in a church is different from other settings, because both social worker and clients are members of the same congregation. She noted that she often initiated offers to help because she knew the life situations of others rather than waiting for the client to ask for services. Connections between the social worker and client were open-ended; contact sometimes continued for many years, often informally and intermittently. Finally, her personal as well as professional self were engaged in the work; the congregation was the faith community for her family, not just the place she was employed (Taggart, 1962).

Ferm's use of the term "parish social work" referred to the tradition where the congregation and its priest or pastor serves a specific territory, or "parish." Financial support for parish social work, as Ferm described it, came from the Lutheran Board of Social Missions. Responsibilities included casework services, consultation with the pastor, developing social ministries for the neighborhood, and consulting with the congregation's pastor and other pastors through the local pastors' association (Ferm, 1962) .

A decade passed before the next publication in 1975. Sister Mary Vincentia Joseph described the congregation as an ideal setting for social work practice, located in the life-space of individual and family life cycle events, and in a setting conducive to community organization and action. She concluded that a congregation's "characteristics as a social unit and its theological orientation combine uniquely in creating an ideal matrix for a social service model" (Joseph, 1975, p. 45). She described the work of parish social work to be accessing services (information, referral, and case management); counseling (individual, family, and group); crisis intervention; resource development (recruiting, training, and supporting volunteers); and developing and nurturing natural support systems (see also Joseph & Conrad, 1980).

By the 1980s, Kenneth Smith was writing about the development and administration of a network of counseling centers based in eleven Methodist, Presbyterian, and Lutheran congregations; the counselors in the network were members of the congregations' staffs and came from several professional disciplines, including social workers (Smith, 1984, 1988).

Based on the work of these early writers in the field, and my (Diana) own work with Baptist congregations through consultation and through the placement of social work graduate students in congregational internships, I (Diana) began to write about this field of practice in the mid-1980s (Garland, 1983a, 1986, 1987b, 1988). In those early writings, I emphasized the distinctive characteristics of congregational social work, which I saw to be the congregation's nature as a voluntary organization, the Christian mission that motivated its social services, its culture as a community, its societal role as one of the few mediating structures found in virtually every community in the USA, and the shared community of social work and client.

I (Diana) launched a research project to study congregational social work in 1986. A group of four graduate social work students, all in field internships in congregations, met throughout the year to share their experiences and questions with one another and with me. They attempted to define goals and tasks for congregational social work, to develop a process for beginning practice as the first social worker on the congregational staff, and to discern appropriate roles. The group concluded its work by designing a structured interview protocol. I then used that protocol to conduct phone interviews with 21 social workers employed in congregational settings (1987b, 1988). The sample for that study came from contacting those congregational social workers I knew and their networks. More than 20 years later, an MSW student at Baylor University's School of Social Work conducted a second study, using the same interview protocol in phone interviews with 30 congregational social workers who responded to an e-mail notice about the study sent to members of the North American Association of Christians in Social Work (NACSW) (Northern, 2009).

The congregational social workers surveyed in both studies had a variety of job titles, as well as job responsibilities, ranging from direct practice to social ministry leadership. Responsibilities included creating and overseeing ministry programs, training volunteers, clinical practice, immigration assistance, children's education ministry, bereavement counseling, and emergency or financial assistance. Their most common titles were "pastor" and "minister." Others were called "director" of a program or ministry. Some of them preached and led mission groups. Virtually all were providing direct services as well as administering programs.

Most saw themselves as social workers and believed that their roles as religious leaders were congruent with their social work identity. Most, but not all, thought that their theology strongly influenced their practice and saw social work practice and their Christian theology as complementary. For example, Northern quotes one social worker who oversaw the congregation's elegant meal for the homeless, with table linens and table service rather than the cafeteria line so typical in homeless feeding programs:

> [The ministry] highlights the grander ideas of social work—respect for the dignity of the individual and the client's right to self-determination. We try to be individualized and personal with each service, influenced by our call to be gracious, not just provide the service (Northern, 2009, p. 276).

After that first 1987 survey, other authors of publications that form the literature on congregational social work have described their own work in and with congregations. For example, Watkins (1992) described the role of the social worker who acts as a consultant to a congregation in developing inner-city ministry programs. Ferguson (1992) described her work as Director of Community Ministries in First Baptist Church of Montgomery, Alabama, an economically affluent congregation that made the decision in the 1980s to stay in its downtown location so that it could serve the city rather than move to the suburbs. First Baptist then hired her to lead them in addressing the poverty that surrounded their congregation and the other challenges of downtown Montgomery.

In 2002, a casebook for teaching about spirituality and religion in social work practice produced by the Council on Social Work Education contained four case studies that are actual accounts of congregational social work practice (Scales, Wolfer, Sherwood, Garland, Hugen, and Pittman (Eds.), 2002). They include the executive director of a Christian housing program who works with congregational groups to build low-income houses and befriend the first-time homeowners (Furman & Aker, 2002); a public child welfare worker working with congregations as supportive communities for foster and adoptive families (Kenny, 2002); a congregational social worker providing clinical services (Harris, Sherwood, & Timmons, 2002); and a congregational social worker working with a state welfare to work program to link "mentors" from her congregation with welfare recipients (Stalwick & Holding Eagle, 2002).

Another casebook for teaching (Wolfer & Huyser, 2010) including an additional four case studies of congregational social work, was published by North American Association of Christians in Social Work. They include a social worker who, as a congregational member, is asked to develop a benevolence ministry, a social work staff member responsible for case management services for clients receiving assistance from her congregation, and two social workers providing counseling services through their congregations, one as an unpaid service and one as a staff member.

The growing field of sociology of religion has also served as a resource for understanding congregations as settings for social work practice. By no means a comprehensive list, some of the leading sociologists that have developed the field of congregational studies include Nancy Ammerman, Jackson Carroll, Mark Chaves, Michael Emerson, James Wind, James Lewis, and Robert Wuthnow.[10]

Despite the historical roots of social work in congregations and religious institutions, as well as the slender thread that we have traced through the social work literature, the social work profession has continued largely unaware of congregations as settings for practice. A handful of social work researchers have made significant contributions to the literature of congregational social work in the past 20 years: Stephanie Boddie, Ram Cnaan, T. Laine Scales, David Sherwood, Bob Wineburg, and Terry Wolfer.[11] Much of the recent attention has come in response to the devolution of public social services in the United States and a consequent looking toward religious institutions to broaden their social service provision (e.g., Cnaan, Sinha, & McGrew, 2004). Nevertheless, congregational social work is still almost never mentioned as a field of practice, at least in introductory textbooks or tracks at professional conferences, with the notable exception of NACSW.

Purposes of Congregations

In order to work effectively in congregational settings, social workers need to understand what congregations are striving to be and to do—their identity and mission. Virtually all congregations have four purposes they pursue: to worship, to be a community for congregants, to provide Christian education, and do missions beyond their own membership. Many congregations often have mission statements that refer to these four primary functions. Here is the mission statement of Calvary Baptist Church in Waco, Texas[12], for example:

> Calvary Baptist Church is a Christ-centered community of faith devoted to the worship of the living God. Committed to a deeper understanding of God's word, we aspire to grow personally and communally, to become a sanctuary for all God's people, and to pour out God's love in the local and global community. (http://www.calvarybaptistwaco.com).

The single highest priority for congregations is participating together in religious rituals to learn about, teach others about, and relate to God through worship.

Worship

Worship is the response people make to God—honoring, rejoicing, and humbling themselves as creatures before their Creator. People express themselves in worship by listening, praying, reading or singing holy texts, making music through instruments and voice, participating in rituals and sacraments, and dancing and kneeling—all ways to communicate devotion to God.

The single highest priority for congregations is participating together in religious rituals to learn about, teach others about, and relate to God through worship. Sociologist Mark Chaves describes this core purpose as "producing and reproducing religious meanings through ritual and religious education" (2004, p. 9). In his extensive study of congregations, he found that worship services use more congregational resources than anything else congregations do. The worship service is the congregation's self-portrait, the way a congregation sees itself and portrays itself to the larger world. Calvary states that its mission is to be "devoted to the worship of the living God." That worship takes place in a "community of faith" that aspires to be a "sanctuary" [i.e., holy, safe place] for everyone.

Ten of the social workers we interviewed preach in the congregations they serve.[13] Many others lead in worship in other ways, leading the congregation in prayer and the reading of scripture, and sharing stories of the work that the congregation is doing in the community. They also teach and interpret scriptures in the educational programs and small group gatherings of the congregation. We will explore further what we learned about social workers serving as worship leaders in Chapter 4.

Christian Education

Faith is not cognitive knowledge alone; Christians also learn by attempting to apply the teachings of Jesus in their relationships with one another as members of families and communities.

Calvary's mission statement affirms that the congregation is "committed to a deeper understanding of God's word," and that it aspires "to grow personally and communally." Congregants learn the beliefs, values, and behaviors of Christian living by learning from one another and from studying the Bible, Christian history, and Christian literature together. Faith is not cognitive knowledge alone; Christians also learn by attempting to apply the teachings of Jesus in their relationships with one another as members of families and communities.

Not only do social workers serve in leadership positions of congregational education, but they also have been authors of denominational and other curricula for the various educational programs of congregations. Their books have been studied in topical series in church schools and seminars. And they have been "experts" invited to address congregations on a variety of topics.[14] Of the 51 social workers we interviewed, 43 led in one or more educational programs. We will explore their roles as Christian educators in Chapter 4.

Community

A community is the people that attempt to give and receive emotional and material support for one another.

The third purpose of congregational life is often called "fellowship," a purpose that has shaped congregational life since the first church devoted itself "to the apostles' teaching and *fellowship*, to the breaking of bread and the prayers" (Acts 2:42; italics added). Fellowship is, in essence, the relationships that form community. A community is *the people that attempt to give and receive emotional and material support for one another.* Communities are the interpersonal networks through which we attempt to find the meaning in our lives, meet one another's needs, accomplish our personal goals, and feel like we belong (W. G. Brueggemann, 1996). Notice that the definition includes the word "attempt." Communities sometimes fall short of this ideal. Like families, however imperfect and sometimes even harmful their attempts to provide material and emotional support for one another may be, they are still communities.

Calvary calls itself a "Christ-centered community of faith." A community "of faith" distinguishes it from a community defined by geography. In a geographic community, people relate to one another because, literally, their paths cross. They interact with one another on a daily basis, whether it is in the hallways of an apartment building, the sidewalks of a neighborhood, or the shop or conference room where they work. A congregation, on the other hand, is a community of people who choose with intentionality to be in relationship with one another, often by going out of the way—outside their daily paths—of home

The term "community" refers to the people who belong to a congregation, and "neighborhood" to the geographic area, recognizing that many congregants may live in the congregation's neighborhood and some neighborhoods still serve as communities where people look out for and support one another.

and work routines to share common faith commitments, mutual support, and shared ideological views in living their faith.

We need language to help distinguish a congregation as a community from the geographical area where a congregation is located, often also called "the community." In this book, we reserve the term "community" for referring to the people who belong to a congregation. We use "neighborhood" to refer to the geographic area, recognizing that many congregants may live in the congregation's neighborhood and that some neighborhoods also function as communities where people look out for and support one another. Many neighborhoods are not communities, however. People may not know the names of their neighbors, much less feel a sense of obligation to be in mutually supportive relationships with those neighbors. Sometimes communities and neighborhoods are the same; often they are different.

The social workers we interviewed are actively involved in developing a sense of community life within the congregation. We will explore their roles as "community builders" in Chapter 5.

Missions

Calvary's mission statement concludes by saying that the congregation is committed "to pour out God's love in the local and global community." The verb "pour out" has connotations of emptying self, of generosity, of "giving it all" more than alternative verbs which could have been used such as "demonstrate" or "witness to" or "represent." To "pour out" communicates that the congregation is totally committed to missions. The congregation intends to give everything it has to serving others locally and around the world, believing that it is the conduit for the love of God. That serving includes a myriad of responses to human need—caring for families in crisis, providing medical services, supporting economic development in impoverished communities, drilling wells for clean water to prevent disease, and so much more. One dimension of human need is to understand the meaning and purpose of life. Missions often includes sharing Christian viewpoints on the ultimate questions of life. We will address this sharing in more depth in the discussion of evangelism in Chapter 6.

As we discussed earlier, congregations often call what they do "ministry"; social work calls it "service." Both terms are used interchangeably in the New Testament, most often in the writings of the Apostle Paul as the following examples illustrate:

- Be a *minister* of Christ Jesus to the Gentiles in the priestly *service* of the gospel God (Romans 15:16).
- The gifts He gave were that some would be apostles, some prophets, some

evangelists, some pastors and teachers, to equip the saints for the work of *ministry* . . . (Ephesians 4:11-12).

- Render *service* with enthusiasm, as to the Lord and not to men and women knowing that whatever good we do, we will receive the same again from the Lord, whether we are slaves or free (Ephesians 6:7-8).
- I am grateful to Christ Jesus our Lord, who has strengthened me, because He judged me faithful and appointed me to His *service* (1 Timothy 1:12).

Both words refer to the work of congregations to demonstrate—or "pour out" in Calvary's language—God's love to their neighbors. Jesus taught that addressing the needs of our neighbors is not optional but commanded, a commandment second only to loving God completely (e.g., Luke 10), or perhaps more correctly, the *way* we show our love for God (Matthew 25:44-46). In talking about congregational social work, however, we often use the word "ministry" rather than "service." We are striving to be clear that congregational engagement in addressing needs of neighbors locally and globally is grounded in Christian mission, which is at the heart of the Christian story.

Congregations call what they do "ministry"; social work calls it "service."

Writings about congregational social work have focused primarily on this function of congregational life, and it is in missions and social ministries that social workers have been most prominent in congregational leadership. We will explore the role of social workers as mission leaders in Chapter 6.

Another Illustration: Riverside Church

Another illustration of the functions of congregational life comes from the mission statement of the historic Riverside Church in New York City:

> The Church seeks to be a community of faith. Its members are united in the worship of God known in Jesus, the Christ, through the inspiration of the Holy Spirit. The mission of the Church is to serve God through word and witness; to treat all human beings as sisters and brothers; and to foster responsible stewardship of all God's creation. The Church commits itself to welcoming all persons, celebrating the diversity found in a Congregation broadly inclusive of persons from different backgrounds of characteristics, including race, economic class, religion, culture, ethnicity, gender, age, sexual orientation, family status and physical and mental abilities. Members are called to an individual and collective quality of life that leads to personal, spiritual and social transformation, witnessing to God's saving purposes for all creation. Therefore, the Church pledges

> itself to education, reflection, and action for peace and justice and the realization of the vision of the heavenly banquet where all are loved and blessed (www.theriversidechurchny.org).

Riverside Church's mission statement contains the same four elements:

- Worship: "...united in the worship of God..."
- Christian education: "pledges itself to education, reflection, and action..."
- Fellowship: "treat all human beings as sisters and brothers... welcoming all"
- Missions: "serve God through word and witness... witnessing to God's saving purposes for all creation... pledging itself to... action for peace and justice"

Some congregations emphasize one aspect of this fourfold mission more than another, but they are typically all present in a congregation's life, whether or not it has a mission statement. These functions dictate how the congregation allocates its resources of funding, staff time, and programmatic emphases. A helpful exercise for congregational social workers is to identify these elements in the mission statement of the congregation where they serve and in the weekly activities that shape the congregation's life.

Congregations as Primary Social Work Settings

As we began our work with congregations, we assumed that we would find congregational social workers engaged most often in that fourth function—leading and equipping congregations for missions in the neighborhood and world. Lynne epitomized our imaginary congregational social worker—a specialized leadership role in congregations large enough and with enough resources to have multiple staff members and a congregation with a heart for community ministry. We had known social workers like Carl and Beth, but we thought they were really outside the realm of the usual. We were wrong.

Congregations may offer human services, but they are not social service organizations.

In the past, I (Diana) have also called congregations "host settings" for social work practice (Garland, 1992). I was wrong again. I realize now that the distinction I was trying to make is that congregations may offer human services, but they are not social service organizations. They have organizational structures—but they are communities. They provide social services, but those services are an expression of their mission. What I have realized in the work on this project is that social work started in the church and still belongs there, even as the profession has broadened by serving the overall mission of many other institutions and organizations in society as well.

Hospitals and schools are examples of other societal organizations where social workers practice, even though the organizations are not considered social service agencies. Social workers further the purposes of hospitals and schools by providing social services and by advocacy in the arenas of health care and education. Hospital social workers help plan for care after a patient leaves the hospital, help families deal with the crises of difficult diagnoses, and facilitate care planning. School social workers address family and community factors that keep children from succeeding in school. The services of social workers presumably help both schools and hospitals to accomplish their stated missions.

Hospital social workers can address the needs of patients and their families, and may even be able to advocate for their needs with community structures and even the hospital itself. They probably cannot expect the hospital to support their spending time working with street gangs in order to decrease the violence in the community, however, unless they can demonstrate that their work helps reduce violent injuries and deaths. If such work is only indirectly related to the health of patients and their families, the hospital will probably see working with gangs as peripheral, not an activity that helps it accomplish its mission of patient health care.

Social workers in schools address factors that have an impact on students' academic performance. They may ensure that children have necessary clothing and school supplies, arrange for tutoring or mentoring for children struggling, provide counseling for children in crisis, and advocate for policies that provide universal breakfasts so that children have the nutrition they need so they can focus in the classroom. But if the school social worker decides to run a support group for children whose parents are divorcing—and pulls children out of math class twice a week for the group—the school is going to object. Perhaps the group can take place after school or during recess or study hall—but not during a subject like math, used to evaluate the school's performance. The focus of the work that always must be primary is helping children succeed educationally—the mission of the school.

Social workers are integrally engaged in all four functions of congregational life, using social work knowledge, values, and skills to contribute to the worship, education, fellowship, and ministry of congregations.

In short, social workers must contribute in direct and measurable ways to the accomplishment of the organization's mission and goals, like they do in any professional setting. Therefore, congregational social workers are central to the life of congregations when they lead in accomplishing congregations' purposes, just as hospital social workers and school social workers are vital to the life of those organizations when they help them accomplish their purposes. We have changed our minds and are no longer using the term "host setting," because it implies that the social services of congregations and the social workers who lead them are "guests" The "host setting" concept marginalizes the social services of organizations like hospitals and clinics, schools, nursing homes, and community centers rather than emphasizing how social services are integral to the accomplishment of organizational purposes. These 51 social workers affirm that they are not guests in congregations, but rather, that their practice expertise is vital to the accomplishment of the overall goals of the congregations. Ministry is one of the four core functions of congregational life. Moreover, we found that social workers are integrally engaged in all four functions of congregational life, using social work knowledge, values, and skills to contribute to the worship, education, fellowship, *and* ministry of congregations.

Chapter 3
Social Workers as Congregational Leaders

In the last chapter, we described the characteristics and functions of congregations as settings for social work practice. This chapter introduces what we learned about the 51 congregational social workers we interviewed. We will explore the leadership roles they carry in congregational life. You will read about how they think of themselves as professional social workers, religious leaders, or both. Finally, we will explore the pastoral role that some of these social workers carry, unique as it is in professional social work practice.

Who They Are

We interviewed by telephone 51 social workers who responded to announcements about the project and a request for volunteers[15] All of them had professional social work degrees and were either working with a single congregation or were employed by an agency that was working with one or more congregations. After analyzing the transcripts over a period of two years, we again interviewed the seven social workers whose stories are told in Chapter 1, in order to explore some of the questions our analysis had created.

Our sample was a convenience sample, not a random sampling of congregational social workers. The descriptions of these congregational social workers should not be construed as representative of this field of social work. We do think we reached a wide diversity of congregational social workers, however, so that we can describe the parameters of this field of practice, at least as we know them now. An appendix provides a brief description of each of the social workers.

Gender, Age, and Ethnicity

These social workers in our study were predominantly female (74%), slightly less than the 80% of professional social workers who are female (Whitaker & Arrington, 2008). At least among those we interviewed, men are somewhat more prevalent than in other fields of social work practice. The median age of these social workers is 45.

The sample is overwhelmingly White (n=47). It includes three who identify themselves as Hispanic and one as African-American. It is not clear why we reached so few non-White social workers. Perhaps they are not connected to the organizations through which we sought volunteers, or perhaps they did not recognize their work as congregational social work. It also may be that there are proportionally fewer non-White congregational social workers for other reasons we cannot determine based on this research project

Geographical and Denominational Locations

These 51 social workers are located in 25 of the 50 states of the United States. Two were located in other countries: Canada and South Africa. Those in the United States are widely disbursed, from California to Connecticut and from Mississippi to Michigan. Three states were represented by more than two social workers; there were 13 from Texas, six from Indiana, and three from Ohio. The larger number from Texas, and to a lesser extent, from Indiana and Ohio, is probably a result of the fact that Texas is home to many large congregations. It is also home to one of the historically Baptist schools, Baylor University, whose School of Social Work focuses on this field of practice, producing a number of alumni in this field; some of these alumni had known the authors as faculty when they were students. Nevertheless, half of the interviewees from Texas were not Baylor alumni (n=6), and most were not Baptist (n=8).

These social workers are working in congregations representing 16 religious groups, with the largest being Baptist (n=16), and nondenominational Christian (n=7). Other groups represented by more than one social worker include Roman Catholic (n=5), Church of God (n=4), Methodist (n=4), Presbyterian (n=3), and Church of Christ (n=3). Since Catholics, nondenominational Christians, and Baptists are the largest three religious groups in the United States (Chaves, 2004), it is not surprising that these groups were more represented than others, although Baptists clearly dominated the sample.

The reasons for Baptists to be so dominant in the sample are probably a mix of factors. In addition to being numerically one of the largest three religious groups in the nation, Baptists have historically prepared congregational social workers in seminary and university programs, as described in the last chapter. Also, the NACSW listserv provided a major portion of the volunteers for this project, and as described in the last chapter, its roots have been in evangelical Christianity, where Baptists tend to be located in the continuum of denominations. Nevertheless, both of these factors have changed in recent years. Other schools of social work, including public universities, are beginning to offer courses in congregational social work, and NACSW includes Christians from diverse traditions. In the future, Baptists may not be so dominant in this field of practice.

Professional Preparation

Most of these social workers had attained a master's degree in social work.[16] We asked for the names of the schools in which they completed their BSW and/or MSW degrees. Less than half (n=21) of the respondents received their highest social work degree (BSW or MSW) in religiously-affiliated college or university settings.[17] The remaining 30 social workers—the majority—attended nonsectarian private and public universities.[18] The listing of schools is quite diverse, including such schools as New York University, Ohio State, and North Carolina (Chapel Hill)[19], suggesting the wide variation of social work educational experiences these social workers have had. The majority did not have a course or a focus in their professional education that addressed congregations as settings for practice.

A large number, though not the majority, have degrees or certificates in religion or ministry. Fifteen have a Master of Divinity degree or another master's degree in theology, three have undergraduate majors or minors in religion, three have certificates in theology or Catechetics, one has a Doctor of Ministry degree, and two are currently enrolled in divinity programs. That leaves 27, however, who did not describe any formal theological preparation. Their only degree preparation was social work and very few of them had any focus in that degree work on congregations.

Their Social Work Careers

These social workers have established careers in congregational social work; they have been serving professionally for a median[20] of eight years, with a range of 2 to 41 years. Most of that time (median=7 years), they have been working in a congregational setting, with a range of 1 to 35 years. Some have worked in the same congregation for most of their careers, with an average of 3 years of service in their current congregational setting, and a range of 1 to 26 years.

Their Current Positions

Their titles are quite diverse. Five have the title "pastor"; four have the title "associate pastor"; and another four have the term "minister" as part of their title (e.g., "Minister of Community Ministries" and "Youth Minister"). The most common title (n=22) was "director" of a program or area of responsibility, such as "Director of Community Ministries," "Director of Social Service Ministries," "Director of Senior Adult Ministries," and "Director of Children and Youth Programs." Four titles included the terms "counselor" or "therapist." Three actually had the title "Social Worker." We could find no trends in preference for one title or another either by denomination or by geographic location.

Over time, congregational social workers shaped that role and the position descriptions based on their own professional experiences and knowledge, as well as their growing relationship with the congregation.

Despite the fact that most are not identified by title as social workers and consequently are not required by law to be licensed as social workers,[21] most (n=33) are licensed as social workers. For example, Inez provides clinical services, part-time, to members of the nondenominational congregation and its neighborhood while she is a full-time social worker in the nearby university. She bears the title "Christian counselor" in her congregation. She noted that she displays her state social work license prominently and makes sure that clients know her professional role.[22]

What They Do

A few of these social workers began their work in a congregation after experiencing congregational social work as a field internship. Beth is one of those; she told us, "I wouldn't be doing what I'm doing if I hadn't had that field placement." As she worked in a congregation as a student, she said she "fell in love with the church." Her field experience engaged her in the congregation's community ministries—she revised how they conducted their benevolence ministries, including using a food pantry for emergency assistance, and she involved the teenagers in mission projects in the community. She is now a pastor in a Baptist church.

Other congregational social workers we interviewed had never seen or heard of "congregational social work." When they found themselves doing it, they thought they were alone. Even for those with experience, congregational social work is not as clearly defined as social work roles in a social service agency. Some of these social workers often began in staff roles familiar in congregational life—associate pastor, youth minister, or director of a program. Over time, they shaped that role and the position descriptions based on their own professional experiences and knowledge, as well as their growing relationship with the congregation. Their roles and positions emerged over time rather than being defined at the outset. We placed three emergent job descriptions in the appendix to give an overview of how congregations come to define the responsibilities of a congregational social worker.

Lois, hired as Director of Senior Adult Ministries for her Presbyterian Church, describes her initial role as "cruise director." It is common for senior adult ministries in congregations to focus on taking senior adults on outings and providing recreation to encourage socialization and engagement, perceiving that senior adults are at risk of isolation. Lois took on the role of directing senior adult activities that reminded her of recreation on a cruise ship because, as she said, "That's what the person in front of me was doing." She was hired to fill a staff position, and she began by doing what the previous director had done—planning activities and outings.

Over time, Lois adapted the position to fit what she perceived was a better use of her leadership—developing a senior adult program called Pastor Aides that trained and supported senior adults in ministry to other senior adults.

Similarly, Beth, the pastor mentioned above, was hired first as a college student minister. Gradually, she engaged the whole congregation, not just college students, in community ministry. Her position was subsequently changed to Associate Pastor before moving to the congregation she now serves as Senior Pastor.

Others were hired to address a specific need, beyond what the congregation was already doing. Lynne's congregation, a large downtown institution, added her position, Director of Community Ministries, because the new pastor wanted to communicate to the city that "the church existed." He prepared the congregation prior to her coming and then turned her loose to lead the congregation in ministry to their city. So although it was a new position, it was clearly seen as a felt need and related to a primary function of the church.

Although these social workers are engaged with population groups that are familiar in social work practice, their work has features distinctive from social work with those same population groups in social service agencies. For example, Carl's work with persons with chronic mental illness is different on his side of the street, in the congregation that he leads in an inner city neighborhood, than what social workers across the street do with the same population group in a day treatment program. He is weaving persons into the community of faith who may otherwise be isolated by an illness that affects social skills and interpersonal connections, complementing and supporting the clinical work of the day treatment program. Glenda provides contractual clinical services to her Catholic parish. Her practice with couples referred by her priest in marriage preparation is different from what she does with couples who come to her for premarital counseling in her private practice. Those referred by her priest know she is conducting an assessment of their readiness for marriage that she is sharing with their priest and that she will address Catholic teachings about marriage and their connection to the Church that are not necessarily part of her private practice with couples.

Lois' practice with senior adults and their families in and through her congregation has a different focus and character from her earlier practice in a geriatric wellness center. The clients may be much the same demographically, and perhaps even the same people, but the practice context, the purpose and mission of the work, and even the clients' expectations of the services they will receive from a congregation shape what these social workers do differently in this setting than in other settings. Congregational social work requires specialized knowledge and skill for work with specific population groups, as well as for work in a congregational context.

The practice context, the purpose and mission of the work, and even the clients' expectations of the services they will receive from a congregation shape what these social workers do differently in this setting than in other settings.

In our first analysis of our interview data, we focused on the array of programs and services these social workers provide or direct. Our initial perspective was that social workers lead a congregation's ministry in its community, and so that was what we were looking to find. Indeed, we learned that these social workers engage in and lead ministries that address immediate human needs (hunger, homelessness), intervene in crises, collaborate with other organizations, and provide the direct clinical services of counseling, support groups and family life educational programming—they do community ministry.

Not all of their work fits into those categories, however. They also engage in activities that we identified as "creating community" and as "leading spiritually"—they preach occasionally or more often, teach Bible studies, and connect people to one another for support and community. Those tasks were square pegs that did not seem to fit our round hole of community ministry. Moreover, the social workers engaged in these activities as a part of their daily routine with all whose lives were touched in some way by the congregation and its leaders, whether they were those within the congregation or those in the neighborhoods the congregation sought to serve.

To create further confusion for us, none of the categories we created to understand social work activity were mutually exclusive. For example, "education" included family life education and support groups similar to what social workers do in the fields of medical social work and family and children's services and so can be considered the social service of "education and counseling." But educational activities also included leading Bible studies and writing curriculum, including writing a family life education curriculum based on biblical teachings. In other words, the array of programs and services that congregational social workers lead not only has a diversity of targets but they also address different and often multiple purposes in the life of the congregation.

We began again, therefore, and tried to understand the functions of these social workers in the life of their congregations. In other words, the focus became "what are the roles a social worker has in the life of the congregation," rather than "what are the services and who are the clients served." The question shifted from "What do social workers do?" to "How do social workers contribute to the mission and purposes of congregational life?" It is a short leap, then, to positing answers to the questions: "How do social workers function as congregational leaders?" and "Why do congregations choose social workers to lead them?"

Leading in the Core Functions of Congregations

As described in the previous chapter, virtually every congregation engages in four core functions: worship, community, education, and missions. Stott (2007) has pointed out these four functions in the life of the first church, as described in Acts 2:42-47. They worshipped together, continuing to spend time together in the temple and praising God together as they shared meals (vs. 46). They were a community—they devoted themselves to "fellowship" (vs. 42); they were "together," and shared everything with one another (vs. 44). They engaged in education, devoting themselves to the apostles' teaching (vs. 42). And they ministered to others "as any had need" (vs. 45). Congregational social workers provide leadership in more than one, and sometimes all, of these functions. In fact, we would hypothesize that the broader their work is in addressing all four functions of congregational life, the more central they are to the life of the congregation. To the extent that the social worker is intentional about relating the work to the congregation's primary functions, the social worker is at the heart of leadership.

The array of programs and services that congregational social workers lead not only have a diversity of targets but they also address different and often more than one purpose in the life of the congregation.

For example, a tutoring program may be seen primarily as "missions," a way to serve the neighborhood. But the social worker preparing mentors to relate to children, particularly children from different cultural and socio-economic groups than the mentors, is doing mentor "education." The social worker facilitates mentors learning the skills of tutoring, how to engage and build a relationship with a child, and an understanding and appreciation for the cultural context of the child and the child's family.

Our own experiences[23] suggest that the social worker also can connect mentoring to Bible study and worship. Jesus taught that welcoming children, those who are small and powerless, is welcoming Jesus (Mark 9:37)—"I was a stranger and you welcomed me" (Matthew 25:35). Mentors are providing care for the "stranger" who is the presence of Christ with us when they tutor a Spanish-speaking child in English or help a child who is from an impoverished community learn the skills to succeed in school.

Formal services of worship begin with a prayer of "invocation," inviting God to be present or acknowledging that God is present. Service, too, is optimally framed as a way of welcoming the presence of God. Dorothy Day said that someone who cannot see the face of God in the face of someone who is poor is an atheist indeed (Forest, 1995).

Just as the mentoring experience can become "worship" for mentors, so is their gathering with one another to share their experiences in mentoring. Their sharing can itself be a form of prayer, and they can also make prayer for children, teachers, families, and one another a part of their gathering. As they convene and lead groups of mentors sharing their experiences, the congregational social worker is weaving them into "community" with one another. One of the most effective ways of building community relationships is engagement in a shared task. As mentors form relationships with children, they are eager to tell others their experiences with those who share their commitment to helping children succeed in school. Mentors learn from and support one another, and become friends—and community—in the process. In summary, although mentoring may be a missions project of the congregation, a congregational leader can also envision and shape that project to serve all four congregational functions, including not only missions but also an opportunity for the mentors themselves to worship, to have fellowship with one another and those they serve, and to learn more deeply about Christian faith as they serve and reflect together on their experiences.

Because congregational activities ideally serve these multiple functions, sometimes all at the same time, it is counterproductive to try to disentangle spiritual and social activities. "People pray together, study together, and worship together and are, at once, creating a community and honoring their god" (Ammerman, 2005, p. 51). We would add that they serve together, too, and that this service—missions—not only is, but also should be framed as worship, as Christian education, and as a way to build community with one another. The most central activities for a congregation are those that ultimately address several of these central congregational functions rather than just one alone.

Service—missions—not only is, but also should be framed as worship, as Christian education, and as a way to build community with one another.

We began our research with the assumption that social workers are engaged primarily in leading congregational mission activities. Those activities are most like what we learned in social work education, and we are guessing that these congregational social workers also began their work with that same assumption—social workers lead in community ministries. As a consequence, although social workers are engaged in the other functions of the congregation, it feels less like what they were professionally prepared to do. There may be less certainty that those activities really *are* social work. For example, Jeanie is the Mission Outreach Coordinator for her congregation. She came to her work from a background in medical social work. She said about her work, "People call in for services. That's when I am a 'pure social worker.'" What she implies is that all the other ways she provides leadership in her congregation may be her job, but they are not really "pure" from a social work perspective.

Not seeing that it is appropriate for social workers to lead in the functions of worship, community building, and Christian education may keep social workers from engaging fully in the leadership of the congregation. Or alternatively, they engage in this leadership, but they define it as "not social work," contributing to a dual identity in their work of social worker and religious leader.

For example, when we talked with Beth almost a year after she became a senior pastor, she mused that she had always seen herself as a minister. In her position on the staff of her previous congregation, her job was "to connect people in the church with people in the community who were in need with ministries that could help transform lives." Now, as senior pastor, she says that focus still "colors" her preaching and the direction she is seeking to lead her congregation, but her days are now filled with worship preparation, administration, and caring for the congregation itself. As a consequence, she said:

> I have had to struggle a little with some guilt. Have I stepped away from some of my call by not being so day-to-day engaged in connecting our congregation with the community? But then, I'm still really using my social work skills, but in a pastoral care way because the pastoral care needs of the congregation are so great.

Beth feels somewhat torn; is it still her calling to social work if she is responding to the needs within the congregation—as pastor—rather than to the needs in the neighborhood? She described what she meant by "pastoral care" with two examples. She had been helping a church member, whose husband is in declining health, decide whether or not to use hospice. She had also been providing support for an adoptive family who had been caring for the infant they were adopting for a number of weeks, when, just before the adoption was finalized, the birth father came forward and the family brokenheartedly relinquished the infant to the adoption agency. She summarized, "Before I saw my role as connecting the church with people who were low income or kids who were at-risk, and now I feel like I'm using all my social work skills with my church members." Clearly, if these two pastoral care situations had been with clients in an agency, they would unquestionably be within the realm of social work expertise.

What she and these other pioneering social workers taught us is that to be most effective as congregational leaders, social workers not only can be, but need to be, engaged in leading in all aspects of congregational life, including worship, Christian education, fellowship/community—and ministry.

Social work is a profession that emphasizes that context helps define effective practice. Not only does Jeanie's work with senior adults look different in a congregation setting from her previous work in a geriatric wellness center, but they both differ from social work with senior adults in Adult Protective Services, or from social work with senior adults in a nursing home serving seniors with Alzheimer's disease. The nature of social work is its adaptation to setting, bringing the knowledge, values, and skills of social work to help an organization achieve its mission as that mission is congruent with social work values.

Social workers not only can be, but need to be, engaged in leading in all aspects of congregational life, including worship, Christian education, fellowship/community—and ministry.

We found that, of the four functions of congregational life, these social workers are, on average, engaged in three of the four functions.[24] Only three of the interviewees described just one of these functions as their responsibility, and that function was "missions." In contrast, 33 social workers described ways in which they address three of the functions in their daily work. As we would have predicted, almost all were providing leadership in the mission and community functions of congregational life. Worship was the least common function we identified; but then, we did not begin this project expecting social workers to be leaders in worship and Christian education in the "traditional" church understanding of what these terms mean. Therefore, we did not ask about these functions—we stumbled across them as we heard the stories of their work. If we had been looking and asking, we may have learned that far more of these interviewees are engaged in three or all four of these congregational functions.

We have been working in the field of congregational social work for almost 40 years—80 years if you add up our two careers! We both have spoken and preached frequently in congregations. We have led Christian education and prepared Christian education literature for others to use in leading. Where Diana was invited to write curriculum and lead workshops on marriage and family life, Gaynor was invited to equip pastors for leading their congregations in responding to persons with HIV/AIDS and to the social problem of pornography. Despite our own professional leadership in worship and education, we did not think to put questions in our interview protocol about these functions of congregational life. We, too, are creatures of an environment that presumes that the focus of congregational social work is the engagement of the congregation in responding to the needs of the neighborhood and world, as though that function can be addressed separately from worship and Christian education, or from the development of the community fellowship. It cannot. If we were slow to come to that understanding as educators in this field, it is clear that these social workers have had little guidance in how to conceptualize their roles in congregational life.

If these social workers had little framework for defining their roles in congregational life, so did the congregations who engaged them as leaders. Many reported that their responsibilities changed and grew dramatically. As Lois said, "I have enlarged my responsibilities and they've come to learn what I can do for them as I've been there longer." Beth's pastor saw the potential for much more than the part-time college ministry she was hired to lead, wanting to expand the congregation's ministry in its neighborhood. Beth began that work in the community from the beginning, taking responsibility for the congregation's benevolence (emergency assistance) ministry. As she led and went from part-time to fulltime, her congregation became known for its missions and ministry, and she said that the result was, "The congregation calls on me for everything." When she left to become a pastor in another state, the congregation sought to replace her with a full-time social worker.

Even Jeffrey, an employee of an agency funded by the Catholic Archdiocese with clear initial expectations, has experienced his responsibilities expanding over time as the archdiocese developed a vision for serving the "total community," not just Catholics: "We offer a vision of life as a gift to the whole community." These social workers provide clear evidence that their impact in congregations is, more often than not, one that emerges as the congregations gain clarity of the social workers' roles and purpose in the congregation. It truly is an emergent process of discovering together, social worker and congregation, how everything can come together in creating and living out a shared vision. Such a shared vision cannot be imposed from outside but develops in relationship and over time.

These social workers have had the opportunity to cast a vision for their work and then pursue it, expanding and defining their roles in relationship with the congregations they lead.

These social workers have had the opportunity to cast a vision for their work and then pursue it, expanding and defining their roles in relationship with the congregations they lead. Often, in addition to little understanding from the congregations they serve, they have had little support from their profession; they have had to figure it out as they have found their way through the work.

Their Roles in Congregational Life

We define role as a particular set of behaviors enacted in relationship with other people; it is who the social workers say they are to others and live out in their actions, and it is who others would say the social workers are as they experience them. Congregations assign some roles to the social worker—e.g., minister with college students, "cruise director" for senior adults. The social worker assumes some roles—e.g., director of emergency assistance, director of ministry to the neighborhood. Most roles are shaped not by one or the other but by a combination of the expectations of others—the congregation, the profession, the larger culture—and those of the social worker. It is the interaction of these expectations over time that shapes the role of a congregational social worker.

As much as the congregations they serve shape the roles of these social workers, the roles themselves are still recognizable as "social work." Three of these 51 social workers actually bear the title "social worker;" many of their roles, however, are familiar in other social work professional contexts. In analyzing the interview transcripts, we identified several social work roles that are common in social service organizations –administrator, advocate, change agent, clinician/counselor, connector/networker, consultant, and researcher (e.g., Popple & Leighninger, 2011; Segal, Gerdes, & Steiner, 2010). Even Carl, with the title "pastor," said that "the majority of the time I am utilizing my social work skills." Jeanie says that what she is doing is "strengths-based social work; old-fashioned social work where I identify needs and find solutions."

A number of the interviewees said that the congregation knows and sees them in the role of a social worker, even though they bear a different title. Inez bears the title "Christian counselor" for her congregation, but she noted that she displays her license prominently and makes sure that clients know her professional role. Most (75%) of these social workers have a state social work license, even though their work setting and state laws vary from state to state, and many exempt those whose titles are not "social worker" as well as any "recognized religious practitioner" (e.g., Texas State Legislature, 2003, Sec. 505.003.4B).

Roles Particular to the Congregational Setting

Despite the commonalities in the roles of these social workers with social work in other settings, there are roles that seem unique to this setting, or at the very least, unusual in other professional social work contexts. These roles fall in two categories: "minister/pastor/religious" and "community member/friend."

Religious Leader

Two thirds of these social workers carry titles that contain words such as "minister," "ministries," "pastor," and "missions" rather than "social worker," replicating earlier research finding that most congregational social workers carry titles that reflect their roles as religious leaders (Garland, 1987b). Their titles locate them in a position of congregational leadership the way the role designation "social worker" might not. At first blush, the use of a title appears to downplay or even sideline their roles as social workers. These titles make it hard to sort out how many social workers there really are in congregational leadership, or who they are. These titles may appear, and in some cases actually may be, a devaluing of their social work preparation as appropriate for the roles they fill.

Upon deeper reflection, however, titling their positions with language specific to the context for practice is not unusual for social workers. In fact, these various titles accentuate their roles as leaders. In other words, a title other than social worker may not be devaluing of the social worker or the social work profession, but quite the opposite. It is recognition that the social worker is in a position of particular responsibility or leadership, just as the leader of a social work school probably bears the title "Program Director" or "Dean," a hospital social worker may carry the title "Discharge Planner," a social worker in a clinic may be called "Therapist," and a member of the state or federal legislature carries the title "Senator" or "Representative." Each of these positions carries role expectations somewhat unique from other settings in social work. For example, the Senator is a politician, a fundraiser, a political party leader. Yet, the Senator who was a social worker presumably still is a social worker, bringing the knowledge, values, and skills of social work to a unique and significant setting for social work practice.

Neither legislative bodies nor hospitals nor congregations are social service agencies, yet their mission and purpose have significance for the profession of social work and the populations whom social workers serve. Social workers bring important knowledge, values, and skills to Congressional bodies as well as to congregations.

Neither Congressional bodies nor hospitals nor congregations are social service agencies, yet their mission and purpose have significance for the profession of social work and the populations that social workers serve.

Many congregational social workers are responsible for leading the local and global missions of their congregations. The social services they provide or facilitate are the current expression of that missions focus. The impetus for service lies in the congregation's religious beliefs about God and what it means to be faithful. Gordon had been working in Child Protective Services, doing abuse investigations, when the Church of Christ congregation called him to be its youth minister three years before we talked. He described to us how his role as a leader in global missions has emerged over those three years:

> The congregation began with pretty low expectations as far as how broad my influence was going to be. They expected me to take care of the students. They were not expecting me to be a part of leading the congregation into outreach, into more global issues .... I think the congregation has benefitted from my social work background because I'm driven to be aware of what's going on not only in our community but also globally.

Gordon illustrates how these social workers developed what we called "role legitimacy," over time, in which the congregations recognized them as providing needed professional expertise to the leadership of the congregation. Role legitimacy for these social workers was seldom ascribed because of the professional degrees they had earned. Rather, it was earned over time, as they demonstrated their expertise and their ability to lead.

Similarly, Kathleen was hired as the Minister of Benevolence and Missions, overseeing the crisis ministries of her congregation and also another congregation in their town. Over time, her responsibilities are growing to a broader mission focus that includes the state, nation, and international mission initiatives. Commenting on how her responsibilities have expanded, she said, "That is something that I am just getting into so I don't know exactly what it is going to look like in the future." Again, it seems to be in the doing of the work that the role of the congregational social worker begins to unfold.

Community Member/Friend

Another role common for congregational social workers is that of "community member" and even "friend" to members of the congregation. Social work is certainly relational in many settings, and congregations are hardly unique in the challenge created by dual and multiple relationships. Anytime a social worker is employed in a setting that is also the social worker's community, such relationships are possible—e.g., the school social worker whose own child is a student in the school or whose sibling is a teacher; the social worker in a mental health community center whose spouse is a community pastor or police officer; the community developer who lives in the community being served; and so forth.

In a congregation, the roles are often not only dual but often multiple. The social worker in this context, we suggest, has to adjust to this ambiguity of roles. They are like ropes of intertwined threads that include not only the professional relationship but also the *expectation* that the social worker is a member of the community. It is often assumed that social workers will join their employing congregations if they are not already members; contribute financially from personal finances; serve as a choir member and/or Sunday School teacher; be present for many congregational activities, not just those the social workers lead; and share personal life as well as professional competence with others in the congregation.

In some practice settings, dual relationships may be considered problematic or even unethical. In congregational settings, however, multiple relationships are inevitable, unavoidable, and important, if managed well, for the overall influence and effectiveness of the social worker. Sometimes they do create dilemmas that have to be addressed and, if mismanaged, dual relationships pose risk for harm. We will explore dual and multiple relationships in more depth in Chapter 5.

Professional Identity

"Professional identity" is the way individuals define themselves in their own internal dialogue, the image of themselves they hold. One's professional identity may or may not match with how others see a person. "Identity" changes over time, often in interaction with changing roles, but it is slower to change than roles. Professional identity includes identifying with the values, knowledge base, and colleagues of the profession (Gustafson, 1982; Netting, Kettner, & McMurtry, 2012; Sullivan, 2005).

The social worker's identity is important not only for understanding self-perceptions but also because the social worker's professional identity influences the scope and tasks of congregational leadership and service provision the social worker seeks or is willing to do. In other words, identity influences role, just as role influences identity.

Several of these social workers indicated how fluid and even amorphous their

Identity influences role, just as role influences identity.

initial job description and responsibilities were, and how their understanding of themselves as professionals has shaped their work over time. Abigail told of how the pastor of the large Bible church where she serves, with a staff of 300 members, hired her to direct the social ministries of the congregation and gave her the responsibility of making a place for herself in the leadership of the congregation. Similarly, Lois said, "I have enlarged my responsibilities and they've come to learn what I can do for them as I've been there longer." For example, instead of just providing direct services to senior adults, she has equipped volunteers to be the direct service providers.

Their congregations placed a number of these social workers, like Abigail and Lois, in the role of social work they understood professionally, that of providing direct services. Although they may have begun the work as direct service providers, *they saw themselves* as *religious leaders* defining the work and not just accepting it as defined. They broadened their roles to that of equipping the congregation for ministry in the congregation's neighborhoods and beyond. They had built trust and shown competence within the work of the congregation so that the congregation affirmed and welcomed this expanded view of the social worker role.

In yet other examples, Austin has used his identity as a religious leader to make community ministries "part of the central mission of the church." Steven, an employee in a denominational agency working with congregations, sees himself as a religious leader and a congregational social worker empowering and equipping congregations to collaborate with agencies who may have a shared vision for ministry/service. He is not solely a social worker using the congregation as a resource for funds and volunteers for his agency's foster care programs, as the agency initially imagined his role.

The professional identities of these social workers are as diverse as their individual journeys, shaped as they are by their experiences. Those experiences include social work education and, for some, previous professional experiences. For most, they include lifelong experiences in one or more congregations in which they grew up and participated as adults. For many, their identity includes education in religion and theology, whether that education took place formally in a university or seminary, or in the less formal programs of Christian education in the congregations of their childhood and beyond– or both. Finally, many described a profound sense of vocational calling that emerged through their spiritual experiences individually or in the context of a faith community. We will explore these shapers of professional identity more fully in Chapter 8.

For some, their professional identities are singularly "social worker." For others, their dominant identity is as "minister," "pastor," or even "spiritual director," and social work is a skills set that they use. Still others see themselves with a complex identity that has dual expression incorporating both religious leader and social worker.

Social Worker

The professional identity "social worker" dominates, although is not always the only identity, for most (n=40) of these social workers. Obviously, the sampling of our research leaned toward those with a social work identity, taking place as it did through professional social work and social work educational channels.

Inez exemplifies those whose professional identity is "social worker." A full-time social work faculty member, Inez is serving as a part-time social worker on her congregation's staff, providing clinical services both to congregants and to those outside the congregation. The congregation pays her salary, so there is no client fee for her services. The current congregation is the second in which Inez has served. Even though Inez' title is "church counselor," she said, "I want to be the church social worker," and she wrote her own job description as "social worker."

Barry's title is Pastor of Care Ministries, the second social worker to serve his congregation in this role. His responsibility is primarily to respond to the needs of his 3,000-member congregation through visiting persons who have been hospitalized or placed in nursing homes or home health care. He also provides counseling and conducts marriages and funerals. Barry says that he identifies himself as a social worker "because of my training and the way I think about things."

Licensure is important to these social workers because being licensed underscores their identity, even though, as religious employees, their states do not require them to be licensed. As Inez said:

> Other community agencies obviously have more respect for someone who has a license. It's not just some person who's doing counseling at this church. It's somebody who actually had some training, and I think that's viewed with respect.

Their identity as a social worker also means that they engage in social work continuing education and carry malpractice insurance. Conferences and workshops are particularly important since most of these social workers are professionally isolated, the only social worker in their employment setting.

Some respondents see themselves *exclusively* as social workers, not as religious leaders, and often the congregational context contributes to that exclusive identity—they are excluded from leader roles. Alice is a social work professor who volunteers in a congregation where women cannot serve as leaders of the congregation itself. She leads a single mothers' group, however, and serves as a mentor and friend to the women in the group. Alice said, "I don't see myself as a minister; I identify as a Christian social worker." Alice does not chafe at the gender restrictions; they fit her own sense of identity as a woman and as a professional.

Because their identities are "social worker" does not mean that their identities are separate from their religious and spiritual understanding of themselves, however. Almost half (n=16) of these 40 social workers whose identity is singularly "social worker" voiced a sense of spiritual calling to social work, even though they may not have initially experienced a calling to congregational social work specifically. One said: "When I started in social work, it was a clear direction from God to go into social work." These social workers believed that God called them to be social workers and that God has directed their paths to the work they do. Lynne says that she has integrated social work into the very core of her identity: "It's a way of thinking, doing, and it works anywhere with anything; it's just the way I function."

Becky is the Director of Special Ministries for her congregation, working with the deaf congregation that is co-located there. Her parents are deaf, and she grew up in a bi-cultural world, at home in both the hearing and the deaf communities. She chose social work from a sense of calling to work with deaf congregations:

> When I went into social work it was because I knew I could be Christ to every person that came to me .... Anything that was at [the school of social work] to me was ministry. Every teacher, every professor, every practicum—everything was ministry. It isn't a program; it isn't a career, it is, simply put, full-time ministry. My calling was always to serve God, and it would be in the social work field.

Like Becky, several interviewees chose to go to social work school very deliberately as a response to their sense of spiritual calling. Abigail was one of those who experienced that calling as a teenager and pursued it into a BSW program:

> I knew I was called to be a social worker when I was a senior in high school. And really it was because I had a relationship with God; I knew I was called to be a social worker. I had no idea what I was going to do with social work. I had no idea I was going to be working in a church. Even when I graduated with my social work degree I did not have any idea I would be working in a church. But I went through the steps and did what I was supposed to do to get a degree and get a license and I said, "Okay Lord, where do I go from here?" Anytime I looked at another field, I was always drawn right back to social work. I knew I was supposed to be helping people and just ministering the love of God's people in whatever environment that meant.

Moreover, that sense of vocation gives ongoing determination to continue when the work is hard. Heather is the Director of the Refugee Program for her Catholic archdiocese, working with congregations to resettle international refugees in this country. She said:

> I'm happy and I feel fulfilled, but there are times when it is really tough. I don't have the energy for this work. And that's when it becomes a vocation, [and I say to myself]: "God put you here and you have to put forth the energy and complete His will."

She finds direction for her days in the words of Jesus: "I was a stranger in the land and you welcomed me."

Pastor or Minister

A smaller group of these social workers (n =16) see themselves primarily, although not always exclusively, as a pastor or religious leader. Ben is the full-time pastor of an ethnically diverse nondenominational congregation. He also is the full-time director of a university's social work program. He already has a Ph.D. in social work, and is now completing a Master of Pastoral Studies degree. He told us, "The pastor piece takes precedence; it is the first thing I think about when I get up." He goes on to say that he sees both of these identities, pastor and social worker, as his "calling."

Some of the women we interviewed have chosen social work as the means by which to be "in ministry" when routes of religious leadership are open to men alone in their tradition. Haley has completed two graduate degrees, a Master of Social Work and a Master of Pastoral Ministry. She now serves as the Spiritual Director of a Catholic residential treatment center. She talks about her identity as one of "priest" in a Catholic tradition that does not allow her that role:

> As a Catholic woman, I'm not able to be a priest, so I wasn't able to even consider that option. So I basically have found the next best thing, to be leading a chapel of children is as close as I'm going to get to being a priest. That is very satisfying to me.

Some of the women we interviewed have chosen social work as the means by which to be "in ministry" when routes of religious leadership are open to men alone in their tradition.

A few of these social workers identify themselves primarily as pastors. Carl says that he sees himself as a "pastor who uses social work skills."

Howard is the associate pastor of his large congregation. When he took on this role, unlike others who deliberately have maintained their state licensure, he relinquished his social work license. He said: "I actually don't even have my diplomas up in my office; that's been a conscious decision on my part." He received his MSW from a public university, and it is possible that he and others who have an either/or identity felt compelled to choose by a professional culture that has not recognized dual professional identities. Howard went on to say, however, "My MSW training provided a broad platform from which I work on a daily basis." It prepared him for working with folks in the congregation "with pretty regular issues in the life of any congregation, whether its substance abuse, or marital discord, or feelings around depression or anxiety." He uses his social work education, but he does not identify himself to others—or to himself—as a social worker.

Dual Identities

A few of these social workers identify themselves both as "minister" and "social worker," yet see them as two distinct identities—intertwined, perhaps, but still a duo. David, an Associate Pastor, says, "I keep my membership in NASW; I will always think of myself as a social worker, but I also consider myself a minister." The key words are "but" and "also."

Ben, the full-time senior pastor and the full-time social work program director, illustrates this duality—he is doing two full-time jobs. He gives an example of his dual identity from the university classroom:

> Like the cartoon, "Cat-dog;" it just depends on what perspective you are looking at it at any given moment. I'm always both .... I'll give you an example. I work with a homeless shelter. In my Human Diversity class, I invite members of the homeless shelter into the class. The individuals from the shelter will refer to me as, "Pastor." In the class, the students refer to me as "Dr." It gets to be somewhat confusing.

The dual identities sometime create tensions and even conflict. Adam served as director of a denominationally affiliated inner city mission that has become a congregation. He is pastor and also directs the social ministries of the mission center. Although he sees social work and ministry as "intertwined," he also notes that the two identities are sometimes dissonant: "It is difficult and there are times that I felt pulled one direction or the other." Congregational social workers live this ambiguity of dual identities.

Adam had completed a dual master's degree program in social work and divinity. Like Adam, virtually all of those who had formal education to prepare them for social work in a congregational setting experienced their education as "dual" in focus. Dual degree programs in social work (Master of Social Work) and theology or divinity (Master of Divinity or Master of Theological Studies) are common in social work education. Not only do 10 religiously affiliated universities offer dual degrees in theology and social work, but a dozen public/state universities have dual degree partnerships with other institutions, often seminaries.[25] Such an educational experience implicitly communicates a dual identity.

It would be interesting to know if social workers who have dual degrees in public health, law, and business also have dual identities; we do not know of research that has

The history of separation of the social work education from a religious identity during the century that social work education was developing has no doubt contributed to a sense of duality.

explored this issue of dual professional identities, however.[26] The history of separation of social work education from a religious identity during the century that social work education was developing has perhaps contributed to a sense of duality more so than in these other fields where it is common to combine degree programs to prepare for particular practice settings.

An Integrated Identity

Most of those we interviewed have a professional identity that integrates the professions of social work and religious leadership as two facets of one whole, seeing them as complementary rather than in tension. We drew our sample in part by contacting social work educators to help us find their alumni. We were surprised when several of the educators we contacted themselves are serving as congregational social workers, working two jobs, like Ben, as social worker educators and congregational social workers. Working in two settings, it is understandable that they would have two identities, yet a number of them, unlike Ben, see their identities as integrated. Earl, a counselor in his congregation and a lecturer in psychology at the nearby college, illustrates:

Sometimes I put the social work hat on the top of the minister hat and social work is at the forefront—like when I am speaking at a professional conference. But the minister hat is always a part of me. Social work gives my ministry direction, history, and connection to other people—a way to understand them and me.

Inez is also a social work lecturer who provides clinical services to persons in her congregation. She also uses "hats" as a way to describe the relationship of religious leadership and social work:

> Linking people with needs with people who have resources is the whole point of ministry—and of social work. It's the same hat, with a different flower in it. Ministers of youth have another flower. They're all ministers and yet have different educational training. They're all ministers' hats, but mine is citron, yellow for social work.[27]

Not all of those with "integrated" identities are social work educators, however. Caleb is a member of a Roman Catholic religious order who felt drawn to work with persons in poverty. He subsequently completed his MSW and now serves a parish in a developing country. He sees the identities of religious leader and social worker as being dual, yet so integrated that he cannot pull them apart: "You can't do one without the other; you can't say you're doing the gospel without doing the social work." We heard a similar refrain from several of these social workers. Daniel, the Pastor of Care ministries for his congregation, describes how these two identities are inseparable:

> I can't separate the two. If I tried, I couldn't get social work out of my ministry or my ministry out of my social work. I say to people that I have professional identity confusion. I'm a pastor; I'm ordained and trained to do ministry, recognized as a minister, a reverend. But I'm also a licensed social worker and I worked in counseling settings for 15 years.

The integration of these two roles does not negate the challenges—the "confusion" Daniel feels—of a congregational context for social work. Nevertheless, challenges do not mean that the two are not integral to one another, according to Gina, the national Director of Church and Community Initiatives for a large agency:

> I have not experienced incompatibility between the two. If I'm doing good social work, it's good ministry as well. And if I'm doing good ministry, there's no reason it can't be good professional social work.

Summary: Who is a Social Worker?

A curious question that has emerged from our conversations with these social workers that has no clear answer is one that seems rather simple on the surface—Who is a social worker? Are these religious leaders we interviewed social workers because that is how they identify themselves professionally? Is it because they completed a social work degree? Is it state licensure? Is it being employed and making money as a professional, or can volunteers be practicing as social workers? If social workers serve as volunteers, are they social workers in that setting? In other words, if we are defining the field of congregational social work, what are the boundaries outside of which we would say that someone is *not* a social worker, even, perhaps, if they think of themselves as social workers? Or if some leaders think of themselves as pastors or priests and not as a social worker, if they obtained social work degrees so that they could use social work knowledge and skills but not "be" social workers—do we call them social workers anyway?

There are costs and benefits to being known as a social worker. In some communities and context, being known as a social worker provides professional credibility and influence, while in others it may raise suspicions or even spark defensiveness. Our own experiences have been that in some congregational settings, social workers are held in high esteem, whereas in others, they are associated with public social policies and programs that are considered problematic rather than helpful.

After talking with these 51 social workers, we concluded that the professional identity "social worker" appears to be the consequence of several factors that reach a tipping point of others' perspectives and one's self identity, and there may not be agreement between the two.

The professional identity "social worker" appears to be the consequence of several factors that reach a tipping point of others' perspectives and one's self identity, and there may not be agreement between the two.

The most important factor appears to be the successful completion of a social work degree, either at the baccalaureate or graduate level. Licensure laws in many states have molded our understanding of the identity of social worker requiring that degree, even if it alone is not enough for licensure. Despite common use of the term "social worker" for well-meaning nonprofessionals, social workers are, in fact, degreed professionals.

A second factor that is not quite as fail safe but still important to so many of these social workers is state licensure. "Title protection"—one cannot publically identify self as a social worker without a state license—is written into approximately 30 states' laws and so into the conscience of professionals.[28] When one of these social workers decided to "give up" the identity of social worker to identify himself as a pastor, he gave up his state social work license. Even so, licensure laws have exception clauses that exempt religious employees from the licensure requirement, so the lack of a license does not deny the identity "social worker" to those who choose to avoid state recognition or just see it as an unnecessary cost of money and effort. Even faculties in schools of social work teaching in states with title protection laws may choose not to be licensed, if they are not also engaged in direct practice with clients. Nevertheless, most of these educators who have social work degrees identify themselves as social workers.

A third factor involves the professional responsibilities that the social worker carries, whether those responsibilities are paid employment or unpaid "volunteer" work. It is this third factor that we are pondering as we explore the work of these congregational social workers. We may think we know when a social worker is "not a social worker"—when parenting a child, when shopping for groceries, when jogging in the neighborhood. Or is our professional identity something we never really lay down, but part of the fabric of our personhood? Parenting a child is a time when we attempt to live what we know about teaching self-discipline and instilling courage and compassion in a child—and many of us learned the theories of child development in social work school. When those parenting experiences and those theories become fodder for developing a parenting course for congregational families, is it then social work? Is someone with a social work degree that chooses to teach in an underserved neighborhood school a social worker or a teacher—or both?

We think of another example related to the above discussion. Shopping for groceries may be a time when we run into a congregational member whom we learn is in crisis. A chance meeting becomes a moment to express compassion and to explore what the congregation can do to be supportive. Standing in the grocery store on a Saturday morning, one is a congregant and the other may be a social worker, depending on how the person sees himself and how the congregant identifies the social worker. As a social worker jogs through the neighborhood, a family in the congregation passes by and waves. And the social worker as a religious leader has modeled a holistic view of the Christian life in which care for the body is a way we discipline ourselves for living into the calling on our lives. In other words, professional identity is not something we put on with our work clothes when we go to work and change out of when we come home, especially if home is in the midst of the community and neighborhood where we serve.

Is our professional identity something we never really lay down, but part of the fabric of our personhood?

We started our research with a simple definition of who is a social worker. They were those who self-identified and so volunteered to talk to us, and they were those with social work degrees. They taught us how social workers are leading congregations. In the chapters that follow, we will explore the professional responsibilities of congregational social workers in more depth—and how writing that parenting course and providing that grocery store support and modeling the importance of healthy disciplines are also professional social work.

Chapter 4
Leading in Worship and Christian Education

Of the four functions of congregational life—worship, religious education, building community, and service—worship and religious education distinguish congregations from other organizations and collectives of people. Sororities, fraternities, professional groups, bowling leagues, and supper clubs gather to be community. Some of those same kinds of groups gather to engage in service together. But the functions of worship and religious education uniquely characterize these gatherings called congregations, which make them unique settings for social work practice. Many of the social workers we interviewed are providing leadership in worship and Christian education, and bringing their professional values and knowledge to that leadership.

Leading Worship

Many Christians believe that any place and any time can be a place of worship, whether alone or with others. The Apostle Paul exhorted Christians to pray—communicate with God—without ceasing, to give thanks in all circumstances (1 Thessalonians 5:16-18). Christians can worship as they sit on the back porch in the cool of the evening, as they listen to music, as they drive down the road, as they sit at the bedside vigil of a dying beloved family member or friend, or as they tutor a child.

Even though Christians can worship by themselves, anywhere, they also have a need to be part of a gathered community of faith. Jesus told his followers that wherever two or three gathered in His name, He would be with them (Matthew 18:20). The doctrine of the Trinity shows us that the very essence of God is community (Byars, 2000). There is no New Testament concept of faith as private, apart from the community. To be a Christian means being incorporated into a body—the body of Christ (Byars, 2000).

The disciples gathered for prayer together in the early days after Jesus' ascension (Acts 1:14). The growing church gathered for daily worship and eating together (Acts 2:44-46). Although one person can pray alone, sing alone, and meditate alone, one person alone cannot be the body of Christ. Paul points out in 1 Corinthians 12:25 that it takes all the members together to complete the body and "there should be no division in the body." The very word "congregation" derives from the verb "congregate," to gather as a group. Even though there is some audience-like behavior in many congregational worship services, there are almost always elements of the service that call for participation together in coordinated ways—standing and sitting, kneeling, singing, clapping hands, dancing, and reciting. Worship in African-American congregations is particularly noted for inclusion of the whole being in responsive celebration, involving voice in singing and calling out, as well as body in dancing, clapping and embracing others. Hispanic congregations also emphasize participation; for example, choirs are not so much performers but leading others as they join in the music of worship (Maynard-Reid, 2000).

Worship as a congregation begins in the basic activity of coming together, of gathering. Some printed programs of worship actually name the first item on the worship schedule as "gathering." The motives of those gathering may be myriad and even conflicting. Some people gather because they want to see their friends, or they want to make friends. Some gather because they want others to consider them as faithful, or because they know *not* gathering will mean conflict with a family member or friend who wants them there. Some gather because they want to encourage others—friends or children or neighbor—to be there, and so they are trying to set an example. Some attend because they seek God's favor or forgiveness or grace. Some worry that God will judge them negatively if they do not participate in this gathering of God's people. Some attend because attendance is a habit formed in childhood that they have continued. Some people go because they are seeking entertainment or inspiration. Some go out of gratitude or despair, or to seek answers or comfort in the challenges of life.

Gathering is an end in itself, an acknowledgement that through Jesus Christ we are supposed to be united as one body.

Whatever the mix of motives, Christian thought teaches that gathering is an end in itself, an acknowledgement that through Jesus Christ we are supposed to be united as one body (Burkhart, 1982). Christians believe that worship is not simply a practice of Christian life, or something we do to fill our "spiritual" tanks to make it through another week—it is the reason we exist. Life's ultimate purpose is to glorify God and enjoy God's presence—worship is an end in itself (Arzola, 2011). Worship embraces all that we are and all that we have—given by God, and returning to God in praise and by worshipful living (Cohen & Parsons, 2010). Some even suggest that there should be no other motive for worship: "God must be worshipped for God's own glory, or worship is idolatry, however worthy its motivations" (Segler & Bradley, 2006, p. 9).

What Worship Is

Worship is acknowledging and praising God as the Lord of all existence, including our own lives. It includes celebrating the acts of God throughout history and in the present. Worship recognizes that God is present with us, as Jacob noted upon awakening from his dream of God coming to him through angels on a ladder from heaven: "Surely the LORD is in this place" (Gen. 28:16). The early Christians reported that every time they assembled for worship, the risen Lord made His presence known to them as they read scriptures, listened to preaching, and ate together. Eating together commemorates Jesus' last supper with the disciples and the banquet that will come when Jesus returns at the end of time (see Luke 24) (Byars, 2000). As Christians gather, they begin their worship with a prayer of "invocation," asking God to be present with them.

Worship activities include reading scripture; singing and/or listening to music; praying; participating in rituals or sacraments; sharing life stories or "testimonies" (personal accounts of a spiritual experience); and gathering the offering, usually money or bank checks in our financial economy, to be used in the work of the church. One or more of these activities may take place whenever an informal group from the congregation gathers, during the programs of the congregation (study and mission groups), as well as during the whole-congregation worship that occurs week by week. In many Christian traditions, when the whole congregation gathers, a leader preaches or otherwise provides a "message" with the objectives of teaching and interpreting scripture, and encouraging and challenging participants to live the teachings of the faith (Jacobsen, 1997).

Sacraments are the ritualized actions that signify the grace of God. The Council of Lyons affirmed the seven sacraments of the Catholic Church in 1274: baptism, confirmation, penance, Eucharist, holy orders, marriage, and the anointing of the sick. Several hundred years later, the Reformers rejected five of these, keeping only baptism and the Lord's Supper, since these are the only two, they argued, in which Jesus directly participated. The Anabaptists included a third sacred act: foot-washing, symbolizing both humility and service (Arzola, 2011).[29]

Although worship is an end in itself, which is the celebration and adoration of God, it also meets basic human needs. In the face of our human limitations and the finiteness of life, worship connects us to the infinite, to the worth and meaning of our own lives. The scriptures and prayers spoken and the songs sung tell us our place of significance in the universe, even when our lives may feel meaningless or chaotic:

When I look at your heavens, the work of your fingers, the moon and the stars that you have established; what are human beings that you are mindful of them, mortals that you care for them? Yet you have made them a little lower than God, and crowned them with glory and honor (Psalm 8:3-5).

In the face of our human limitations and the finiteness of life, worship connects us to the infinite, to the worth and meaning of our own lives.

In times of insecurity and fear, worship offers refuge and stability; "God is our refuge and strength, a very present help in trouble (Psalm 46:1). Worship offers companionship with God and with others in the face of loneliness. Guilt can be absolved by the forgiveness we can experience through confession in worship. Worship can confront sickness and grief with experiences that are comforting and healing (Segler & Bradley, 2006). When people sing and recite scripture together, they find their faith strengthened—we sing and speak ourselves into faith. When some in the congregation are too heartbroken by grief or disappointment or too angry to sing through gritted teeth, the community sings and recites the words for them, interceding for them, carrying them to God "when they cannot carry themselves" (Segler & Bradley, 2006, p. 87).

How Congregations Worship

Congregations differ in how they think about the nature of worship. Some Christian traditions prescribe a "liturgy" that shapes each worship service and special occasions such as weddings, baptisms, funerals, and holy day celebrations. The liturgy may include set prayers, the lighting of incense and/or candles, recitations of creeds, singing, designation of scripture to be read, offerings, sermons, and ritual acts such as greetings exchanged and sharing in bread and wine that commemorate Jesus' meal with the disciples the night before His crucifixion. The attire of leaders (robes or stoles), who can lead in which aspects of the liturgy, and the use of worship resources such as prayer books and hymnals, all are ritualized and have meaning to individuals and to the community as a whole. We symbolize our connections with the larger Church through the use of such resources as the *Book of Common Prayer* or the *Methodist Hymnal.*

Some congregations consider themselves "non-liturgical." They do not have a prayer book but instead individuals lead with prayers they have written themselves or that they create spontaneously. A lectionary, shared with other congregations, does not define the scripture text but the one preaching chooses the scripture, often in response to the current life of the congregation. Some congregations have songs for singing that come from a variety of sources, projected on a screen, perhaps including but not limited to the hymnal produced by a denominational publishing house. Clothing of leaders may be jeans and a t-shirt instead of clerical robes.

Even in so-called "non-liturgical" congregations, however, worship is ritualized, with a set order of worship that may not vary from week to week, with a stylized language used for prayer and learned from oral tradition, and with the use of music that congregants know and can sing. Rituals may include everything from dancing and clapping to listening to children's sermons, and from incense and moments of silence to a time of greeting one another when people cross aisles and shake hands or hug one another. Greetings may consist of brief conversations or stylized phrases such as "Christ be with you," responded to with "And also with you."

Some large congregations with large professional staffs and a broad diversity of members have divided themselves for worship along generational lines or by cultural groups. "Contemporary" worship services with worship bands and drums meet at one hour and may attract teenagers and young adults. "Traditional" worship services with pipe organ and hymnbooks meet at another time; older adults may prefer these worship services that use the hymns and instruments they have known for decades. An ethnicity-oriented worship service meets at yet another time; in some locations, different ethnic groups may meet in different spaces or at different times in the same building. Children have a separate "children's church." A consumer-oriented culture has seeped into expectations for what worship is, and congregants may "shop" for a worship experience that is most comfortable or inspirational for them (Ammerman, 2002).

Some leaders are reversing this trend. Congregational worship needs to be inclusive of the congregation's diversity. Worship needs to be a participatory response to God, not a performance of worship leaders with the congregation in the role of audience. York (2003), for example, argues that worship "performers" should be the whole congregation, with God as the "audience" whom the congregation has gathered to worship, and the gathering should be the whole body, not as groups segregated by generation, ability, or culture. This is not a new call to integration; almost two centuries ago, Soren Kierkegaard said that people come to worship as though they were going to the theatre, as an audience for the cast of preacher, choir and musicians. God is offstage in this metaphor, the prompter, occasionally helping the performers with their lines. Kierkegaard said that although theatre is an appropriate metaphor, God is the audience; the people are the performers, and the leaders are the prompters (Kierkegaard, 1948 (original 1847)).

The rituals and practices of Christian worship communicate home to those who know them.

Whether liturgical or non-liturgical, and no matter how dire the times, the rituals and practices of Christian worship communicate home to those who know them. When people gather and pray, "Thy kingdom come; Thy will be done on earth as it is in heaven," they are claiming the promise that God will act and right all wrongs, that God is not finished yet. Hope is active, expectant, and empowering (Byars, 2000).

These rituals serve a boundary function. They communicate belonging and inclusion for insiders and strangeness to outsiders. No matter how much a congregation strives to make newcomers feel included, its rituals make those new to a congregation, and especially coming from no congregational experience or from a different denominational tradition, feel left out or at least "strange" when they do not know when to stand up or sit down, and do not know the words and melody of the congregational song everyone else has memorized.

Genuine worship puts our hearts in rhythm with the heartbeat of God and gives us the courage to join in God's work in the world.

The Bible issues sobering cautions about worship. It rails against worship that God finds unacceptable, due not to liturgical errors but to failure to live justly with neighbors (Cohen & Parsons, 2010). Genuine worship puts our hearts in rhythm with the heartbeat of God and gives us the courage to join in God's work in the world. Christians gather to praise and thank God, to listen for a Word from God, and to draw strength. But then, they are to go and serve. The church shares in Israel's mission to be a blessing to all the families of the earth and to be a servant people (see 1 Peter 2:9; Byars, 2000). It is here that social workers in a congregational context may find themselves practicing with a shared purpose with congregations: living justly with neighbors, creating community, building on strengths together, and ultimately, in service to one another. This focus on worship as preamble for service is where social workers have a vital and unique role as worship leaders.

The Role of Leader

All the baptized in the early church could lead in the rites of worship, such as the celebration of the Eucharist; it was not a role reserved for the apostles. By the third century, a ceremony of ordination had developed, installing leaders to office. By the sixth century, worship leadership had been restricted to priests (Talley, 1990; White, 2006). The role of leader has continued to be defined and redefined as different Christian traditions developed—Roman Catholic, Orthodox, and Protestant—and continued to evolve through denominational identities.

Because worship is the most important function of congregations, those who lead in worship have roles imbued with respect and authority. Normally, they are considered qualified for congregational leadership based on an inseparable mix of both interpretation of biblical teaching and on congregation or denominational tradition. In American congregations, a diversity of qualifications may—or may not—include ordination (ordained for church office), education (seminary), gender (whether or not women can lead), marital status (only celibate or married and never divorced), and sexual orientation (only heterosexual).

These qualifications are usually fairly clear for the role of pastor but may be less overt for other roles of worship leadership, such as the staff member or congregant who leads in prayer or scripture reading. These qualifications and roles may be so subtly communicated that the congregation is not aware of them, at least until they are broken in some way. In some congregations, for example, women may speak or pray or read scripture, but only from the "floor" of the congregation, and not from the pulpit. In other congregations, women are permitted to bring a "message" or a "testimony" but not a "sermon," which is a term still reserved, in some traditions, for male leaders only. Still other congregations have women serving as pastors.

Leadership varies not only based on the qualifications of leaders but also in how leaders define their responsibilities. In his interviews with religious leaders, Witvliet identifies four terms that define leadership. "Craftspeople" focus on making words come to life through dramatic reading, or sewing banners, or writing music. "Directors and coordinators" recruit and rehearse others, providing them with resources for their leadership like new music or readings. "Performers" play the organ or preach a sermon. "Spiritual engineers" attempt to create moments of spiritual power and holiness (Witvliet, 2003, pp. 280-281). He argues that none of these is sufficient—that the first three do not aim high enough, and the fourth overshoots. We cannot make a moment holy by our own creativity or effort; God's presence is a gift. Instead, planning and leading worship is a task for leaders, which, like the cook in the family who controls the family's nutrition, shapes the spiritual nutrition of the congregation.

Given the importance of worship in the life of a congregation, social workers

Social workers who participate in worship may be considered by others to be "part of" the congregation more than those who fulfill a function in the congregation's programs during the week but do not attend worship.

who participate in worship may be considered by others to be "part of" the congregation more than those who fulfill a function in the congregation's programs during the week but do not attend worship. Those social workers who occasionally or regularly lead elements of the congregation's worship may be recognized as leaders in the congregation and have more authority and influence than those who do not.

Social Workers in the Pulpit

The most visible and traditional leadership role in congregations is that of preacher or proclaimer. Although worship leadership was not a role in the work of all the congregational social workers we interviewed, 10 of them preach at least occasionally and those who are pastors, like Carl and Beth, do so every week. Of those who do, 8 are men and 2 are women; there are 37 women and 14 men in the sample. That is, 60% of the men we interviewed preach whereas only 5% of the women do.

Given the history and current polity of the denominations and congregational traditions where some of these social workers are serving, where women are not permitted to take leadership roles, especially those considered to be traditional male pastoral roles, these percentages are not particularly surprising. The sample is heavily Baptist, and the largest Baptist denomination in the USA is the Southern Baptist Convention, which explicitly states as essential doctrine that the role of pastor is limited to men (Rogers & Baptist Faith and Message Study Committee, 2000). In fact, it was the development of this limitation, which had existed in practice in many Baptist congregations but not in a formalized denominational doctrinal statement, that created the conflict between denominational leadership and the leadership of the Carver School of Church Social Work (The Southern Baptist Theological Seminary) that resulted in its closure in 1997, as described in Chapter 2 (Garland, 1999c).

Beth is one of the two women among our interviewees who preach. In her previous church, where she served as the Minister to College Students, she preached whenever the pastor was out of town or on vacation. She loved having the opportunity. Now as a pastor, preaching is a major part of her responsibility.

Others have opportunity to lead through preaching, even though they are not the weekly preaching pastor. Earl was teaching in the psychology department of a college when he learned that his congregation was planning to hire a counselor. He applied and was hired. As "Counselor Minister," he provided counseling to those in the congregation and preached monthly. Gordon is a youth minister, also in a Church of Christ congregation, where he occasionally preaches and has responsibility every week for helping to plan worship and reading and sharing ideas for sermons that the senior pastor can use in his sermons. Melinda is often invited to be a guest speaker in the worship services of congregations who sponsor the prisoner re-entry program.

Obviously, many of these social workers do not preach, however. Although the 15 social workers who have masters' degrees in theology or divinity probably had one or more graduate courses in preaching, social work programs—even the few who provide a track or specialization in congregational social work—do not provide coursework in preaching. On the other hand, many pastors/preachers have not attended seminary nor taken graduate coursework in preaching. Because it is such a significant and vital role in the life of many congregations, perhaps those preparing or already in roles of congregational social work should consider seeking professional education for this role, if it is open to them in their tradition.

... Or Not

Lynne's congregation is not open to a woman preaching, but she does lead the congregation's worship in other roles, such as leading in prayer or reading the scripture lesson. Her congregation has not been open to ordaining women to the leadership role of deacon either. Lynne has experienced the exclusion from leading by preaching as a "personal loss":

> Most of the time I go along and just accept it, but then things will come up that remind me all over again and it's like opening up an old wound. I said many times over the last few years, had I been younger when I started out as a social worker, I probably would have fought it more, but considering my age, I just decided that was a battle I wasn't going to fight. I actually had a minister on the staff here who volunteered to ordain me, and my husband's church volunteered to ordain me before he died, but I just weighed the cost and decided that, right or wrong, I would just go with the status quo.

The cost would be the real potential for conflict in her congregation, and conflict with and even expulsion of her congregation from its denomination. Still, it continues to be a painful exclusion for her. For example, she has very close relationships with congregants who serve in the programs she supervises, and she thinks, consequently, that she is more qualified to provide them with pastoral care than her pastor, including worship rituals such as funerals:

> I could do their funerals better than our pastor could in many of those cases because I knew them better. That hurts. The thing about it is it just didn't occur to the family to even ask me. I had one very wonderful volunteer that I was very close to. He confided in me a lot about his illness. We were close, we prayed together and everything, but then when he died, it didn't even occur to his family to ask me to participate in his service.

Lynne has led other funerals for members of her congregation, she told me, because the person dying specifically requested it.

Both of us have experienced rejection of our leadership because of our gender. For Gaynor, the invitation to preach at an annual gathering of congregations offended some who thought preaching is an inappropriate role for a woman. The gathering subsequently developed a policy prohibiting women from preaching to the annually gathered body of congregations. On another occasion, Diana was invited to preach at a national gathering of Baptist women. When the time came in the worship service for her to preach, a number of people stood and walked out, communicating their rejection of women in the role of proclaiming. Those experiences of rejection, painful as they were, have been rare in careers that have included many other times in which we were invited and welcomed in the preaching role.

The Processes of Worship

The processes of worship include how the context for worship together is designed.

Social workers bring a particular set of skills and valuing of diversity that can help congregations who seek to be inclusive in worship. Congregations face the challenge of welcoming people to worship together who are differently abled, of different generations, and of different cultures. Carl's congregation, for example, is located in an ethnically diverse inner city neighborhood, across the street from an agency that serves persons with chronic mental illness. As a consequence, the congregation has learned to embrace a diversity of people. Carl described a "typical" Sunday morning worship service:

> A woman came and her children were making all kind of noise. And then they left. I was relieved, and then one of the ushers raised his white-gloved hand, and said "Pastor, their father just died." We prayed for them, and then I went back to my sermon. . . . And then Larry on the second row said, "I'm convicted." And he got on his knees and proposed to his girlfriend. So I didn't need to preach that Sunday; we had it all. This is like heaven is going to be. We have so much diversity. We have African-Americans, Puerto Ricans, Jamaicans—you name the culture. We have hymns and drums. Everybody is uncomfortable at least some of the time. But we have it all. I come expecting chaos. Laughing helps me to manage it. Other pastors say "I could never handle this." Because of my background [as a social worker] I understand this congregation and how to lead them.

In his small congregation, Carl describes the inclusion of persons who are coping with chronic mental illness, of different generations (noisy children), and of different cultures. Leading his congregation requires careful planning, flexibility to alter plans, sensitivity to the dynamics of the congregation, skills of connecting with and including a diverse gathering of people who may or may not know one another or the leader, knowledge of the various cultures and personal challenges represented, humility, comfort with self so the focus can be on the visual and verbal communication of others, and a ready sense of humor. As Carl says, being part of a diverse congregation gives the experience of "heaven," of what it means to be part of the eternal Church.[30]

Being part of a diverse congregation gives the experience of "heaven," of what it means to be part of the eternal Church.

The Content of Worship

Preaching has two basic elements: the message of the biblical text and illustrations that show how the message makes a difference in the way we live (Jacobsen, 1997). In some traditions, a lectionary controls the text chosen. In others, the leader may choose. Whether the scripture is a given or the leader is given the freedom to decide, the emphasis and focus is in the hands of the leader. The biblical text may be given but the leader has the freedom and responsibility for deriving the interpretation and focus. Beth said that her identity as a social worker "colors the way that I read scripture." She finds herself drawn to themes of justice and inclusion as she prepares messages for her congregation. She is responding to their sense of calling to be a congregation actively engaged with the needs around them; she believes that the search committee who brought her to the congregation sought her out because they believed she could lead them to a deeper engagement in missions.

Preaching is sometimes topical, beginning with a theme and then finding text to support that theme rather than following a text and deriving themes from it. A few examples of topics include understanding God (Willimon, 2004), family relationships (Achtemeier, 1987), the daily workplace (Jacobsen, 1997), poverty (Myers, 1999), and social justice (Burghardt, 1997; McLaren, 2004; McNeal, 2009). The opportunity to shape the message of worship is a powerful opportunity to guide the life and work of the congregation to be celebrating and participating in the narrative of a God of compassion, love, and justice.

All power creates opportunities for abuse as well as good, however. With this power to shape the agenda of worship comes the ever-constant danger of misusing the opportunity, hijacking worship to accomplish the leader's own agenda.

Jeffrey readily acknowledges and is respectful of the opportunity and the ever-present challenge that leading in worship creates. He and his staff annually facilitate a Catholic mass in the congregations to which his agency relates, to pray for ending the abuse of women. His city has immigrants from a wide diversity of people groups; worship is celebrated in more than two dozen languages in the Catholic congregations

With this power to shape the agenda of worship comes the ever-constant danger of misusing the opportunity, hijacking worship to accomplish the leader's own agenda.

of the city each Sunday. Many of those who attend come from cultures that expect women to be subjugated to men. If there is trouble in the family, the first person from whom the family seeks help is their priest. Jeffrey and his colleagues have prepared a liturgy that is designed not only to speak about this issue to the congregations but also to educate the priests who lead the liturgy. "It's amazingly powerful if the priest, when talking about marriage, will say abuse is wrong."

In one sense, Jeffrey is using the planning of worship to promote a message, as part of a strategy to bring justice to women and families. Jeffrey says that they have to be cautious; it would be easy to "go off track" and use the worship experience for the purposes of the agency. The Roman Catholic Church considers teaching on social justice as an appropriate function of the liturgy. "You don't preach what your own doctrine is; you preach the teaching of the church." Jeffrey is passionate about reducing the abuse of women in his diocese, recognizing that his agenda must be grounded in church doctrine.

Jeffrey uses a worship liturgy to promote the safety of women and nonviolence in families as teaching church doctrine. In fact, even though worship is an end in itself, even though worshippers engage in worship to celebrate and bring glory to God, one outcome of worship is the second function of congregational life, which is Christian education. Although there are distinctive programs of worship and education in congregational life, the *functions* of worship and education are actually interwoven in much of congregational life. The weekly worship services of the congregation are contexts for education as well as worship. The sermon and texts of music intentionally teach Christian beliefs and values. The sermon may be a "teaching series," and is almost always designed not just to lead the congregation in the worship of God but also to teach about God and to apply biblical texts to daily living. Other elements of the weekly worship service are also educational at the same time they are calling forth worship. Perhaps most overtly educational is the sermon, which is based on a biblical text. Congregants may passively listen to the sermon, but in some congregations, a religious leader encourages them to take notes, supported by a "notes" page in the service bulletin.

Hymns not only call forth the worship of those singing, but singing the same songs year by year leads to memorization of texts and melodies that set to music scripture and theology, hope and despair, joy and grief. Music aids memory; think of the popular music you listened to as teenagers and can still sing from memory when school lessons have long been forgotten. Parents may subsequently find themselves singing hymns they learned in church to crying babies in the wee hours of the morning; adult children sitting vigil by the bed of a dying parent may sing the songs of faith to carry the loved one through the transition of death. Social workers who work with older persons who suffer with cognitive conditions often recount how the older persons can sing, often with no texts or music, the hymns that they learned long ago, when they were children.

Similarly, educational programs such as study groups almost always include elements of worship such as a time of prayer and sharing of personal concerns and joys with God and with one another.

Leading Christian Education

The congregation is a community context for learning and living the life of faith. Education includes learning about and also engaging in the practices and disciplines of faith together (Dykstra, 1986, 1991, 1999). Christian education is not just knowledge; it is putting that knowledge into practice. Christian education is ongoing formation that continues throughout life, not something that we provide for children alone; it is an ongoing discipline of learning and living together. Participants may complete a particular program and "graduate," but only to the next expectation for learning and living faith in the context of the community. Christians are "born" when they decide to become followers of Christ, but they are also "formed" in the lifelong journey of attempting to live their faith (Dykstra, 1999; Hawn, 2003; Lee, 1990; McNeal, 2009)

The learning is never complete because the Christian life is a way of life, not just cognitive knowledge. Jesus taught us to love our enemies (Matthew 5:44), for example, which we cannot simply learn to do and then move on to the next skill set until we have all Christian knowledge and related skills. As our life unfolds, the congregation provides a context for applying Christian teachings to the unfolding life experiences that confront us. Many people garner support and encouragement from others who are traveling through the same, or similar, experiences and learning.

The learning is never complete because the Christian life is a way of life, not just cognitive knowledge.

Christian education shapes much of the programming of congregational life. Many Protestant congregations have "schools" with classes for everyone, often divided by age and sometimes by gender and taught by congregants themselves. Classes can become communities that may last for years. A well-worn subject of congregational humor is the adult class full of persons 10 years older than the class age level but who refuse to be "promoted" out of the class to the next age level because the class is where their friends are. Not only do members study Christian teachings together week by week, but members share life's ups and downs with one another, pray for one another, and may develop friendships that extend into their daily lives. Class projects may engage members in ministry to those in the neighborhood or simply be the collection of funds to support a mission organization they have chosen. In some congregations, the Sunday school classes may be more faithfully attended and have more people involved in them than the weekly worship service. In other traditions, the weekly school experience is limited to children and teenagers and takes place at the same time as an adult worship service, where, as we have seen, the functions of worship and education are blended.

Many congregations have augmented or supplanted Sunday morning schools with small groups that meet during the week, either at the congregation's site or in the homes of members or a lunchtime or breakfast restaurant near members' workplaces. These groups may include a meal, but there is almost always a time of prayer together and then study of a curriculum or a book the group has chosen to study together.

The Christian education programs of our (Gaynor's and Diana's) congregations shaped our lives as children and teenagers. We attended worship both in the morning and in the evening every Sunday. Sunday school for designated age groups preceded the Sunday morning service, where we studied the Bible. The Sunday evening service was preceded by "Training Union," with its own curriculum designed to prepare us as future leaders for the church. The content included church history and doctrine. Characteristically, the weekly Training Union sessions involved participants reciting their assigned parts of the lesson to the group, giving everyone the opportunity to learn group leadership skills.

Music education is also common, usually through choirs for different age groups. The adult choir practices each week to lead the congregational singing and to perform one or more pieces for the worship service; children and youth choirs sing more occasionally as part of congregational worship. Youth and adult choirs may also go on "tours," visiting and singing in other congregations. Music education may also include learning musical instruments, from rhythm instruments that accompany the choir, to playing hand bells, or even orchestral instruments, which are then played in worship.

Christian education programming also typically includes weekly education about missions. In our tradition, mission education has its own curriculum as well, often emphasizing the mission organizations of the denomination that sends career missionaries to people groups in the United States and around the world. In Protestant denominations, women's organizations often carry the responsibility for mission education and have their own publishing houses. These women's mission organizations are the same organizations that developed the training schools described earlier. Some of these organizations are settings for church social workers; social workers can be found leading these organizations at the state and national denominational level, as well as authoring their curricula and other publications.

The curriculum for Protestant Christian education in many congregations is prepared at the denominational level, with guidebooks for the lay teacher, so that the same "lesson" is being learned across all congregations. One of the closest ties between congregations and their denominations has been this provision of literature for the congregation. The curriculum may be based on a methodical study of a portion of the Bible, sometimes varied by a foray into church history, traditions, and theology. In recent decades, other publishers have been providing curriculum for church schools and programs. The choice of alternative curricula is both a result of and contributing to weakened ties between congregations and denominations. Some congregations allow adult classes to choose their own literature for study.

Finally, Christian education takes place through special events—seminars, workshops, and retreats. These events may provide more in-depth opportunities to study a book of the Bible or to explore how Christians live into life experiences and challenges—parenting, marriage, budgeting, relationships, or retirement. These special events may be a group studying prepared materials together or be led by an "expert" from within or outside the congregation. That expert is sometimes a social worker. Beth's congregation had just offered a course in financial wellbeing. She said that participants who have become burdened by credit card debt learned together how to live their faith by the way they manage their finances. Beth said that Christian education is not just delivering knowledge about Christian scriptures and teachings, but taking a more holistic approach of helping Christians apply those teachings to the challenges of their daily lives.

Depending on the resources and size of a congregation, a paid staff member—"Minister of Education"—or lay leaders may organize and support Christian education programs. In some congregations, there are multiple staff members responsible for the educational programming, often defined by the age groups for which they are responsible. Beth's first employment by a congregation was as a minister with college students, for example.

Education in congregations also takes place through self-directed learning with resources the congregation provides or congregants find on their own. These resources may focus directly on studying scriptures, or on life issues viewed from a Christian worldview—the vast world of Christian devotional and self-help literature. In addition to individualized and self-directed study, Christian education also takes place in one-on-one tutoring relationships such as spiritual direction and mentoring, as well as in learning groups, in teacher-directed classes, in whole-congregation settings, and in large audiences at special events (Elias, 2012).

Content of Christian Education

The content of Christian education usually includes a combination of: (1) knowing and interpreting scripture; (2) understanding and drawing principles from the history of the Church, denominational life, and the lives of saints—either Catholic saints or the "saints" of Protestant life like Lottie Moon, Jim Elliot, William Wilberforce, Corrie ten Boom, or Martin Luther King, Jr.; (3) applying scripture and historical experiences to today's life challenges and decisions; and (4) understanding and being equipped for service and vocation. It would be relatively ineffective to lead a Bible study group in learning about and interpreting the scripture without including ways that scripture can be applied in daily living. The reverse is also true; preparing congregants for the living of their daily lives and for service and vocation—to serve in the outreach ministries of the congregation—needs to connect to an understanding of Christian scriptures and teachings.

The content of Christian education ranges far more broadly than Christian scriptures and doctrine and their application in life. Congregations have provided important education in general life skills for people historically. Sunday Schools were originally developed in the late 18th Century to teach reading to working children, preceding and leading today's model of public education and originally using the Bible as text (Little, 2004). In the USA, the clandestine Black church provided education for adults as well as children at a time when it was unlawful for slaves to receive an education. After the collapse of the Confederacy after the Civil War, it was the Black church that led African-American communities in education, economics, and politics (Billingsley, 1999).

Today, many congregations not only provide literacy education but a variety of other life skills courses from auto repair to computer skills. A sampling of the wide range of congregational education programs includes teen pregnancy prevention, marriage and parenting education, anger and conflict management, human sexuality, health education, cooking and nutrition, English and other languages, exercise and wellness, job skills, re-entry after imprisonment, becoming foster parents, care-giving for family members with health challenges, and preparation for retirement (e.g., Ammerman, 2005; Blank & Davie, 2004; Chaves, 2004; Clerkin & Gronbjerg, 2003; Cnaan, Boddie, Handy, Yancey & Schneider, 2002; Cnaan, Boddie & Yancey, 2003; Garland, 2012a; Garland, Hugen, Myers, Sheridan, Sherwood, & Wolfer, 2002; Isaac, 2012; Polson, 2006; Pritchett, 2003; Unruh, 2004). Christianity is a worldview with implications for every aspect of human experience, including family life, finances, physical health, community relationships, and vocation.[31]

Congregations have provided important education in life skills for people historically.

Social Workers as Christian Educators

The congregational social workers we interviewed lead programs designed to teach the knowledge, values, and practices of the congregation's religion to congregants as well as to those neighbors the congregation serves through its missions and ministries. Even those educational programs that one might find in other settings for social work practice—parent education, addiction recovery, and grief support –use a curriculum explicitly or implicitly based in Christian teaching. For example, Lynne teaches adults in her congregation's Sunday school and other educational programs, usually on topics related to community ministry, such as poverty, homelessness, and mental health and illness.

Sometimes these social workers are leading a group using a curriculum or resources others have developed. Sometimes they develop their own curriculum. Or they may find themselves adapting the already existing curriculum or resources because the content assumes a familiarity with Christian faith that participants may not have. They also write informational pieces and resources for dissemination in their congregation, such as weekly newsletters and blogs. Some disseminate the curriculum they develop beyond their congregation to be used in other congregations as well. I (Diana) began my work with congregations by writing curricula on parent education, marriage education, and child advocacy.

Several described the focus of their educational work to be content related to social justice. Social justice topics are often highly charged emotionally and politically. In Caiden's congregation, gay marriage became a "hot issue." So Caiden prepared a program of group discussions over a period of six weeks. She put the biblical passages that are often referred to in their original historical context. She discovered that "proscriptions against homosexuality in the Bible really had to do with sexual abuse of slaves." It was the hardest issue she has faced, she said, because she had to work out her own beliefs as well as worrying about how her leadership would be perceived. Even after she had worked through her own position, she said, "It wasn't my role to tell them what is right or wrong but to give them the best information possible to make their decision." The social work value of client self-determination echoes through her approach to Christian education.

Addressing emotionally charged topics like sexual orientation from a Christian education perspective are common tasks for congregational social workers. In my (Gaynor's) first year as a congregational social worker more than 40 years ago, I was working in an inner-city ministry supported by a denomination and located in an old church building. One day, the man whose family lived in a brownstone row house across the street from the church building knocked on the agency door and said that I must go and talk with his family. He and his family considered themselves to be congregants because they attended every program and activity that was offered through our ministries, even though there was no longer a congregation located in the church building. I walked with him across the street and found the family sitting around the kitchen table smoking; everyone was crying, some wailing out loud.

At first, I thought someone in the family had died, but then I learned that one of the man's daughters, who was married and the mother of four children, had announced to them that she was leaving her husband and children because she was a lesbian. They were asking me to help them understand their daughter's decision from a Christian perspective. As a Christian educator—and a social worker—my responsibility was to help them decide how they would respond to their daughter. As I did so, the daughter and her partner also asked me to help them through the changes in their relationship with one another, with the daughter's children, and with the daughter's estranged husband. Reconciliation became the focal point of my work with these different family units. The relationship with this family started because of my work at the church.

Whether they are leading a group or preparing written materials or responding to persons in crisis, like the family across the street from Gaynor's denominational agency, the focus of the education these social workers are facilitating includes one or more of these dimensions: (1) Christian discipleship, (2) life skills training, and (3) relationship education. These categories are not exclusive; to some extent, virtually all of the life skills training and relationship education programs congregational social workers lead include an application of Christian discipleship to the topic at hand and have an implicit or explicit goal of helping participants apply those teachings to their lives.

Christian Discipleship

These social workers are deeply engaged in providing Christian discipleship education. In addition to leading in worship, they are engaged in mentoring relationships, in leading occasional and regular educational programs of the congregation, and in camping and mission trips. These various formats for discipleship education are hardly exclusive but one activity may lead to another over time. For example, when Carl began his work to plant a church in an inner city, he began with a community needs assessment that found that the community was troubled by prostitution, drugs, and a lack of constructive activities for children. He said:

> So we found an abandoned park. We didn't think we could do anything about prostitution and drugs right away, but we could do something for children. So we did a day camp.... On this vacant lot, we put sheets down on the ground and had a weeklong day camp.

A day camp is a half day or full day activity program for children during the summer months when they are not in school. Activities include learning Bible stories, arts and crafts, sports and games, and snacks. From that day camp grew a regular Sunday school for children that later became the congregation he pastors today.[32] He brought to his work the skills of community organizing.

Not only do a number of these social workers lead discipleship groups, but some carry responsibility for the entire Christian education program of their congregations. Others are responsible for particular age groups—children, teens, or older adults. Gordon, with the title "Youth Minister," describes his educational program for teenagers:

> I'll try to keep an eye out for what students are dealing with. I try to do that a couple of ways. One is to just give them blank pieces of paper and say, "What is it you're wrestling with? What do you want to hear about? Is there anything you are curious about what God might have to say?

He said that the topics have "run the gamut" from the meaning of salvation to issues of sexuality and pornography.

It was the focus on social justice in their work that made their education roles "social work" in the minds of several of these social workers. For example, Beth, at the time "College Minister" in the first congregation she served, explained that she took the college students she led to the grocery store, assigning them the task of planning a week's menus for a family based on the allotment for food stamps that an impoverished mother with young children receives. Her educational goal was for them to understand the realities of poverty in the US.

Fay writes curriculum on social justice issues and speaks in congregations. She is advocating for congregations with the denomination, arguing that the denomination should not tell congregations what social justice issues in which to engage and how, but rather, that the denomination allow congregations to develop their own agenda for their own context. She is applying the concept of self-determination to the community level. She developed a Bible study curriculum that includes an overview of biblical content addressing poverty, what congregations can and are doing in response to poverty, and a visioning process to guide the congregation toward action. She has also developed a game for congregational groups, to guide them in discussions about issues like poverty and hunger. She believes that "Often we don't move forward to act upon our faith in just ways because we don't spend enough time talking to one another." She sees her job as a facilitator of conversations that will lead to action for social justice.

It was the focus on social justice in their work that made their education roles "social work" in the minds of several of these social workers.

We heard the knowledge and values of social work in a somewhat different way from Catarina. She serves as a "mission trip teacher" when her congregation sends short-term missions teams to international sites. She states that her goal is to help congregants develop a holistic understanding of what it means to share their faith in those settings, an understanding that involves the whole person in the context of the larger community. The focus on broadening the understanding of evangelism was a common one that we will revisit in some depth in Chapter 6, when we look at how these social workers lead in their congregation's missions and ministries.

Leadership in Christian discipleship education is one of the few areas documented as a role for social workers leading in congregations. Students who complete a dual-degree program in social work at the University of North Carolina and divinity at Duke Divinity School take a required capstone course, in which they select a contemporary social issue and develop an educational program for their congregation, an annual denominational meeting, or other settings such as a conference of pastors. Examples of past project topics include abortion, autism, substance abuse, sexual orientation, domestic violence, sexual abuse/incest, gender disparities, pornography, and mental health (Roberts-Lewis & Armstrong, 2010). In a published example from this course, one student developed an interactive book that tells the fictional story of a person living in poverty. The book is used in small groups, where participants put themselves in the character's shoes and make daily decisions that lead them through the story (Turner, 2010).

The educational focus for the social workers we interviewed was not only within their congregations but also beyond. For example, Ben leads a Bible study in the nearby prison and community correctional center. Carl leads worship and Bible study in a nearby nursing home. He bases his engagement with the residents on what he learned in social work school about the importance of life review in the late stages of life as a means of consolidating identity and the sense of purpose and meaning in life as health fails. So as he does Bible study, he also draws out of the residents their memories and life stories.

Many of these social workers are teaching and training congregants to teach others as a significant dimension of Christian discipleship. These social workers, particularly those preparing congregants for service beyond the congregation, did not often define their work as "Christian education"; they were simply applying their profession to the work of congregational leadership. Studying their roles in congregational life has caused us to reflect on our own careers and work with congregations and realize that as we have sought as social work educators to provide leadership in congregational life, we have been in the roles of Christian educators.[33]

Life Skills Training

These social workers also lead educational programs that are focused on life skills that are much like those offered by social service agencies, although the underlying values of the congregational programs are Christian. They lead and/or facilitate educational groups designed to provide knowledge, values, and skills for life around a diversity of issues: survival skills for women (Denise), decision-making based on religious values (Haley), healthy life choices (Glenda), GED preparation (Megan), computer skills (Megan), and financial management (Barry). They also lead support groups for persons whose lives are affected by wide-ranging issues: single mothers (Alice), alcohol addiction (David), mental illness (Glenda), same-sex orientation of adult children (Glenda), release from imprisonment (David), pornography and sexual addictions (Earl), grief and loss (Jeanie), immigration issues (Jeanie), Alzheimer's disease (Lois), divorce recovery (Barry), coping with cancer (Barry), and loss of custody of children (Melinda). Daniel has led workshops on topics like eating disorders, sexual abuse, suicide and its prevention, and child safety.

Some of these services take place one on one rather than—or in addition to—group educational programs. Formalized programmed services like tutoring take place in the schools children attend or in the prisons and jails where inmates are learning reading or parenting skills. A major focus of Beth's early work in her first congregation was their adoption of a nearby elementary school, where members of her congregation provided weekly tutoring for children who needed the extra help and attention of a loving adult. Scheduled sessions at the church building or in other settings provide education for immigrants learning English, welfare recipients learning budgeting, or single mothers learning car repair.

Mentoring is often less structured and may take place according to the needs and scheduling opportunities of the mentor and the recipient of mentoring. Daniel, a Pastor of Care Ministries, prepares members of his congregation to be mentors for others based on experiences they have had that can be useful for others—recovering from an addiction, coping with the imprisonment of a family member, or living with a chronic disease. He says that mentoring is based on a specific skill-set the mentor has, or an area of life in which the mentor "has suffered well."

The mentor role is not limited to adults. Joy is the director of an organization that grew out of her congregation and now is a separate legal entity. The program equips more than 450 teens annually, teaching them to reach out to children who need spiritual and emotional support in experiencing life's issues. The teens commit to spending two hours a week for six weeks to work with a child in a scheduled group as well as in informal interaction.

In our own work in Christian education, we have used the term "befriending" rather than "mentoring."[34] "Mentoring" implies that one person serves as an example for the other, and that the older and wiser person gives and the younger or novice person receive the lessons of the mentor. Mentoring is a term that has been carried into congregational leadership from the social services (e.g., Blinn-Pike, Kuschell, McDaniel, Mingus, & Mutti, 1998; Branch, 2002; Calhoun, 2004; Freedman, 1993; Jucovy, 2003; Trumble, 1999). The term does not fit comfortably with a Christian worldview, however. In biblical stories, God often chooses persons as guides who are full of flaws, perhaps, in fact, so that they will *not* be pointed to as being exemplary. One biblical example of an important adult-youth relationship is Eli, the priest, raising Samuel. Clearly, Eli's life was not exemplary; he did not encourage Samuel to follow his example but instead helped him to listen to God (1 Samuel 3:1-19).

We have found that a more helpful concept for congregational programs than "mentor," then, is simply "friend." "Friend" is very different than the connotations that have come to be associated with the beginnings of social work in the late 19th Century in "friendly visiting." A friendly visitor was a volunteer or professional who made home visits to persons in poverty, assessing how their behavior contributed to their distress and then guided them to improvement (Segal et al., 2010). In contrast, the role of friend empowers both persons to receive as well as to give, not to have the answers and sometimes to say, "Don't do like me; do better!" Moreover, many times children and teens can be important resources in the lives of older adults, or what Earl Creps calls "reverse mentoring" (Creps, 2008). The role of congregational social workers is making the connections between potential friends, supporting these mutual relationships, rather than themselves taking on ongoing roles of "friend" or "mentor" with those they serve.

Relationship Education

These social workers in our study also lead educational programs that focus on forming and living in primary relationships, including the challenges those relationships present, such as premarital education, marriage enrichment, parent education, grandparents raising grandchildren, managing conflict and anger in family life, and relating to adult children. Two examples stand out. Gordon, a youth minister, writes material for his students on Facebook, and web articles for their parents, as well as for others that are in youth ministry. He finds he can reach more parents with online material than if he tried to schedule a meeting with them. Earl organized a weekend camp for children whose parents were going through divorce, with the theme "how to be a kid in a divorced family." Becky provides educational programs for parents of deaf children, helping them to learn the ways they can support healthy, productive, joyful futures for their children.

These social workers also lead educational programs that focus on forming and living in primary relationships, including the challenges those relationships present.

Social Workers as Worshippers and Learners

Even those social workers leading in worship or the congregation's educational programs are not in leadership positions all the time. Even small congregations usually have multiple programs during a given week, and it is not typical for one person to lead in all of them. In congregational life, it is not only acceptable but assumed that leaders will "show up" as participants in congregational programs, even if they are not leading. In larger congregations with multiple programs each week, where it is expected that congregants will choose one worship service instead of attending all three on a Sunday morning, and one Bible study group instead of the 20 that are offered, leaders, too, are expected to make those choices and "show up" at least as often as the active congregants do.

"Showing up" is what members of a community do—they are present with one another, living life together, even when they are not "doing for" one another. To the extent that social workers are congregational leaders, they need to be community members—present and engaged in at least some of the community's worship and educational programs. Congregational social work is not necessarily a Monday to Friday job, 8-5; to be effective as a leader, the social worker may need to be a part of the life of the congregation that takes place on Saturdays, Sundays, and weeknights. Participation is the foundation for community building, which we will explore in Chapter 5.

Because a congregation is a community, the line between leader and participant is a permeable one. The social worker brings the leadership role into the setting, even when the social worker is not the up-front leader. When a social worker participates in an educational group being led by a staff or lay leader of the congregation, the leader or the group may call on the social worker for expert opinions or advice related to topic they are discussing. Or the leader may look to the social worker for help in other ways, such as conversations about how to handle group interaction or group norms.

Ethical Opportunities and Challenges[35]

"Showing up" is what members of a community do—they are present with one another, living life together, even when they are not "doing for" one another.

Serving as a worship and educational leader creates both opportunities that are congruent with the ethics and values of social work as well as the possibility for challenges. The broad ethical principles of the profession include helping people in need, addressing social problems, and challenging social injustice. A social worker in the pulpit and in leadership of education programs is uniquely positioned to accomplish those purposes of the profession.

At the same time, the functions of preaching and teaching create the potential for ethical dilemmas, depending on the other roles of the social worker in the lives of congregants. Ethical problems and dilemmas are most salient and challenging when the social worker is providing counseling and other direct services to members of the congregation.

When a social worker has more than one role with another person— for example, as both a friend and teacher, or as a teacher and religious leader—the professional is in a "dual relationship"—like being members of the same congregational community. Dual, and multiple, relationships are virtually unavoidable, so the issue is to "separate the professional relationship from other relationships" (Dolgoff, Loewenberg, & Harrington, 2005, p. 142). In other words, the social worker should not use the professional relationship with a client to meet the social worker's professional or personal needs. In other settings for social work practice, keeping separate means avoiding friendships and romantic relationships with clients and not doing business with clients, especially if the client offers a "special deal" because of the professional relationship with the social worker.

Because congregations are communities, however, *not* to give business to other congregants or relate to them informally as friends in the various activities of the congregation would be a breach of the norms of community life. When the social worker is relating to congregants within the functions of congregational life—leading in worship, education, community development, and ministry—dual relationships may create challenges on occasion. Inez likened congregational social work to rural social work, both involve living in the community where one works: "When you do church social work where you attend, you have to think rural; there are going to be dual roles."

Serving as a worship and educational leader creates both opportunities that are congruent with the ethics and values of social work as well as the possibility for challenges.

These challenges are akin to those faced by others in professional leadership in the congregation and community. The experience is like living in a fish bowl, where a leader's personal life is lived with boundaries as transparent as glass, where it seems the whole community knows all about one's personal life. The symbol of that transparency is the church parsonage, the house the church owns, often located next door to the church building, where their leader's family lives in full sight of everyone.

My (Diana's) own experience as a newlywed pastor's wife was in a church parsonage with the chair of the deacons as a next-door neighbor and other church members living up and down the street. I remember distinctly the experience, now more than 40 years ago, of slamming out the kitchen door in utter frustration at my husband/pastor, muttering under my breath, only to find myself not fifteen feet from the chair of the deacons, who looked up from working on his car motor and said, "Is something wrong?"

As interesting and challenging as life may be as a leader living one's personal life steeped in the community of a congregation, the ethical challenges are concentrated when the social worker is not only a community leader and educator but also has the professional role of counselor or therapist. It is when the social worker is a provider of direct clinical services to congregants that the challenges of dual relationships become dilemmas that have the potential for harm.

The therapeutic environment requires a high level of trust, vulnerability, and confidentiality. In counseling, clients share their thoughts, feelings, and experiences that they would never want shared with the larger community. Therefore, clients whose social work counselor also serves on a congregational committee or project may wonder if the information shared in counseling contributed to the counselor's response to them verbally or nonverbally in their work together in the larger community.

Because church staff members are often considered friends, spiritual advisors, and shepherds to congregants, they must be able to quickly adapt to different social expectations, circumstances, and levels of intimacy (Parent, 2005). This flexibility is necessary for the social worker as a congregational leader, but it creates challenges for the counseling relationship, which needs to be governed by well-defined boundaries. Boundaries help to maintain the client's privacy by establishing rules for confidentiality, but they also serve a variety of other functions. Boundaries provide a sense of safety for the client and the needed emotional distance for effective therapeutic work (Welfel, 2002).

The dual relationships of counselor and community member do indeed create the possibility of the social worker violating boundaries and confidentiality. The nature of congregations as networks of friendships and communities of care make it challenging, but also important, to protect confidentiality (Yancey, Kilpatrick, & Stutts, 2010). The client may wonder or worry about the social worker sharing with other staff or friends, perhaps not deliberately if confidentially was promised, but perhaps accidentally, not remembering what was shared behind the closed doors of the counseling setting and not knowing what may be common knowledge in the community. That may limit the client's ability to share with the social worker in the counseling relationship, or the client's sense of safety in the life of the congregation. Or the opposite may happen; because of their social worker/client relationship, the client may presume that the social worker is available in the clinical role at other times. The client may stop the social worker before or after a worship service to say, "Can I just have a minute with you privately?"

Others in the congregation also imagine that the social worker knows what is going on in the private lives of congregants and, out of concern or curiosity, may ask about how someone else is faring or how they can be supportive. Even though the social worker may not intend to break confidentiality in a given situation, casual conversations with others outside the therapeutic relationship provide opportunity for an innocent slip-of-the-tongue. Even when such a slip does not occur, the congregant may be anxious that it might happen. When a social worker chooses a congregant for leadership of a church project or mentions a concern from the pulpit, a client may assume a connection of those decisions and conversations to information disclosed in a counseling session, whether or not that assumption is accurate.

The role of congregational leader is quite different from that of counselor. A religious leader may exhort a congregation to believe or act in specified ways. Social workers who provide counseling, on the other hand, are diligent to protect the client's right to self-determination, even if the client's choices are contrary to the beliefs or actions to which the religious community adheres. Wearing both roles of religious leader and counselor, then, place the social worker in ethical dilemmas.

Religious leaders are not always aware of their influence over their congregants, who often regard them as spiritual authorities. This discrepancy in perception may result in the leader minimizing or ignoring boundaries, creating an environment in which a leader can intentionally or unintentionally misuse the power they have to exploit the vulnerability of congregants. Religious leaders are in a position to influence not only the decisions of congregants but also their beliefs about God, about forgiveness, and about eternity. The representation of the presence of God can provide the power to absolve behavior or promote behavior. A social worker unaware of this ascribed power can easily and unintentionally misuse that power. It may be hard for a congregant to say no to a religious leader, even if the request is innocently asking for free tax advice from a tax advisor, an informal medical consult from a physician, or to borrow a tool or vehicle.

The most egregious violation of boundaries is when a relationship between religious leader and congregant becomes romantic and/or sexualized. Our research on clergy sexual misconduct, based on a nationally representative sample, has found very high rates of sexual boundary violation by religious leaders (Chaves & Garland, 2009). In a qualitative study of victims of clergy sexual misconduct, we found most of them had been in ongoing individual counseling relationships with the religious leader whose religious authority became an entrée to sexual misconduct (Garland & Argueta, 2010).

Although the studies of clergy sexual misconduct we cite above did not identify congregational social workers as offenders, the dynamics of dual relationships are similar if the social worker is in a pastoral role. Moreover, the high rates of sexual boundary violations suggest that there may be other kinds of boundary violations also taking place at high rates; other violations of the trust of religious leaders have been less well studied.

Therefore, it seems most prudent for congregational social workers who preach and teach in their roles as leaders to consider carefully the potential confusion of also providing clinical/counseling services to congregants. Not all ethical problems and dilemmas can be totally avoided, but when they happen, social workers can seek consultation and develop accountability structures to help them find their way through in ways that, above all, protect the clients and congregations they serve.

Chapter 5
Weaving Nets

We define a congregation as the body of people who come together regularly and voluntarily for worship at a particular location. The term "body of people" brings to mind the body of Christ and Paul's teaching that we are all members of Christ's body; we suffer and rejoice together, as parts of a whole (1 Corinthians 12). Stanley Hauerwas (1981) has said that being Christian is not a set of beliefs embraced but a calling to follow Jesus, and to follow Jesus means to become part of a community.

On Being a Community

A community is a group of people who know and are a part of one another's lives. In Chapter 2, we drew a distinction between the term "neighborhood," or a geographic area where people live and work, and a community. A community is an association of people who attempt to find meaning in their lives, meet one another's needs, and help one another accomplish shared goals (W. G. Brueggemann, 1996). *All* persons, both children and adults, need to be known by others, to be members of one or more communities. In our world of increasing independence, of more adults living alone than with others and more children in single-parent households, one of the most powerful contributions congregations can make in the lives of people, both those in the congregation and those in the neighborhood, is being a community for them.

We have identified four characteristics of congregations as communities that inform congregational social work—(1) congregations are networks of kinship and friendship; (2) people are part of the congregation more or less voluntarily; (3) congregations have distinct cultures; and (4) congregations are mission-driven.

"Family" is the relationships that endure over time and contexts, through which persons attempt to meet their needs for attachment, belonging, and sharing.

Networks of Kinship and Friendship

Congregations are communities bound together by interwoven networks of kinship and friendship. We define kinship (families) using a functional rather than a legal/biological definition; that is, who functions as family for each other, whether or not they are related biologically or legally by marriage or adoption. This functional definition is useful not only because of the myriad ways people organize themselves into families in our society, but even more importantly, because it is congruent with the life and teachings of Jesus about families. Jesus promises that those who follow Him will find a new family within the community of His disciples (Matthew 12: 46-50)[36] and fulfills that promise on the cross, as He turns His beloved disciple and His mother into a new mother-son relationship (John 19:25-27).

Defining Family

We define family as the relationships that endure over time and contexts, through which persons attempt to meet their needs for attachment, belonging, and sharing (D. R. Garland, 2012a). A family is the group of people with whom we share our troubles, our money, and with whom we eat on a regular basis, if not daily. A family takes care of each other during illness and sticks together year after year, despite geographic moves and other changing life circumstance. The words "attempt to" in the definition communicate that families are not always successful in fulfilling these functions. Nevertheless, these are the relationships through which people try to live out what it means to be family. The definition includes three functions of families: attachment, belonging, and sharing.[37]

Attachment—Comfort and Protection

We normally think of attachment in the context of the primary attachment of an infant to the caregiver. When a child is distressed or anxious, she seeks to be with the caregiver as a source of comfort, even when the other cannot really "fix" what is causing the distress. When a toddler falls and skins his knee, he may start to cry but at the same time, searches with his eyes and then runs to the parent with arms outstretched to be picked up—even though the parent's embrace does not heal the scrape.

Separation itself causes distress, as any babysitter will attest as a parent attempts to leave a child with an unfamiliar adult (Bowlby, 1969, 1975, 1988). Attachment does not end with childhood, however. Adults retain childhood attachments to family (Mikulincer & Shaver, 2005, 2007). Adult attachment figures may or may not be sexual partners; they may be friends who over time function as a family, in that these are the people we seek out to share joys and distresses, and to share the daily activities of life. These attachments form over time, as we experience comforting and caring for one another (Garland, 2012c).

Belonging—Identity

The second aspect of family bonds is a sense of belonging, the group expression of attachment. A family is the web of attachment relationships among members. Some attachments may be stronger than others, but all are strengthened by the webbed nature of the relationships. Families are bounded groups—it is clear who is an insider and who is not.

Family members see one another and know they are seen by the others as family, even if they do not necessarily like one another or "feel close" to one another—they still belong to one another. They may get mad and leave, but anger or leaving cannot dissolve this sense of belonging. To belong to nobody is to *be* nobody. "We know who we are only when we know to whom we belong" (Smedes, 2001, p. 21). The pictures we carry of one another in our billfolds or smart phones, the phone numbers we have in our "frequently called" list or committed to memory, the place at the table that is "ours"—these characterize belonging.

Entitlement—Rights and Responsibilities

A third facet of family bonds is that family members can make claims on one another; they are "entitled" to expect certain behaviors from one another and to give advice or comment about the life and ways of one another in ways that would be considered meddling or socially inappropriate interference by nonfamily members. Family members have chores, curfews, and other expectations—and they are entitled to expect similar behaviors of others in the family. Family members are expected to tell one another when they have spinach stuck in their teeth, a joke was inappropriate, or they are about to make a stupid mistake—the kinds of social indiscretions that strangers and even acquaintances are supposed to overlook.

Defining Friendship

The boundaries between friendship and kinship are permeable—family relationships may begin as friendships and become family ties over time. Friendships, too, are characterized by attachment, belonging, and entitlement.

Endurance seems to be the often subtle distinction between friendship and family—the definition of family above states that they "endure over time and contexts." The boundary between family and friendship is a fuzzy one, but it is still a "real" boundary.

Friendships, too, are characterized by attachment, belonging, and entitlement.

Friendships are often location-specific; retirees often attest to their surprise that long-term friendships in the workplace often fade on retirement. Obviously, sometimes friends go to extraordinary lengths to maintain friendships when distance intervenes, and sometimes friends become more family than some biological relatives. For example, we allow relationships with our least favorite cousins or aunts and uncles to drift for years, perhaps losing addresses and phone numbers. Alternatively, some relationships between family members may take on salient characteristics of friendships. These overlapping descriptions simply indicate that the boundaries between friendships and family are not crisply defined, not that there is not a difference between the two kinds of relationships.

The defining distinction between friendships and family is the covenant that characterizes family to continue the relationship despite whatever challenges may come—families endure. There is an understood or spoken commitment to "be family" for one another no matter what happens. A cross-country relocation for employment, a major interpersonal conflict, or a drifting of interests sometimes result in an end to friendships, but not usually to family relationships. The commitment to "be family" means figuring out how to bridge such chasms—whether it means everyone moving across country, seeking counsel from others to address the conflict, or finding ways to reconnect despite diverging interests.

Friendships experience no socially sanctioned expectation to repair such relationship rifts. When friends choose to let life circumstances or differences create distance in a friendship, there may be hurt and loss, but there is less a sense of betrayal or social pressure to make reparations. A family covenant commits persons to continue being family unconditionally even when their expectations of one another are not met. It is the promise we make to be family for one another, even when we are disappointed. Love does not hold families together; promises—and covenants—do (Doherty, 2001).

Family of God

Many congregations describe themselves as "family," and indeed, the concept of being part of the "family of God" has theological warrant in scripture. Jesus said that whoever follows Him would be His sister, His brother, His mother—followers become part of His family (Matthew 12:46-50). At Calvary Baptist Church, when persons present themselves to become members at the end of a worship service, the congregation recites a welcome—printed in the worship bulletin—that includes the words, "We promise to be the family of God for you in this place."

The congregation's function of fellowship is to ensure that everyone is enfolded into these networks of special relationship—friends and family.

The expectation that 300 people become family for one another is an important one, but it does not mean that each of us adds a place at our kitchen table for the new family member, or clears out a closet and makes space in our homes. Realistically, we are more like an extended family—cousins, aunts, uncles, and nieces—than we are brothers and sisters to one another.

A careful look at the examples Jesus provided suggests that within this larger family of God, there are intimate friendships and family relationships. For example, the Gospel of John says "Jesus loved Martha and her sister and Lazarus" (11:5). Mary, Martha and Lazarus were special to Jesus. The Gospels also reveal that Jesus had an inner circle of disciples (Mt 26:37; Lk 9:28; Jn 13:23). This inner circle likely functioned as family for Jesus.

A congregation is an extended family—or community—of friendship and kinship. The congregation's function of fellowship is to ensure that everyone is enfolded into these networks of special relationship—friends and family—like those Jesus had with his closest friends and disciples. In her study of congregational life, Becker found that the attachment people feel for their congregations is not the same thing as having an active social life or a group of friends, although they may have those relationships in a congregation. But she found that a congregation provides a sense of belonging, a knowledge or important events in each other's life and support in times of crisis—like a family provides (Becker, 1999).

Koinonia

The Christian scriptures use the Greek word *koinonia* for community, illustrated in Acts 2:42-47a, by the first church:

> They devoted themselves to the apostles' teaching and fellowship, to the breaking of bread and the prayers. Awe came upon everyone, because many wonders and signs were being done by the apostles. All who believed were together and had all things in common; they would sell their possessions and goods and distribute the proceeds to all, as any had need. Day by day, as they spent much time together in the temple, they broke

> bread at home and ate their food with glad and generous hearts, praising God and having the goodwill of all the people.

The way these early believers lived together day by day was a picture of what it meant to follow Jesus and continues to serve as an ideal for Christian congregations. The picture is one that looks like an extended family—spending time together on a daily basis, eating together, and sharing resources with one another.

Kinship and friendship are the domain of communities—of koinonia.

Being a community, an extended family, distinguishes this setting for social work practice from others. The congregational social worker's task is to strengthen the bonds of friendship and kinship, and to find ways that everyone is woven into these primary relationships. These bonds can be supplemented but not replaced by professional care. Social service professionals can provide services to clients; medical service professionals can provide surgical interventions, prescriptions, and expert advice; educational professionals can provide learning opportunities. But professional organizations do not provide kinship and friendship for clients. Kinship and friendship are the domain of communities—of *koinonia* (Brueggemann, 1996; Garland, 2012a; Saleebey, 2004).

"Voluntary"

Participation in a congregation is generally voluntary in the United States; everyone is more or less a member of the community because they have chosen to be there. Religious freedom is a hallmark of American society and institutionalized in the First Amendment to the U.S. Constitution (Congress of the U.S., 1789), which states that religious faith shall not be legislated or prohibited.

That freedom to participate voluntarily has been broadened in the norms of our society to congregational life. No one can tell American adults which congregation they must attend. If they do not like what is happening in one congregation, they simply move to another, or stop participating altogether. Even among Catholic congregations, which historically have defined membership by geographic parishes, the Second Vatican Council established a process that has led to the decoupling of residency and church membership, so that the territory is no longer the congregation—a Catholic no longer has to attend their parish congregation but can drive across town to a congregation they like better (Gamm, 2001). Large church complexes are built near expressway interchanges, with congregations coming from miles away, rather than nestled in a residential neighborhood to serve that neighborhood.

The voluntary nature of congregations is relative, however. Children attend because parents bring them. Teenagers and reluctant adults come because family members expect or demand their participation. Extended family, friends, and business customers may exert pressure to attend. Some believe that congregational leaders have the power to petition God for help, forgive or withhold forgiveness for sin, and even to assure or deny life after death for self and loved ones—so they attend to stay in the good graces of religious leaders. In short, participation in a congregation may not be coerced or denied by government agents in the United States, but that does not negate the power of social relationships and religious beliefs about its importance. Moreover, if congregations are genuine communities, then leaving one congregation and joining another can be a wrenching process for those who leave as well as for those who stay.

Large congregations may be defined by the expressway interchange that gives access to large parking lots for congregants from a broad area rather than by the neighborhoods in which they are located.

Within these parameters, the regularity with which adult congregants attend the various services and programs of the congregation is generally voluntary. If a program is not fulfilling expectations, people can simply stop going. As a consequence, maintaining interpersonal relationships and addressing conflict constructively have much greater import for social workers in congregations than those in other professional settings. If the congregational social worker is responsible for the social service outreach programs of the congregation, it is likely that congregants do much of the actual work. They are the tutors, the mentors, the activity leaders, the worker bees. Consulting with congregants who may decide to stop participating at any time is dramatically different than supervising employees. Congregants have to continue to feel the significance of what they do in order to be motivated; there is no paycheck at the end of the week that keeps them coming even when they are busy, tired, angry, hurt, or discouraged.

The American culture of religious voluntarism has also influenced the relationship of congregations with their Protestant denominations. In some denominations, the congregation's financial assets and facilities belong to the denomination; in others, however, congregations are free to associate, or not, with the denomination. If the congregation does not like what the denomination is doing, it may choose to withdraw and to affiliate with another denomination, to remain independent, or simply to withhold its financial support from the denomination. Or congregations may take partial steps in this process of exercising their freedom, by removing the name of their denomination from their name or downplaying their affiliation, even though it still exists.

Congregants have to continue to feel the significance of what they do in order to be motivated; there is no paycheck at the end of the week that keeps them coming even when they are busy, tired, angry, hurt, or discouraged.

Congregational Culture

The third characteristic of congregations as communities is that they have distinct cultures. They have their own language, nonverbal symbols, norms, and patterns of relationships. Terms may be fraught with nuances of meaning beyond their universal understanding, terms such as grace, blessing, evil, sin, shepherd, sanctified, sacrament, saved, and redeemed. Brian McLaren summarizes wide divergence in beliefs and traditions among Christian tradition on even basic Christology, or the nature and mission of Jesus Christ, all grounded in the same biblical text:

> For conservative Protestants and Roman Catholics, Jesus saves individuals through the cross and resurrection; for Eastern Orthodox followers, Jesus saves the world through the incarnation; for liberal Protestants and Anabaptists, 'Jesus saves' [quotation marks added] uniquely emphasizes Jesus' role in convening and leading a community of disciples. For them the church is not at heart an institution, as it has tended to be for the other groups ... with hierarchies and policies, headquarters, and bureaucracy (McLaren, 2004, p. 62).

Congregations have historical identities that shape their current understanding of themselves. Like families, congregations develop over time, going through stages that shape the community's life together.

The Bible, theology, and doctrine are central repositories of beliefs and values that are central to a congregation's culture and are touchstones for charting life together (Ammerman, 1997, 1999, 2002). For example, the concept of hospitality provides a foundation for social action on behalf of persons who are homeless and isolated, as well as social ministry programs designed to include them in the community. Biblical teachings on the value and role of children provide impetus for child welfare services and child advocacy.

Congregational social workers need to develop fluency in the beliefs and traditions of their communities.

All social workers, including congregational social workers, need to develop fluency in the beliefs and traditions of the communities they serve. In our own Baptist context, that means being able to use biblical stories and teachings, with appropriate biblical citations, as well as historic Baptist principles, programs, and ways to define our congregational work. Congregational social workers who do not have formal theological education can take or audit seminary and university courses in theology and explore the congregational leadership literature most relevant to the religious faith of the congregations with they are serving. A large number, though not the majority, of the congregational social workers we interviewed—24 of the 51—have degrees or certificates in religion or ministry.

Like social work in any cultural setting, as important as preparatory education about the culture can be, social workers sift and refine their cultural understandings by learning from those they serve. As valuable as seminary and other Christian education is for congregational social workers, they then use their skills of cultural learning and adaptation, "learning the ways," just as they would in an unfamiliar ethnic community.

Although congregations are shaped by the cultural values of society, such as religious voluntarism, they nurture and celebrate values and beliefs alternative to mainstream culture. They are not only conservators of culture, but also challengers of culture. The history of African Americans has been shaped markedly by the role of many Black congregations that served as alternative communities where ordinary people found respect instead of the dehumanization of a segregated society. Some Black congregations were seedbeds of cultural change during the Civil Rights era even as other congregations sought to maintain the status quo or at least stay uninvolved in cultural conflict. Similarly, ethnic congregations can serve as enclaves where people speak the first language rather than English and embrace ethnic cultural ways. For the poorest persons in our society, congregations are one of the few communities available that give access to resources and opportunities, including opportunities to develop leadership skills such as chairing a meeting and speaking in public. They link people with others who can provide a wide variety of resources—employment opportunities, informal child care, and a sharing of everything from yard tools to camping equipment (Ammerman, 1999).

Mission-Driven

Jesus used the image of fishing to call the disciples who were fishers by trade to follow him, saying "Follow me, and I will make you become fishers of men" (Mark 1:17). The fishing image is a rich one for understanding the missional nature of congregations.[38] I (Diana) have asked several congregational groups what they need to go fishing. Inevitably, they answer a line and a pole, bait, and a hook. Fishing means catching one fish at a time for most Americans. In conversations about providing ministry programs for the congregation's neighborhood, there are sometimes lively conversations about whether these programs should be considered "bait" to evangelize those being served, or simply as ministry with no "strings" (i.e., fishing line) attached.

The previous verse, however, says that Simon and Andrew were "casting a net into the sea, for they were fishermen" (Mk 1:16). The early disciples fished not with lines, hooks, and bait but with large nets of strong ropes that were thrown out into the water and used to gather in many fish at one time. A congregation is like a fishing net—it is a great web of relationships for folding people in, gathering them into the net, into the community of faith. Jesus calls followers not to fish by sitting alone in a rowboat or by donning hip boots and wading into swift water alone. In our individualistic, community-deprived culture, it is this promise of community—a network of relationships—that has the greatest potential for drawing others into the fellowship. Jesus said that the world should know us by our love for one another (John 13:35). This is the good news for our world: God intends for none of us to be alone, but rather, folded into a community (*koinonia*)—a network– known for its love. There we have pushed the picture as far as it applies, because a congregation is not a net used to entrap those who are unwilling but rather an open network, inviting rather than trapping into community.

The community itself, then, has a mission. A congregation is not simply a nurturing home base where individuals are taught, supported, encouraged, challenged, and then sent out on individual missions, like an air force base from which pilots and their planes leave to conduct their mission and return to for rest and fuel. The congregation itself has a mission and purpose, which is to fold others into the fellowship.

A congregation is a fishing net.

Social Workers as Community Builders

Congregations are or strive to be communities. Social workers who serve as congregational leaders engage in community formation and development. Using the image of fishing, they lead in (1) weaving nets of relationship, (2) repairing the frays, and (3) casting the net into the neighborhood and world.

Weaving the Net

A social worker brings knowledge and skills of group and community development to lead in the congregation's task of weaving itself into a strong net of relationships. That weaving involves connecting the nodes of kin and friends to one another so no one is left "dangling" or unconnected. The heart of the work of the congregational social workers we interviewed is forming relationships with congregants, clients, volunteers, community members, community leaders, and even among community organizations. As this list indicates, some of their weaving takes place within the congregation, forming community among congregants, among congregants and their neighbors, and in the world beyond the congregation, so that the social worker is leading the congregation in building a larger community with neighbors, other congregations, and other organizations.

The heart of the work of the congregational social workers we interviewed is forming relationships.

Weaving Self into Community

A primary task for these social workers is building relationships between themselves and others, which is a different approach to professional relationships from the time-limited, contract-for-service-focus with clients in a social service agency. Brandi described how different this was for her when she began her leadership as the Congregational Care Minister from her previous practice experience, with both positions involving work with senior adults:

Initially it was about connecting with people. A lot of what I do is about building relationships and that takes time. So I am in a continual journey with people on relationship building. With a congregation this size, new families are always coming in. New people are always stepping into that picture. My role is really trying to walk alongside each person, reminding them that they matter to this body of believers.

Her role is more personal and ongoing than is the norm for agency-based social workers:

> Every few days, I do some calling on some people to stay connected with them, especially if they do not have family in the area or if I feel there is no connection going for them. I want them to know that the church feels that interest in them and responsibility for them. So, I am that person.

In church language, this personal caring for congregants is called "pastoral care" (Holifield, 1983; Howe, 2000; Oates, 1970, 1985; Shelp & Sunderland, 2000). It includes visiting members in their homes, workplaces, or while they are in a health care facility as a representative of the congregation's care. In this role, the social worker listens to the other as a demonstration of caring for the other. As Beth said, "On my good days, I lay aside the tasks and just listen to people."

These social workers described how they sought to be in key places for relationships to develop. Becky describes her decision to drive the mini-bus that picks up deaf children and their parents for the congregation's summer American Sign Language camp. For the twenty-minute ride to the summer camp, she has opportunity to interact with parents and children while they ride the bus together.

> The majority of these parents do not sign. A typical day in the summer for me would be that I pick up kids and hear from parents, "Would you please talk with my child for me? Would you interpret for me?" One of the dads has a lot of doubt about the deaf community, and signing. His child is profoundly deaf. Two weeks ago he said that he knew he gave me a hard time last summer. His son is seven and came last year for the first time. He was really appreciative of me being patient with him, and helping him work through some of his own fears and concerns.

Forming relationships means getting out of the office and into the places where congregants are, as we see with Becky climbing on that camp bus each day. Sometimes, it means just being available during odd hours, with the office door open, so that congregants can drop in. When Sue began her new role in a congregation, she stayed late some evenings when there were programs taking place in the building, even though she was not leading or participating:

> There were nights that they have different activities and I would stay late because I knew some of them were going to walk by my door. I got to know them. They would come in and chat and visit with me. I would intentionally stay especially those early years when I was trying to get to know people in the congregation so that I could talk to them and visit with them.

Like social workers employed by social agencies, congregational social workers seek to be culturally competent in their context of practice. Beth, for example, describes how she led her congregation in responding to the grief of adoptive parents who had to relinquish the child they thought they were adopting when the birth mother changed her mind—she organized others to "bring in meals they could put in the freezer." Frozen casseroles carry the warm message that the congregation wants to nourish and care for them in their grief; a macaroni and cheese casserole is a symbol of that care.

Forming relationships means getting out of the office and into the places where congregants are.

The relationships that social workers develop are ongoing, often for as long as the social worker stays in that congregation, quite unlike time-limited professionally contracted relationships. Carl mused on his role as a "church planter" for his denomination. Church planters move into a neighborhood and through the formation of relationships, start a new congregation, as Carl did when he organized that first group of children into a Sunday school in a neighborhood park.

> We have not started one church; we've started many churches from generation to generation to generation. My dad was a tree farmer, and he showed me how to see the different rings of life of a tree when it was cut. You can tell when there was fire or drought. Those events affect the whole tree the rest of its life. In the starting of this church, every decision that was made and everything that we've done, I've not only thought about immediate growth for the church but how we will affect the faith community generations from now. Those are thoughts I wouldn't have had, I don't think, if I were not a social worker.

Connecting Others

In addition to forming personal relationships with congregants, these social workers also connected others to one another informally, as well as in short term and ongoing groups and coalitions. As one said, if she were going to use two words to describe the tasks that fill a typical day, they would be "making connections."

Much of the activity in congregational life takes place in groups. As a result, these social workers spend much of their time leading and serving in groups. Groups conduct the business of the congregation (staff, finance committee, deacons, elders), provide opportunities for Christian education (study groups, fellowship groups, Sunday school), prepare and lead in worship (choir, band, orchestra), and engage in missions in the neighborhood and world (ministry teams). As they go about their work together, members of these groups form friendships and weave themselves into small communities, or friendship groups, that have interlocking relationships with members of other small groups.

One of the most common ways of building community in a congregation is through the creation of small groups.

The congregational social workers we interviewed lead and/or facilitate educational groups designed to provide knowledge, values, and skills for life around a diversity of issues, as we described in the previous chapter.

Several of the social workers describe how they use camp—day camps, overnight camps, family camping—to build community. Lois does so between children and the older adults she serves:

> The fourth, fifth, and sixth graders have "Grace Camp," a weeklong day camp at Grace Presbyterian Village, which is a continuous care senior adult residential facility. Everybody loves it. The kids love it and the folks love it. They eat lunch there, and each day we invite senior adults who live there to come and share their gifts. We have one Grace Village resident who is an architect. Every year he teaches the children something new about architects. Another one teaches them how to make fudge. I work with the kids to prepare them to visit and spend time with those in the Alzheimer's unit. It's phenomenal how those kids interact with the older adults and how those older adults just love those kids.

These social workers have connected congregants—and those from the neighborhood—who share a life challenge into support groups, which the social worker may or may not facilitate. Life issues they have addressed with support groups include Alzheimer's disease; addiction to alcohol, drugs, or pornography; cancer; care-giving for a dependent parent or spouse; divorce; financial difficulties; grief and loss; immigration from another culture; incarceration and release; sexual abuse; and parenting as a single adult.

Weaving Congregation into a Larger Community

These social workers also weave their congregations into a larger community of congregations and other organizations in town. One social worker said that the heart of her responsibilities is "linking with other services in the community, connecting with other churches, trying to just pull churches together and share resources." They described developing relationships across lines that normally divide the community—political, cultural, and even religious—and using their relationships to form bridges and collaborations.

A big focus of Carl's work has been locating his congregation as an important hub for the neighborhood and the community of neighbors. That focus permeates much of what he does, including thinking about the physical location of his congregation. After the beginnings in the neighborhood park and the café where he held the memorial service, they rented an old gay bar that had been abandoned; he said wryly that they were the only church in town with a liquor license. Once they began to outgrow that space, an Anglican church with a beautiful facility offered them the use of space in their building without charging rent. Carl worried, though, that the gothic architecture of the beautiful facility would inadvertently make his congregation of folks from the neighborhood, some homeless and others living in a single-occupancy hotel, feel like it was not "theirs."

> Once you have them on folding chairs, how do you get them on pews? So once a month, we had church outside, to symbolize that we belonged in the community. Symbols like that are very important.

That belonging to the larger neighborhood is carried out in Carl's work to connect with other leaders in the city to form collaborations for the sake of neighborhood residents.

> I work with everybody, regardless of whether they are Christian or not. We have to work together. I trust that God will accomplish God's purposes. We can't get caught up in theological differences that prevent us from working together to help people.

Ben is the full-time pastor of an ethnically diverse nondenominational congregation, in addition to being a full-time social work program director in a university. He also sees developing and participating in city partnerships as a primary focus of his work:

> I spend a lot of time networking. I have a volunteer position with the city as a liaison for the African American and Latino communities, building bridges between those existing communities and the city. I spend a lot of time doing that. I have lots of breakfast meetings, lots of lunch meetings. It's about building the individual relationships first so that the individu-

> als trust me and are comfortable with me, and then will introduce me to their congregations without worrying about losing their mission or their culture. It's about finding places where we can have joint ventures.

Again, Ben focuses on building coalitions around common causes, even as he is respectful and protective of the differences across the various congregations and organizations.

As an example of such work across organizations, Howard, an associate pastor, described how he connects the lay leadership in his congregation with organizations in the community to help families who are homeless. His congregation provides housing several times a year as part of a consortium of congregations that partner to provide a crisis family shelter, moving the program from one congregation to another so as not to overtax the resources in any one.

Like Howard, many of these interviewees describe ways they lead their congregation to collaborate with other congregations in the community. David describes his role in a program for homeless families in ways very similar to Howard's role:

> Our community doesn't have a shelter for the homeless, so the churches cooperate together to provide shelter through the winter. When our church's time came, I coordinated and enlisted the volunteers. I also gave input and suggestions at the community level. The jail washed the linens every day. There were also congregations who wanted to participate but didn't have the facility so I worked out for them to use our facility when it was their turn.

These social workers also build collaborations with social service agencies as well as with other congregations. Brenda, the Director of Social Service Ministries for her congregation, describes how they have built partnerships with both congregations and social service agencies in their community to make sure that their resources are used most effectively. This kind of communication and experience with community partners led to greater trust that social service agencies could better provide emergency assistance than could the volunteers in her congregation, leading to her congregation's decision to discontinue their emergency food pantry and instead contribute to and collaborate with a social service agency in town that provides emergency assistance:

> My volunteers were getting burned out because people would come in with these long stories of woe, and they felt overwhelmed. They also thought some people were taking advantage of us. Now we're taking the food to a social service agency and social workers can take food in their car and just take in a bag of groceries when they run across a need. So we know that the food is getting to people who need it. So that's why we closed our food pantry.

Many of the interviewees describe organizing and leading community boards and committees. For example, Carl is chair of the community's "prevention committee" of the interfaith committee. They formed a group of all those providing emergency food assistance to coordinate and together stretch their resources. Others serve on Homeless Coalitions, United Way Committees, and city-formed Community Service Committees, as well as on the advisory and governing boards of community organizations. Sue describes her work with the local United Way:

> I chair the social services committee for United Way, and our committee decided what we needed to focus on is to get our community to work together so we hosted a workshop that we called "We are all in this together." We invited all of our churches and agencies in town and said we are going to have a brainstorming workshop to see how we can work smarter and work together. We had about 65 people that came from churches and agencies. We ended up with four subcommittees that are still meeting to work on those four community projects.

Some of the ways these social workers build relationships with the people they serve reflects the nature of congregations as communities or voluntary organizations. Social workers' relationships have more fluid boundaries than they would with clients in a social service agency. For example, they reported providing transportation for volunteers or clients or meeting them in restaurants for coffee of lunch. The professional role is, paradoxically, also a personal one, as Kylie explains:

> It's easier for mental health social workers to know who the client is because they're actually involved in therapy or the case manager role, but the things that I do here are more activity oriented. My activities with [congregants and neighbors] don't set me up as a professional who is working with you. I'm a Christian who wants to be in relationship with you.

The challenge, of course, is that the social worker must be clear about the professional nature of the relationship and the social worker's professional responsibilities toward clients in this less formal context.

Using Humor to Strengthen Relationships

Several of these social workers use humor to manage and reframe their work, and the humor is often aimed at themselves. Humor, devoid of any sarcastic tone that implies diminishing the other, can turn awkward or difficult moments into endearing ones—and can strengthen bonds between people. Carl is especially adept at using humor. For example, he describes one of his parishioners who is a client at the day treatment program for persons with chronic mental illness that is located across the street from the congregation:

> One day Steve was knocking on the door and said, "I want Jesus for my savior. And I want to be a minister." We talked, and I asked what he meant by wanting to be a minister. He said, "When you take your robe off, I want to fold it. When you need a drink, I'll bring you water." One Sunday he brought eight rolls of toilet paper. I asked what he was doing with all that toilet paper. He said that when he bought it, there were all those rolls and he only needed one so he brought the rest to the church. That's what we all ought to do: keep only what we need and give the rest away. Little things like that happen, and God teaches me so much.
>
> I started coughing one Sunday during worship and he asked if I needed a drink of water. So he brought me orange stuff in a glass. I asked what it was and he said "Slimfast; I figured you needed that more than water." I'm a little large.

Instead of being dismissive of a call to the ministry of folding the pastor's robe and bringing him a drink, instead of being inconvenienced by needing to find a cabinet for eight rolls of toilet paper, and instead of being embarrassed or humiliated by a glass of Slimfast in the middle of a sermon, Carl tuned himself to God's teaching through these "little things." His humor was joy at the treasure of these moments; one can hear his affection for Steve in his telling of these stories.

In a follow-up interview more than three years after the interview in which he told these stories, he informed us that he started working out at the gym and has lost 100 pounds. Perhaps Steve's glass of Slimfast encouraged him to hear God calling him to care for himself. In fact, that care has become yet another expression of his ministry:

> Health is not something that urban people think about a lot. They are attacked by the cigarette companies. They are attacked by these juices that are cheap and they drink all the time and there's no nutrition in them. Mindfulness about nutrition is just not a part of the culture. Also, now I have a whole group of friends at the gym who know me as Carl, not as Pastor. I didn't know how much I needed that, to be Carl again, and not Pastor. I'll go out bowling with them. I train with these people; I run with them; I bike with them.
>
> I told the church I was going to do this. I was preaching on a series of sermons, and I used the Greek word that means "overcome." Paul said, "Be not overcome by evil, but overcome evil by good," so I printed that verse and put it on a bracelet. I wore the bracelet and put the verse on all my workout clothes. That became my ministry also at the YMCA, even though that wasn't my intent. People started coming to me and asking me for prayer there, or they were asking me for a bracelet. I have this whole group of friends there that know that I'm a pastor, but they're of another faith. Sometimes they'll volunteer to help at our work. They've become a part of the ministry that I do.

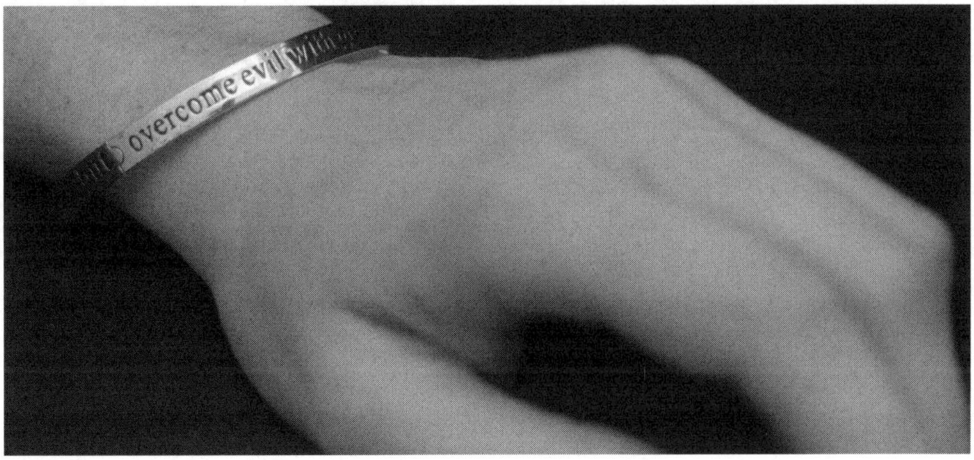

He now sees his ministry as including modeling care for the physical self for his congregation, as well as networking into his congregation the new friends he has made at the gym.

Repairing Frayed Nets

Simon and Andrew were fishing when Jesus called them (Mark 1:16), and James and John were mending their nets (Mark 1:19). Nets fray with use and have to be repaired. Communities—including congregations—have conflicts that have the potential for relationship frays and rifts. If addressed with respect, tolerance for a diversity of viewpoints, and willingness to compromise and learn from other another, conflict can actually strengthen the community. Several social workers we interviewed expressed their surprise at the prevalence of conflict in congregational life, and the challenges they face in addressing it. David is serving as an Associate Pastor in a congregation after decades spent in a career with a denominational agency. He said:

Nets fray with use and have to be repaired.

> Even though we are a small town church, there are strong personalities on the staff. There is more open expression of conflict than I've ever experienced. I'm certainly having the opportunity to be stretched. I don't really relish conflict, but I enjoy helping us to find common ground.

He went on to say that it is skills he learned as a social worker—understanding systems, mediation and forming community—that have helped him lead his congregation through conflict. Another social worker was not so positive in her description of the prevalence of conflict in her congregation:

> There are a small number of self-centered, narcissistic, demanding, arrogant people who think the world revolves around them and everything should be done exactly their way, or they're going to take their marbles and go home. I'm just really tired of that group of people.

David, too, sometimes feels worn down by the conflict:

> I go home sometimes feeling like there is too much drama. Our business meetings sometimes are two hours.... Folks are very free in expressing their positions.

These leaders identified a variety of sources of conflict that illustrate the commonness of conflict: three frequent examples are disagreement about the use of congregational resources, worship styles, and the limits of hospitality.

Use of Resources

Kylie runs a basketball program for five year olds in a basement room. This upset the congregation's trustees who feared that the building might be damaged by the children's rough play. The program targets children in their neighborhood, children of a lower socio-economic level than the long-term members of the congregation. I (Gaynor) had a similar experience with a congregation that was excited to bring people from a low-income inner city neighborhood on a bus to their suburban congregation for Sunday church activities; the congregation named it their "bus ministry." The children from the bus were not sent to the "regular" Sunday school classes, however, but to the gym in a separate Sunday school. Congregational leaders' reasons paralleled those of Kylie's congregation—they thought the children did "not know how to act in church" and might "tear up" the building. Such segregation communicates that the physical property is more valuable than forming community with newcomers. From the perspective of the congregational leaders, however, they are simply being good stewards of the resources with which they have been entrusted.

It is common for congregations to seek to serve their neighborhood and yet for some members—and leaders—to be resentful of the cost of success, such as the wear and tear to the building. In point of fact, it is rarely "just a building," but because a congregation is like an extended family, the building has the emotive feel of "home." People are attached to the physical surroundings (Becker, 1999). Others may define protection of property over inclusion of others as inappropriate or even racist. Conflict results and it is often seasoned with emotional heat because the issues are important to all.

Chris experienced similar interpersonal conflict when a group in the congregation proposed that their congregation use their building as an extreme weather shelter for persons who are homeless.

> Even with all of the contact [through our] ministries with persons that are homeless over the past several years, it was still a process and struggle for the church as a whole to embrace that ministry. There was [concern about] the idea of people sleeping overnight in the church's facility, and we heard people at general church membership meetings say things like, "They're going to clog up the toilets" and "What if they hide in the closet and jump out the next morning?"

One woman suggested they raise money for the shelter so that it could be placed separately from the congregation's facility. Not only is there concern about the use of the building, then, but also a distrust and even fear of the neighbors they are attempting to serve.

Worship Styles

Conflict over styles of worship, often expressed most overtly in music—use of "traditional" hymns with organ accompaniment versus praise choruses with drums and guitars—is arguably the most heated and common of conflicts in congregations today (Bader-Saye, 2004; York, 2003). David has searched for the underlying hurts and unmet expectations that have created this conflict in his congregation:

> I'm surprised by the extent of the conflict. I think some of that is grief expressing itself with seniors who see that the church is different from what it once was. We have two services, one contemporary at 8:30 and then the more traditional at 11:00. The contemporary service is growing.

But dividing into services has not ended the conflict:

> There is distrust, a fear that resources are going one way or the other. Some older folks feel pushed to the edge.

David described how he has used his social work skills as a congregational staff member in managing this conflict as an ongoing dynamic of congregational life. Moreover, this conflict is refreshed when the congregation's ministries result in neighbors joining in congregational life who bring their own expectations about worship styles.

Limits of Hospitality

An issue that creates perennial conflict for many congregations is the extent to which they welcome persons they perceive to be different from themselves. Even the early church leaders experienced conflict over whether or not to welcome non-Jews into their fellowship (Acts 15). This conflict is an umbrella for the two above; conflicts over hospitality often underlay concerns couched in other terms, that "they" will misuse our building, or whether or not to embrace worship styles that are different from "ours."

One limit of hospitality that is hotly debated in some congregations is that over whether or not to welcome persons who are gay or lesbian. As David talked about conflict in his congregation, he described the conflict he feels about this issue and believes others do as well. He is struggling with knowing how to address this topic, knowing that he has a responsibility to "help my congregation know that every human being is of worth, to know that their words can be hurtful to gays and lesbians in our congregation, or parents [with gay/lesbian children]."

Organizational Practices

A congregation's policies and practices are often based at least in part in interpretations of sacred texts and historical traditions, so that differences in interpretations may lead to conflict over practices that are based in differing understandings of God and truth. Such issues have the potential of splintering congregations. Extending hospitality to persons who are homosexual may be one such example, but there are certainly other life circumstances that at least a few people in some congregations may think warrant exclusion from the community, such as persons who are cohabiting or single women who are pregnant. Another organizational practice that is anchored in beliefs about ultimate truth include whether or not women, divorced people, or married people can serve as religious leaders. Chapter 4 discussed this issue from the context of the social workers' role in the congregation, but it also is a broader conflict in many congregations. For others, there may be conflict, for example, over whether or not to change the language in familiar hymns to gender neutrality, not referring to God as male and people as men, or to use biblical translations that use gender-neutral language.

These social workers also experienced and had to work through value conflicts with other congregational leaders or leaders in the community. Adam's congregation runs a "store" at Christmas time, selling toys and other gifts for children to parents in poverty at steeply reduced prices. The program expresses the congregation's valuing of the dignity of parents, recognizing that it is humiliating to have well-meaning others give gifts to their children that they cannot provide. Paying a portion of the price makes the gift from the parent, and not a "handout," preserving the parents' role as giver of gifts. He describes a conflict with a workers' union in the community over this program:

> A union representative came to me and said, "We want to fund all of your toys, we want to give you ten or fifteen thousand dollars worth, we will triple what you're doing, we want to do it all, but you can't sell it; we don't want you to sell them; that's not right." And I said, "no this is part of how we do it, and there are very logical reasons." And she said "Well that doesn't matter; do you want it or not." I said, "no." She was mad and couldn't believe that we turned that down.

The Role of Mediator

These congregational social workers told us that they frequently serve as mediators of congregational conflict, not only seeking to repair the fraying network of relationships in the congregation but also, in the process, serving the function of Christian education—teaching constructive conflict management. In other social service settings, conflict may be tolerated; staff may not agree with the policies and decisions of management, but they learn to cope for the sake of employment if nothing else. In a congregation, people may simply leave and join another congregation or simply drop out. Managing conflict effectively is important to maintaining the health and wellbeing of the community.

Social workers have ample opportunity not only to model conflict management but also to equip congregational leaders and members in conflict resolution skills.

Moreover, managing conflict is not only an important challenge but a common one. Becker (1998) studied 23 congregations over a five-year period and the 65 identifiable conflicts that took place over that time period in those congregations. Of those 65 conflicts, the most common reasons for conflict (n = 37) were administrative in nature—staff, money, and programming. Thirteen had to do with worship styles. Nine focused on conflict about the role or behavior of the pastor. Ten were over gender and sexuality issues. There were 19 conflicts in which factions were composed largely of longer-term versus newer members. Clearly, social workers have ample opportunity not only to model conflict management but also to equip congregational leaders and members in conflict resolution skills.

Casting the Net

Finally, a congregation as a network of relationships has a purpose, which is to "cast" itself into the neighborhood and world to draw in others. The most powerful resource a congregation has for missions is that it is a network of kinship and friendship with a purpose of folding others into itself. Congregations can complement professional agency-based services with care for congregants and neighbors that reflect their identities as a community—mentoring, tutoring, support groups, and other programs that emphasize informal, open-ended relationships between people rather than professional-client contractual services.

The most powerful resource a congregation has for missions is that it is a network of kinship and friendship with a purpose of folding others into itself.

For example, Lois had previous experience in providing professional services in a senior adult center. When she became a congregational staff member charged with ministry to senior adults, however, she recognized the potential of her congregation becoming a caring community for vulnerable older adults and their families. By developing the pastor aide program, she complemented the professional services she provides with the care and love of a community through congregants trained to offer friendship and support. Similarly, we have already seen that, through the 13 programs she has developed over the years, Lynne has extended the community care of her congregation to thousands of people. Her responsibility is training and supporting congregants to be "neighbors" through those programs.

Congregations can and do offer professional social services; several of the social workers we interviewed provide counseling services through the congregation or in an agency sponsored by one or more congregations. Ginger, for instance, works part-time as a clinical therapist in a three-person pastoral counseling agency where she is paid a salary, in addition to her full-time job as the director of field education in a university's undergraduate social work program. Her clinical practice reflects the community nature of congregational life; she describes her work as "building a healthy community." She leads workshops in the congregations on a variety of mental health topics. She had a client who was a single mother coping with high medical bills from repeated bouts with cancer. Ginger's congregation provided some groceries, financial assistance, and a support group. When the woman shared her situation with the support group, they had a "barbeque fundraiser" to provide further financial assistance, with her permission. Ginger said that in her social work experience, this kind of "wrap-around support" makes a congregational setting unique in its ability to reach through the isolation of the crises her clients face.

Although social workers are leading in all of the functions of congregational life, as we have seen, it is this missions function—casting the net—which is at the center of what most of the social workers we interviewed do on a daily basis. Chapter 6 will explore leadership in missions more fully.

Social Workers as Community Members

In Chapter 4, we began exploring the unique ethical challenges created by being a worship and educational leader when the social worker is providing counseling and other direct services to members of the congregation. We went so far as to caution congregational social workers who do serve in these leadership roles not to create dilemmas by considering carefully before offering clinical services to congregants. The challenges are broader, however, than those that are particularly sharp for those social workers who serve as worship and educational leaders. Congregational social workers are embedded in the network of kinship and friendship that is a congregation, and that creates challenges even for those who are not preaching or teaching Sunday school.

Counselor in the Community

Beth and Carl are both pastors—and they both do counseling. They limit their counseling to brief crisis counseling, however, and then refer to counseling professionals. Carl says that it is important that he stay in the role of pastor and not counselor, even in the short term. Moreover, he has had to structure even the crisis counseling; he said that people would be lined up to talk with him during the Sunday school hour that preceded worship. He found himself concerned that whatever he had prepared to preach about, they would imagine that he was speaking in response to whatever crisis they had just shared with him. Or he would be distracted by what they had just shared. Therefore, he turned the Sunday schedule around to protect himself, so that they started the morning with worship and then had their Sunday school, the time when members drift into Carl's office for conversation.

Still, he struggles with the challenges the crisis counseling creates for him. The week before our last conversation, one of Carl's members had shared with him that he is addicted to pornography and it is negatively affecting his marriage. A day later, Carl was leading the men's Bible study, and the topic was holiness and what it means to be set apart:

> I'm thinking that this person just talked to me yesterday. Is pornography a good topic to use in exploring holiness, or do I avoid it? I went ahead and got close to it, then he voluntarily shared his situation, and we went with it. I've been here 20 years; if I say the wrong thing or make mistakes, they still know I care about them. If I'm their pastor and someone is talking to me about pornography and they're having trouble, I'm not going to bring up their issue, but do I skirt it every time? I don't know if that's what a pastor should do. One thing about this church—there's no pretense. They are very open about their struggles.

For Carl, that is gratifying, because he has tried to create that kind of openness by being transparent about his own struggles:

> I decided a long time ago that they would also see who I am. The church is the land of the misfit toys. We're all waiting for God to fix us. As a community we come together and we can be the body of Christ. Some of that healing comes from each other as we're the body of Christ, but that won't happen if we're pretending there's no brokenness. It's definitely a culture I've tried to develop here, good or bad, and it seems to work for us.

Beth has noticed that when she counsels people, they put distance between themselves and her. For example, after worship they go out a different door so as not to greet her, the pastor, standing at the front door as people leave. That seems appropriate and not necessarily a problem:

> I just try to give them the space to do that. I don't pursue them. If they need space, I allow them to have the space. After a period of time, they reengage with me.

Like Carl, she has tried to stay in the role of pastor rather than counselor:

> Even though they withdraw, when they do come back, there is a deeper sense of relationship than there was before. They told me this information, and I haven't rejected them. I haven't disowned them or whatever they thought I might do.

In the role of pastor, Carl and Beth represent the acceptance of the community rather than judgment or rejection. This role distinguishes counseling in the role of religious leader from counseling in the role of social worker.

Glenda only rarely sees persons for counseling who are members of her congregation, and it makes her uncomfortable when she does, although she thinks her clients like being part of the same community with her. She describes an experience with one of her clients:

> We commemorate the seven last words of Christ during Good Friday services. They asked me to pick one and comment on it, and I totally forgot that she was probably going to be there. I spoke, and then I saw her receiving communion. I realized that I had revealed a part of myself that I would not have revealed otherwise. But I don't know that it was harmful in any way. I think she liked the idea that I was a person of faith and that she could rely on me. We certainly brought in a lot of her religious and spiritual life into the therapy I was providing. Maybe she just saw it as a part of me that was syntonic with the rest of the therapy. If I had thought about it [sharing in the Good Friday service], I probably would not have chosen to do it because it was very exposing.

Glenda's discomfort mirrors Beth's congregants who put distance between themselves and Beth for a time after sharing in counseling. But Glenda is the leader—although she feels exposed, she cannot slip out a side door. She has a responsibility to continue to work with her client and figure out how to cope with her client knowing more of her inner life than she would normally reveal in a professional relationship.

Melinda, too, is made uncomfortable by the thought of providing services to people with whom she has a personal relationship, although it is not much of an issue since her congregation numbers 2000 and she serves in a counseling center where she can easily refer to others. She compared counseling people she knows to her own discomfort with the fact that her doctor has joined her congregation, and "he knows everything about me." She is coping with it, she says, but she feels "violated." She gave an example of how she maintains boundaries with clients and former clients:

> Just a few months ago, I was in a fast food restaurant and a young woman looked at me and said, "Hi, do you remember me? Aren't you so and so?" I said, "Yes, I am. Help me with your name." I recognized her as someone that I had worked with before as a client, but I didn't particularly try to engage her in conversation. I would just smile no differently than I might as a warm greeting to a stranger, but she wanted to connect with me, pulled out her wallet, and showed me pictures of her baby. She said, "I'm here because my husband works here," and she wanted to introduce him to me. It's interesting because that's just a reminder to me that I played an important role in her life at a very vulnerable time,

> but another person might see me and choose not to say anything. I'm okay either way.

At the same time, Melinda welcomes clients from the prisoner re-entry program to come to her congregation and even to sit with her in worship; the difference is that she is not in a role of providing counseling services.

> If I'm working with them directly, then we talk about what it means to come to my church. My purpose isn't necessarily that clients come and worship where I worship, but that clients have opportunity to look at different ways that people worship and choose a place that really fits their needs and where they feel welcome and where they can blossom and grow. I have to be very careful that it's not a dependency that's growing, but it's a healthy kind of transitioning along the developmental lines so that the person ends up connecting with friends. Then the church community provides a wonderful opportunity for them to find their own safe place and their own place to grow and be when they can't do that for whatever reason in their biological family. I don't want to actually hinder their growth by encouraging someone to be overly dependent on me.

In other words, Melinda is using her relationship with her clients to connect them to the congregational network of relationships, a particularly poignant need for many of her clients who are ex-prisoners who have lost connections to biological family and friends.

Jeffrey has taken a different approach, which he can do, since he is working in an agency setting with congregational referrals. He says he learned from his father, a physician in a small town, how to provide confidential services in the community where you live and worship. He simply never acknowledged any patient outside the clinic setting. Jeffrey says that he, too, tells clients:

> If I see you on the street, I won't say hello because if I say hello to you my wife is going to say, 'Who's that?' and I tell her 'Somebody I know' and then she will say, 'Oh, a client.' So I will not say hello.

Jeffrey carefully explains these boundaries to his clients and maintains confidentiality as a strict discipline in his agency. Occasionally, in an emergency situation, he will see someone he knows in a counseling relationship one time, but then he refers.

Beyond 40 Hours

As we saw in Chapter 4, social work in a congregation is not a typical 40 hour, weekday job. It involves becoming part of a community that primarily gathers during after-work hours and on Sundays, with special events on Saturdays. The social worker becomes a part of that community, known to others as a community member and leader, not just a weaver of community for others.

Congregational social work involves becoming part of a community that primarily gathers during after-work hours and on Sundays, with special events on Saturday.

Many have made the decision to relocate, to live in the neighborhood of the congregation, particularly when the congregation sees itself as belonging to and serving a particular geographic area. Whether geographically in the neighborhood or a member of the congregation that is community for people from a larger geographical region, social workers find themselves "on" all the time as members of the community who also lead that community. One social worker said, "You become your function, and that is really hard."

Yet participation as a community member is an important asset the social workers can use in their work. Earl, a congregational social worker in a rural community, went hunting with a man "who wanted to know what kind of man I am," which was the first step that led to the man allowing Earl to work with his family through some difficulties. Like Becky, who reached out to form relationships with parents of children with hearing impairments by riding the bus with them, many of these social workers describe ways they sought personal relationships with members of the congregation. They visit those they serve in their homes, in the hospital, and in the workplace. They are present with families in times of crisis, illness, and death.

Some describe this leadership role of visiting and phoning members in times of crisis, illness, or bereavement as "pastoral care," contrasted with "congregational care," defined as congregants themselves providing this ministry of presence. Both grow out of, and contribute to, the community nature of the congregation. Brandi is the Congregational Care Minister and says that her congregation sees her "as the mother of the church in some aspects, that person that they can trust and come to and know that I'm going to be there to take care for them."

In our first interview, Earl told us that most of his friendships were with fellow church members. A number of months later, however, he contacted us to let us know that the funding for his position was no longer available. Because he was not included in the decision to terminate his role, he said he was "very surprised, hurt, betrayed, and angry." Congregations are human institutions that can be hurtful as well as helpful. They are not only communities but also organizations that hire—and fire. This experience of losing a job is not unique to congregations, of course, but a sense of betrayal and anger may be much more overwhelming whenever the workplace is also one's community.

Given the communal nature of congregational life, a task that falls to many of these social workers is setting appropriate interpersonal boundaries for themselves and for others. Social workers in these sections have multiple roles with congregants and community members. They may find themselves expected to be counselor, worship leader, religious teacher, and neighbor/friend—all with the same people. They juggle the contradictions that come when their community is also their employer. Dual, and multiple, relationships cannot be avoided; they are expected and so these social workers have sought ways to manage relationships that protect community members/clients and themselves from exploitation.

The social work *Code of Ethics* primarily deals with the most blatant of boundary violations, such as engaging in a sexual relationship with a client. It does not provide such explicit prescriptions and proscriptions for the daily challenges that may arise in congregational social work, such as finding yourself sitting with your family across a church supper table from a client's family. In a critique of the *NASW Code of Ethics,* Freud and Krug suggest that there is inevitable blurring of professional, social, and business distinctions, and engaging in a "social work relationship" can be an integral part of social work in communities like congregations. In fact, "purposeful cultivation of 'dual relationships' may be necessary for successful entry, professional legitimacy, and knowledgeable intervention" (Freud & Krug, 2002, p. 486).

Several of these social workers describe the ways they relate informally in friendly ways with those they serve. Catarina took a young mother whose husband was unemployed to the hospital for chemotherapy for her cancer. The mother shared that there were no groceries at home, so Catarina bought groceries on the return trip to the woman's home.

One of our students, while doing an internship in a congregation, wrote in her learning log:

> I am learning that congregational social worker often involves relationships that are personal and intimate ... Professional does not equal detached. But it does mean you can never step out of role. I am encouraged by the intimacy of the relationships between the members of the congregation and the community but am anxious about the appropriateness of these relationships for a social worker. Not only are dual relationships inevitable but might be necessary to gain trust of congregation and other church leaders. Boundary crossings are not necessarily boundary violations. Very important to remember! (personal communication, MSW student, February 12, 2008).

Setting Boundaries

The boundaries of congregational social work are rarely set by any organizational policy as they are in many agency settings. It often falls to the social worker to define the boundaries to protect congregants as individuals, the congregation as a community, and themselves and their families.

Boundaries for Congregants

An extended example shows how complicated relationships can become for congregational social workers, and the resultant complexity for these social workers to sort through in deciding how to think about relationship boundaries. Austin spent two hours taking a homeless client, Sam, in his own car to an appointment at the mental health center, to get his medication for schizophrenia renewed.

> The psychiatrist was very grateful that I was there, to help facilitate communication between the two. After the appointment, we went to lunch and talked over sandwiches.

One of Sam's difficulties is maintaining his medication, not taking too much and then running out by the end of the month, or losing it. So the congregation's community center locks them in the safe for him, and Sam comes to the community center and dispenses himself a week's worth at a time. That way, if he loses his medication, he only loses a week of medication and not two months' worth, which was what he had been carrying around with him.

The dispensing arrangement also gives him a way of being accountable. Austin mused that he is not technically Sam's case manager, but they are even closer than that; "I am his minister and friend." That relationship, and the medication dispensing strategy, developed over time, as a result of a crisis in their relationship. Austin had seen that Sam was in a process of "spiraling down into a self-destructing pattern of not taking care of himself and not taking his medication:"

> I sat him down and said, "Sam, this is your choice to do this and to make some of the decisions you've been making, but we're not going to sit by and watch you do it. I'm either going to be here to help you and for us to work together on this, or you're going to have to do this somewhere else, and you can't come to church here." And I knew that church was very, very important to him, and it was pretty much the only thing I had to hold out there was his church attendance.

Sam made his choice, and his choice was to continue in a pattern of refusing medication and to ignore the other conditions Austin had placed on congregational participation. So Austin acted:

> I had to say, "You can't be here." And that was one of the hardest things that I've done since I've been at this church, to tell someone that they can't come to church.

Three months passed, and when Sam did not return, Austin went looking for him in the woods, where he knew Sam camped:

> He knew that my door was open, that he could come and meet with me to renegotiate his church involvement, but he hadn't come through the door. So I went back out there and found him. I actually taped a note on a tree in the woods on a path that I knew he took, and he found it and he showed back up.

Austin's "conditions" for Sam's involvement in the congregation amount to program boundaries and establishing behavioral expectations as the conditions for service.

Several of these social workers described similar challenges in setting such boundaries. Beth had to ban a man from church attendance when she learned that he was stealing food from the church. When we interviewed her, she had just dealt with a marital couple that had separated and both people were still attending the congregation. During a fellowship time after a worship service, one partner approached the other with a big hug, and Beth "watched the people around them recoil; it felt like a violation of the sacred space and of boundaries." She called them both and told them that she wanted to see them together to talk about appropriate public boundaries. Congregational life, she says, is "very messy."

"Congregational life is very messy."

Boundaries for the Community

A number of these social workers have the responsibility of ensuring the physical safety of their congregations; they deal with physical threats and consider ways to prevent or respond to sexual and physical abuse (Garland, 2013c, 2013e; Harder & Haynie, 2012; Oxford, 2012; Pohl, 1999; Westerhoff, 2002). The church elders asked Earl to figure out what to do with a man who was "grooming children sexually." After consulting a lawyer, Earl offered the man counseling and told him he had to be monitored at all times when on the congregation's premises.

> He refused, so we escorted him off the campus. And then I walked the perimeter during worship.... My job is to keep children safe. After that, we got windows put in all the doors to spaces where there are children.

Carl, in his role as pastor, learned that a church member had had sex with a child. Carl reported the incident to the police; the man went to jail. Carl says that he has to be minister to both the man and the child.

> He came to me for counseling; my mistake was that I didn't tell him that I had to report that. I just didn't expect it. I was not happy to be me that day. Somebody told me that a pastor shouldn't report. But of course I had no choice.

After his jail term, the man returned to the congregation.

> He came back angry, but he came back. The church had to vote to let him come back. He can't be around children at all. We watch and make sure. There was a time we had three registered sexual offenders. It's tough to know what to do. I let the whole community know and we decide together.

It often falls to the social worker to develop and carry out policies that protect the congregation and its people—both children and adults—from abuse of the considerable power that religious leaders have in the lives of others.

Most religious leaders are highly caring and ethical. Nevertheless, the continuing media coverage of the sexual abuse of children by religious leaders—Protestant as well as Catholic—has brought attention to the need for protective policies and strategies. Our own research discovered that more than 3% of women in the U.S. who are active in a congregation (i.e., have attended in the last month) have been the target of sexual harassment by a religious leader at some time during their adult life. In the average American congregation of 400 persons, with women representing, on average, 60% of the congregation, there are an average of 7 women who have been the targets of sexual harassment by a religious leader and 32 persons who have experienced clergy sexual misconduct (Chaves & Garland, 2009). Of course, that does not mean that clergy sexual misconduct occurs in every congregation, but it occurs in many, and when it does, it often occurs multiple times. Further, we found that it is the nature of congregational life that allows abuse to occur—(1) the trust people have of their leaders; (2) the fluid structures and lack of leaders' formal accountability that characterize most community life; (3) discomfort with conflict and confrontation, or what we have called a culture of "niceness"; and (4) the opportunities for private and intimate communication that provide a context ripe for abuse (Garland, 2013c; Garland & Argueta, 2010). The congregational social worker brings an understanding of social systems and communities that can help congregations recognize risks and develop ways of making congregations true "sanctuaries"—safe places (Garland & Kabat, 2013).

> *The congregational social worker brings an understanding of social systems and communities that can help congregations recognize risks and develop ways of making congregations true "sanctuaries"—safe places.*

Boundaries for Personal and Family Lives

Another important task for these social workers is managing the impact of their vocation on their personal lives and their families' lives. Of course, that is true in every setting of social work practice, and for that matter, in every other profession as well. But the challenges for these social workers are unique in some ways. For example, a few of those interviewed said that they believe that a social worker should be committed to living in the congregation's neighborhood long-term; if the social worker makes that commitment, then it has major impact on their families and on their relationships with extended families and friends. In essence, the neighborhood and community they serve becomes their community and their family's community. Their calling determines where their children will go to school, who their friends will be, and what risks they do or do not face by living in the neighborhood.

These social workers did not all reach this conclusion, and those that have done so have come to their commitment over time. Adam is one of those who have made this commitment as the pastor of an inner-city congregation and director of the agency that grew from the congregation. He explains:

> For me, this inner-city work is really a long term commitment—helping a community and being part of a community that has in most places seen 40 or 50 years of deterioration. The encouraging part for me is that almost all our teenagers that we have grew up in our programs as little kids. We are just on the cusp of that generation of getting them into college and adulthood. Part of our success will be help them to realize that they can stay here and be a part of the positive.

Carl made a different decision because of the challenge of boundaries with his congregation. He and his wife bought a home outside the neighborhood of the congregation, "so people are not knocking on our door." He does not give his congregation his cell phone number, and he screens his calls to his home landline. Even so, his involvement in the congregation has been a source of family contention. He felt he had to cut a vacation short when someone in the congregation died, and he delayed joining his wife, who went without him, to be with her mother who was dying; Carl felt he had to do a funeral for a member of his congregation first, before attending to his own family's crisis.[39]

Many of those we interviewed stressed the importance of personal boundaries and caring for themselves. We earlier described how, in the years between our interviews with him, Carl joined a gym, lost a significant amount of weight, and began training to do triathlons. Beth said that she is diligent about taking her allotted days off and limiting the number of evening meetings she has to attend.

For others, boundaries are much more permeable, perhaps even nonexistent. Lynne says her life is her congregation. She lives with her adult daughter, who runs one of the programs Lynne supervises, so she is her daughter's work supervisor. She considered and then rejected retirement, now that she is in her 70s: "What I do brings me more pleasure than anything else I could imagine."

Beth and Lynne are both apparently very much appreciated by their congregations and happy in their work. Their situations are quite different, however. Beth is a pastor; Lynne is in a congregation where women are not allowed to preach. Beth's focus is on pastoral care for her congregation; Lynne's focus is on overseeing a multitude of congregational programs of service to the congregation's neighbors and beyond. Beth is a wife and mother of a preschooler; Lynne is a widow and grandmother. These differences in their stages of life, family circumstances, and professional responsibilities underscore that there is no one way to be a congregational social worker. Each must work out what works best, given the congregational setting, the roles they fill, and their own personal needs and family situations.

There is no one way to be a congregational social worker.

Chapter 6
Leading in Missions

Although social workers serve as leaders in all the functions of congregational life—worship, Christian education, fellowship, and missions—leadership of congregational missions is the primary focus for many of the social workers we interviewed. Various terms for this function of congregation life reflect distinctive church traditions and beliefs. The term "outreach" implies that this is activity that attempts to reach those outside the congregation through service. Similarly, "community ministry" refers to service to those in the geographic community of a congregation, or what we are calling the "neighborhood." emphasizing local rather than distant neighbors. "Missions" also often connotes the support of or direct engagement in international service programs. "Social justice" and "social action" imply that activity focuses on social systems that hinder human flourishing rather than or in addition to addressing needs on an individual basis (Davidson, Johnson, & Mock, 1990; Davis, 1997; Kysar, 1991).

"Missions" refers to all the ways that Christians and their congregations address the needs of neighbors wherever those needs exist as a way of responding to God's calling, whether the focus is individuals, families, neighborhoods, social systems or society.

Missions—Responding to God's Call to Serve

We use the term "missions" as an umbrella that encompasses *all the ways that Christians and their congregations respond to God's call to address the needs of neighbors wherever those needs exist , whether the focus is individuals, families, neighborhoods, social systems or society.* The definition of "mission" connotes a person receiving a task or assignment from a superior—think of military missions, espionage assignments in movies, and the old television show *Mission Impossible.* Jesus "commissioned" His disciples—sent them on the mission—of sharing what they had experienced as His last act after His death and as He ascended into heaven (Acts 1:8-10).

The concern of Christian missions is neighbors who are outside the congregation, both nearby and continents away. We see missions as a subset of "ministry," which includes service to those inside the congregation as well as those beyond the congregation's boundary.

The Focus is Neighbor and Neighborhood

The focus of missions is to reach outside the congregation to address the human needs of local and global neighbors. Although neighbors are the primary focus of service, mission activity also frequently includes service to congregants as well. When we began studying the transcripts of our interviews with these social workers, we attempted to organize their leadership in social service activities by the target of service. That is, we tried to identify those services targeted to members of the congregations and those that are targeted outside the congregation to the geographic neighborhood and beyond. Quickly, we learned that dichotomy does not work for rather obvious reasons. Congregants are themselves neighborhood residents, whether they are from geographically close neighborhoods or more distant neighborhoods; they often share the same needs as neighbors who are not congregants. A grief support group, for example, can be an effective ministry for both those within a congregation who are grieving as well as those in the neighborhood. Thus, mission also contributes to one of the other primary purposes of congregational life, that of fellowship.

In fact, many mission programs that target the neighborhood may begin because of a felt need of one or more congregants. Carl gave the example of his congregation's feeding program through which neighborhood residents can receive groceries to take home. Some of the congregants who volunteer to distribute the groceries are themselves recipients—they need the groceries, too.

Nevertheless, congregational programs of service are often designed to draw nonmembers from the congregation's neighborhood to join the congregation. A congregation may evaluate the "success" of its mission activity by the number of neighbors served who become Christians and/or members of the congregation.

Missions is Also Worship, Christian Education, and Fellowship

"Missions" is not a discreet function, separate from the other functions of congregational life. Activities and programs that are designed as missions contain at least some elements of worship, Christian education, and fellowship. In fact, they may be more effective and sustainable when they include these other functions of congregational life.

Activities and programs that are designed as missions contain at least some elements of worship, Christian education, and fellowship.

Worship

Missions may contain explicit worship elements. Christians may pray together or alone as they begin or reflect on a service activity—or while they are engaged in it. Jesus taught that acts of service to neighbors are acts of devotion to Him; "just as you did it to one of the least of these who are members of my family, you did it to me" (Matthew 25:40). If His followers want to welcome God into their lives, they care for the smallest and most powerless of people, symbolized by a child (Mark 9:36). Service, then, is a form of worship, of seeking, recognizing, and celebrating God's presence.

Christian Education

The mission function of a congregation may involve collecting funds to support others—professionals and lay persons—as they go and do mission work locally and globally. Even when congregants are not themselves directly engaged in the mission activity, however, congregations provide education about missions. As we saw in Chapter 2, mission education organizations were the birthplace of congregational social work, with their focus on preparing career missionaries, supported by congregational missions organizations who learned about their work and prayed for them as "their" missionaries (see also Wuthnow, 2009).

I (Gaynor) was one of those career missionaries serving through the Home Mission Board (now the North American Mission Board) of the Southern Baptist Convention. A printed monthly calendar from the Woman's Missionary Union, SBC included the names of all the missionaries who had birthdays that month and was distributed to all the congregational missions organizations in our denomination. For over 30 years of missionary service, I could count on the consistent prayers of people in Southern Baptist congregations, particularly the women of the Woman's Missionary Union. They also gave to mission offerings that paid our salaries and in other ways supported our work.

Congregations also involve their members directly in serving others in short-term and ongoing programs, and in today's world of rapid transportation, both locally and globally. Engagement in mission programs is integral to Christian education, in at least some respects like field education is integral to social work education. Christian education is not just a classroom activity designed to teach biblical and theological knowledge for the sake of knowing it. Rather, knowledge becomes complete when it is enacted through application. Christian education is a cycle of learning based on studying, living life, and reflecting on the interaction of what we know and believe with our lived experiences.

Mission activities provide opportunity for forming and deepening relationships between congregants—fellowship and community building.

Community Building

Finally, mission activities provide opportunity for forming and deepening relationships between congregants—fellowship and community building. Team members often become friends as they work side by side preparing food to be distributed in a food pantry or Meals on Wheels, or building or refurbishing a house, or tutoring children together. Likewise, friendships also may develop among team members, among recipients, and also between team members and the recipients of service, so that relationships become mutual rather than one way.

The Desire for Mission Engagement[40]

Christian leaders want to engage their people in missions, recognizing that it is through serving that Christians grow in their faith. Rick Rusaw, a leader in what has been called "the externally focused church movement," and pastor of Lifebridge Church in Longmont, Colorado, said in a sermon at a conference:

"People don't grow until they serve."

> People don't grow until they serve. One of our members was serving in a halfway house and a man there asked him to pray. He said 'I don't know how, but I'll go get one and be right back.' He came to me to ask for a prayer. And so I helped him learn to pray (Rusaw, 2008).

The doing of faith through service drives us to prayer and Bible study and worship, as this servant in the halfway house illustrates. Jesus called the disciples and engaged them in ministry almost immediately—and then taught them as they walked the journey together, as they healed and served, as they ran into challenges and failure (e.g., Mark 9:14-29). Rusaw believes that a church is not really a church "if it is not engaged in the life of the community through ministry and service to others" (Rusaw & Swanson, 2004). He continues:

> The biggest factor in our church's retaining people is not personal follow up or joining a small group; it is being involved from the very beginning in service to others in the community. It is mobilization that equals assimilation (p. 80).

Rick Warren has astutely observed that a congregation's strength is not its seating capacity, but its sending capacity—the deployment of members into ministry (Warren, 1995). Reggie McNeal offers a similar refrain. He says that "externally focused ministry leaders take their cues from the environment around them in terms of needs and opportunities; they look for ways to bless and to serve the communities where they are located" (McNeal, 2009, p. 7). These religious leaders' advocacy for service as the heart of a life of faith sounds like something a social worker would say.

What We Learned from Congregations

In the early 1990s, I (Diana) developed an assessment tool called The Church Census (CC) that has been revised over and over in the subsequent 25 years. The CC surveys all the teenagers and adults attending a given congregation during a specific time period in order to provide leaders of the congregation with a comprehensive description of congregational demographics, family strengths and stressors, life crises, and felt needs that congregants want their leaders to address. We added the "How the church can help" section in 2001. Topics in that section include communication skills, romance and sexuality in married life, romance and sexuality in single life, roles of men and women, managing time; managing money, family worship and prayer, coping with crises, parenting children, single parenting—and the list goes on, 52 topics in all (Garland, 2002d, 2004a; Garland & Yankeelov, 2001; Garland & Yankeelov, 1998).

In a different research project taking place during those same years, I (Diana) asked a diversity of families who are active in Christian congregations to tell me about their faith life together, taping and transcribing their conversations with me and then coding the transcripts so I could understand the role of faith in these families' experiences (Garland, 2001a, 2002a, 2002b, 2003). I was surprised to hear how many of those families told me stories about their shared faith being expressed in service together to others in their neighborhoods and cities. Because of what I learned from those families, I added another item, number 53, into the "How the church can help" section of the CC. The item I added was "help in serving others outside our family."

The CC has been conducted in Presbyterian, Lutheran, United Methodist, Southern Baptist, Cooperative Baptist, Unitarian, Episcopal, "Christian," Disciples of Christ, Church of God, and nondenominational congregations. Almost without exception, in the more than 50 congregations we have surveyed since adding that item, "help in serving others outside our family" is the most frequent need felt by every category of family type in every congregation. Congregants with all kinds of family structures and at different places in the family life cycle are asking their congregation's leaders to help them find ways to engage in service to their neighbors together (e.g., Garland & Edmonds, 2007).

Congregants with all kinds of family structures and at different places in the family life cycle are asking their congregation's leaders to help them find ways to engage in service to their neighbors together.

The CC findings also indicated that, in fact, these families are already engaged in service together. The survey includes a section entitled "how we live our faith together." We found that these families were already more likely to be engaged together in service as expressions of their shared faith than to be engaged in studying the Bible together. Yet they still are asking their congregations to guide them in that service; why is that?

We are a society known for volunteering; opportunities are everywhere. Families can go to any number of social service agencies and find ample opportunities to serve their communities. There are a myriad of "walks" and "runs" to raise money for various causes, community cleanups, and children's programs that need leaders. What these families said to us in the survey is that they want to ground what they are doing in their lives of faith.

What We Learned from Christians Serving in Missions[41]

In yet another research study in this same line of inquiry, a group of colleagues and I (Diana)[42] conducted research with 35 congregations, surveying 7,300 church attendees.[43] The surveys showed Rick Rusaw is right in saying that engagement in service is related to growth in the life of faith. Those involved in service to their community reported that they prayed, came to worship services, and gave financially significantly more than those not involved in service.

In fact, we found that being involved in service in a congregation's neighborhoods as often as once a week was significantly related to other measures of faith, such as prayer and Bible study. Active engagement in service to others had a more profound relationship with Christian faith than any other faith activity, even attending congregational worship. This finding applied to teenagers as well as to adults. It suggests that to encourage the deepening of a life of faith, programs that engage Christians in service should be at the heart of congregational life and not simply a once a year mission trip or project.

A congregation's theology motivates and shapes the nature of its missions. Some emphasize caring for the needs of neighbors whatever their religious faith may or may not be, and without expectation that the service will include an opportunity for conversation about religious faith. Others emphasize service as a way to gain opportunity to talk about matters of faith in the hope of evangelizing service recipients who are not Christian. Some emphasize addressing human need through charity—feeding persons who are homeless and providing emergency assistance to those in need. Others emphasize addressing human need through advocacy for justice—strengthening educational programming for children and adults in poverty, leading economic development in an impoverished community, advocating for fair trade with disadvantaged global farmers. Social workers need to understand not only the congregants they lead and the geographical neighborhoods a congregation feels called to serve, but also the motivations that shape the congregation's understanding of mission. Motivations are often complex; congregants will have different and perhaps even conflicting motivations and understandings of their mission together.

Active engagement in service to others had a more profound relationship with Christian faith than any other faith activity, even attending congregational worship.

In the Service and Faith Project described above, Christians engaged in service told us about four motivations for their work that were primary and overlapping: (1) response to God, (2) obligation to respond to human need, (3) beneficial relationships, and (4) other personal benefits. "Evangelism" per se was actually not a primary motivation for them, even though it may motivate their congregations.

Most of these Christians talked of their service activities as a *response to God.* They spoke of their service as doing what Christian scriptures instruct Christians to do and thus they are fulfilling what they sense to be a general obligation to God. An African American Assemblies of God postal worker, who purchases food and distributes to the elderly, said:

> I'd like to think that what I'm doing pleases God. I'm trying to fulfill the mandate that he's given to each of us, and that is to help our brothers.

This sense of obligation continues to motivate beyond the first blush of serving, as this Anglo-American Baptist who had been involved in organizing inner city programs for years indicated:

> I became more and more convinced that this is what everybody ought to be doing. The main thing that Christianity was about was ministering to the poor and changing their situation.

Second, they felt *an obligation to respond to the needs of their neighbors and communities.* Seeing the need obligated them to try to help. Moreover, some identified how their own marginal socioeconomic status or personal misfortune in the past sensitized them to the needs of others and obligated them to help as they had been helped.

Moreover, these Christians believe that they have responsibility to respond to spiritual as well as physical needs they perceive in those they serve. Some see their service as an opportunity to share their faith with service recipients, but how that sharing takes place varies from loving actions to verbally conversing with recipients about faith. A Presbyterian journalist teaching budgeting skills in a homeless shelter explains that for him, faith is meeting the other's needs, whatever they are:

> It's like the blind man when he cried outside the gates of Jericho, "Jesus have mercy on me, Jesus have mercy on me!" Jesus walked over to him and said, "What is it you would have me do for you?" That is the question I am always asking myself. What is it that Jesus would have me do for this person? That's it. We come from all different circumstances and situations, and some of us have a better role and position in life than others by whatever circumstance, but you strip all that away and we are just brothers and sisters together. And so then how do you choose to respond to one another?

Others saw their service as an opportunity to share their own stories as a means of encouraging others, as this African American Baptist grandmother who delivers food and clothing to homeless persons on the streets explains:

> Because of my exposure in my own family with chemical dependency and its impact it had on my family structure, I have a testimony that I can share with others. God lets me know when I need to share that testimony. When I see others at a certain point in their lives then I can pull them aside, and I can testify about the goodness of God.

While feeling obligated to respond to God or to human need often motivated Christians to get involved, some spoke of *personal benefits* they discovered in serving, primarily the satisfaction they found in the relationships with those they served. These satisfactions apparently served more to motivate their continued service than they did to initiate it.

Christians are asking their congregations to show them where and how to live lives of meaningful service.

In fact, most of the motivations include some indirect personal benefits, such as the satisfaction that comes from believing that one has been obedient to religious teachings or that one has responded appropriately to need, as well as the beneficial relationships that develop. None talked of job skills or other material benefits from serving, however. Rather, they talked about the positive emotions and personal identity that serving provided them. They spoke of their service as an experience that has deepened their religious faith.

To summarize, church leaders are telling one another that to lead Christians in the faith, they must lead them in service. We have research that suggests strongly they are right. Service is highly correlated with an active life of faith. Moreover, Christians are asking their congregations to show them where and how to live lives of meaningful service.

Evangelism

The role of evangelism in missions is of particular importance to social workers. We define evangelism as *teaching others about Christianity and attempting to attract them to become Christians and/or members of a congregation.*

Social Work Practice and Evangelism

In their professional relationships with clients, social workers value the protection of a client's ability to make their own decisions about how to live life as much as possible, limited only by the protection of life itself—their own and others—and by the rights of others. Professional standards explicitly identify religion as an area in which social workers need to exercise particular caution that they not take advantage of clients' dependence on them for the services clients need:

> Social workers should not take unfair advantage of any professional relationship or exploit others to further their personal, religious, political, or business interests (National Association of Social Workers, 2008).

In other words, social workers have to exercise caution not to explicitly or implicitly exert pressure on clients to adopt the social worker's religious beliefs and practices. David Sherwood has written extensively and wisely about the ethical issues of social work practice and evangelism:

> The key is that we must [discuss religion and spiritual issues] from a client-focused and client-led perspective. This normally means that we may not ethically engage in evangelism with our clients…It is always ethical and appropriate to demonstrate the gospel to our clients, but it is seldom ethical to proclaim the gospel to them in our professional role as social workers…The profession of social work provides us all with unique opportunities to demonstrate the gospel of Christ…It can be a form of "pre-evangelism," preparing the soil for the good seed of the gospel proclaimed (Sherwood, 2012b, p. 4).

At the same time, Sherwood defines the avoidance of spiritual and religious issues as "professional incompetence" (p. 329). He asserts that the agenda must be the client's, addressing the client's concerns, not the needs of the social worker to steer the conversation to a discussion of religion and faith. Sherwood makes the point that this is not simply a social work ethical principle, but also a Christian one, since the principle of self determination derives from the freedom God gave humanity in creation, including the freedom to make wrong and harmful choices.

Self determination derives from the freedom God gave humanity in creation, including the freedom to make wrong and harmful choices.

To say that social workers should not engage in evangelism in their practice with clients does not suggest that it is inappropriate for congregations to have evangelism as a goal, nor even that congregational social workers should not lead the congregations they serve in evangelistic activities. Organizations where social workers are employed often have goals that are appropriate for the organization and for the social worker's professional leadership, but not necessarily for direct social work practice with clients.

An example from another organizational context may help clarify. A health care organization may launch a major "stop smoking" campaign, with the very appropriate goal of diminished health care costs and deaths due to tobacco use. A social worker in the organization may engage ethically and appropriately in developing and launching the campaign. At the same time, it would be inappropriate for that same social worker, in her direct practice with a family seeking help in coping with a family member's terminal illness, to try to convince an adult in the family to stop smoking. Clearly, all the research points to smoking as health harming. The social worker may certainly set boundaries that there will be no smoking in her presence to protect her own health, but despite her knowledge of the health costs of smoking, it is not her role to try to influence clients to give it up, especially when that is not their purpose in seeking her services. In our society, they still have a right to engage in smoking.

The ethical issue is not the organization's goals of preventing tobacco use. Rather, the issue is the social worker's role and purpose in helping the organization achieve its objectives. It would rarely be considered ethical to deny services to clients unless they committed themselves to a no-tobacco-use pledge. Similarly, evangelism may seldom be appropriate in a social worker's counseling role with clients. Both are examples of attempts to limit clients' abilities to make their own life choices, even if the social worker personally considers the choices "good" or "bad." Helping a congregation accomplish its goals of evangelism—or preventing tobacco use—in ways that are consistent with both Christian and social work ethics is quite appropriate social work practice.

Evangelism as a Congregational Goal

Christians and Christian leaders believe that they have truth that others can benefit from knowing and a lifestyle that others can benefit from living. Therefore, their mission includes teaching others their faith and attempting to attract them to become Christians and/or members of a congregation—evangelism. Inviting neighbors they serve to join the faith is not only appropriate but the heart of what it means to love neighbors and to be faithful to the teachings of Jesus, "being his witnesses . . . to the ends of the earth" (Acts 11:7). Jeavons (2004) indicates that this propensity of having such an absolute truth is one of the reasons that makes faith-based service suspect to the social work profession.

The evangelism goal is akin to any organization's attempt to grow its members/followers. The question becomes what the role of the social worker is in leading that work, and how to ensure the self-determination of those served, as dictated not only by social work but also by Christian ethics. Congregations approach this goal with differing perspectives on how missions and evangelism should be connected. On one end of the continuum are those who believe that Christians are called to serve whoever is in need, that the act of service itself is the demonstration of Christian belief and does not need words of explanation, nor should service be done with the expectation of response from the other, including the response of choosing Christian faith. On the other end of the continuum are those who believe that the primary responsibility of Christians is to influence others to become Christians, so that acts of service should always be accompanied by invitations to join the faith. Unruh and Sider (2005) and Rogers, Yancey, and Singletary (2005) identified strategies that fall along this continuum from no expectation for sharing faith to the requirement that service recipients participate in religious activities.

Inviting neighbors they serve to join the faith is not only appropriate but the heart of what it means to love neighbors and to be faithful to the teachings of Jesus.

Conservative and evangelical Protestants and churches in the historic African American denominations emphasize evangelism as a primary goal, whereas Mainline Protestant congregations are more likely to emphasize seeking social justice through economic and political change and less through conversion of people to Christianity (Ammerman, 2005). This divide peaked at the turn of the 19th century, when the Social Gospel Movement encouraged work for institutional changes over personal evangelism, a movement rejected by conservative and evangelical Protestants (Chaves, 2011a; Evans, 2001; Hart, 1996). The only missions activity considered legitimate for many conservative congregations is preaching (Ammerman, 2005).

Our own research with 946 Christians serving for at least a year through community service programs found that, even though most of them were members of evangelical and conservative Christian congregations, 87% reported that they saw actions as more important than words in sharing their faith. In addition, 77% reported that working for social change was a way to share their faith (Garland, Myers, et al., 2008).

These Christians, most from conservative congregations, made it clear that they see service as a way of sharing their faith—as evangelism. It is not as though service and evangelism are different activities, but they are one cloth with two sides. Service is an enactment of Christian faith—evangelism. Sharing Christian faith with another is providing something other people are perceived to need—service.

Those who sew know that fabrics often have a "right" side that is supposed to go on the outside of a finished sewn article, and a "wrong" side which is the underside. Which side of the fabric of evangelism/service is the "right" side? It is a matter of differing perspectives. McNeal argues that evangelism is a natural by-product of living a Christian life. "When evangelism is a program, it often involves questionable methods that commoditize Jesus and Christianity and frequently involve some ploy to get people to connect to church" (McNeal, 2009, p. 59). In other words, overt evangelism can actually be a disservice. Others would argue that service alone without words is not evangelism; Christianity modeled can be enhanced by a verbal presentation of Christian faith. For example, Unruh and Sider write that it can be appropriate to make "an honest, respectful attempt at persuading someone to accept a different system of belief, particularly when the dialogue is motivated by genuine concern for the person's current and eternal well-being" (2002, p. 312). For the social worker in this setting, the appropriate role is helping the congregation achieve its goals, along the lines of helping a health organization with its anti-smoking campaign. The social worker in the congregational setting has unique opportunities to equip congregants in issues of the appropriate use of power, for example, in evangelism by offering seminars that focus on appropriate relationships. Additionally, the match of social worker and congregation is crucial so that the expressed values of each are congruent especially on the efforts focused on service and evangelism. This is also a primary example of role and values congruence of the social worker with the theological and ideological perspective of the congregation.

Congregational Social Workers and Evangelism

Understanding the congregation's motivations is part of the larger task that social workers face wherever they serve; they have to know the world views of communities and organizations in which they are employed, whether the setting is public or private, religious or nonsectarian. They also need to have examined their own religious frameworks in order to know how their own world views inform, conflict with, and can be used in their work setting. For example, the various motivations of congregational missions create emotive responses in us—some of them we appreciate, others set our teeth on edge. We need to know that about ourselves if we are going to use ourselves most effectively in leadership.

The congregational social workers we interviewed serve in congregations that range the spectrum on the relationship of evangelism and service. Abigail is the social worker in a large evangelical church with a staff of 300. She expressed confidence that she will not violate social work's ethics because of the informed consent persons seeking help from her congregation must sign prior to services. The form indicates that the helper may use the Bible and pray with the client as a part of the helping process. If the potential client is not comfortable signing the consent form, Abigail makes referrals to other community resources. Barry, the Pastor of Care Ministries, said it this way: "Our job is to let them know what the Bible says and who we believe Jesus is."

For other social workers, however, the expectation that their work include evangelism has created a significant professional challenge, whether the expectation was their own, the congregation's, or even the clients they serve.

A Personal Challenge

For some, the challenge is one they wrestle with personally as they attempt to define their role in a congregational setting. Ingrid is the social worker responsible for a federally funded, faith-based initiative grant that focuses on children of prisoners. Her role is to be a case manager for the families served and to develop and train the mentors from the congregation. She told us that she debated with herself, wanting to recommend to incarcerated parents that the mess they were in could be addressed most effectively if they became followers of Christ:

> I want to say, 'If you give your heart to Jesus and begin to walk a different kind of a life, then there are some things that will improve and change.' But we have to be careful how we do that. I know that my role is really to love people where they are and connect a mentor to their child. We know we can have impact without having to be overtly evangelistic. But I just want to help a parent know that your life can be better if you choose righteousness.

Social workers want clients to choose a life path that they perceive to be "the best." Wanting a client to make a particular choice, however, is not the same as telling a client what to do. In this case, Ingrid feels the constraint not only of the federal guidelines for this grant-funded program but also the boundary of her professional role with these clients. The purpose of the program is to provide children with mentors from her congregation. She knows that if a mother in prison believes that having a mentor for her child could really be helpful, then she may think she has a better chance of obtaining that mentoring service if she pleases the social worker by following her advice to "choose righteousness." As a consequence, Ingrid refrains from giving the advice she wants to give, and hopes instead that the ongoing relationship with a mentor from her congregation will be a Christian influence. It is Ingrid's role to help those mentors understand their role and the place—or not—for evangelism in their work with the child and parent.

Kathleen is the Minister of Benevolence and Missions in her congregation. For several years, the pastor of her congregation and another pastor had the vision of collaborating together to meet the needs of the people in their small town. After utilizing social work interns over a period of several years, the pastors agreed that one of the churches should hire a social worker to direct this work; Kathleen was the first person hired to oversee this ministry. She directs the food pantry and clothing ministry. She also uses funds provided by the congregation to help people in financial crisis to pay bills. Kathleen told us that she has struggled with whether or not she should speak of faith matters to clients and is more comfortable with doing the work before her and trusting her professional instincts:

> I had such a fear of doing something wrong and getting my license taken away. I guess over the last year I've begun to relax and be myself. I struggle with the opportunity to tell other people about Jesus, but then recognizing the need to meet the person where they are and that some people aren't ready for you to share the gospel with them when they are asking for help with their rent. I would imagine that I wouldn't be either.

The struggle for Kathleen was initially between her personal beliefs—that knowing Jesus would help the people she is serving—and what she believed the professional licensure board would say is an appropriate role for a social worker providing emergency assistance. As she has considered the issues, however, she realizes that the conflict is not so much with the licensure board, but that it is her own personal struggle. She realizes, like Ingrid, that her wanting to tell clients about Jesus comes more from her own beliefs and experiences than from what her clients are asking for from her in the time of their crisis. Again like Ingrid, Kathleen has material resources her clients need, so that she has considerable power to influence their behavior. If she "tells them about Jesus," they are likely to listen if they believe that is what is required to get the needed resources. But being willing to listen is not the same as wanting to listen. Kathleen recognizes that, even though she is working in a congregation and not a federal program as Ingrid is, making access to needed resources contingent on hearing a message about Jesus is not sensitive to her clients' situation and may even violate their right freely to choose—or not—to embrace her religious perspectives.

A Challenge in Relating to the Congregation

Other congregational social workers we interviewed find themselves in conflict with the congregation or other congregational leaders about the role of evangelism in their work. Kathleen told us:

> There probably are some members of our congregation that feel that I am not evangelistic enough, that I don't share my faith verbally enough, especially with our food pantry and our clothing ministry. But I don't really feel comfortable doing that. I feel comfortable doing that personally, but professionally, as a social worker, I want to meet people where they are and build relationships with them. I don't really want to go and stand on a box and preach at them. I've tried to teach my volunteers that the ministry is an opportunity to meet physical needs and to build relationships. If those relationships result in people coming to know the Lord, then that is the ultimate goal. But my job is not to shove Jesus down their throat; my job is to feed them and to clothe them like Jesus talks about in the Bible.

Again, Kathleen echoes Ingrid. Sharing faith with clients does have a role in their work, not in their own professional relationship with clients but rather as they work with members of their congregation who are forming relationships with the clients they serve. Kathleen has come to this understanding for herself; the challenge before her is helping her congregation and its leaders understand that sharing faith can take place more effectively through caring relationships than through "preaching at" people who are in crisis. What she is leading her congregation to understand has less to do with professional ethics and much more to do with Christian ethics. As she says, the foundation for her approach to evangelism is the teaching of Jesus.

Jeanie is Mission Outreach Coordinator for her congregation after a previous experience in medical social work. She sees a focus on evangelism at the expense of relationship with someone seeking their help as simply ineffective, as well as unethical, but she is in conflict with the pastor about her perspective. He believes in starting with talk about his faith, "unconcerned

> *Sharing faith with clients does have a role in their work, not in their own professional relationship with clients but rather as they work with members of their congregation who are forming relationships with the clients they serve.*

about whether or not the other is already a Christian," or whether or not this approach offends those seeking help. His approach to evangelism is based on his motivation to tell others about faith, not on connecting with them in their life situation. She recognizes that Christians find themselves in crisis, too, and that clients may be offended by the assumption that because they are in crisis of some kind or another, that they are "without faith." She is candid about how difficult this conflict with her pastor has been:

Clients may be offended by the assumption that because they are in crisis of some kind or another, that they are "without faith."

> It's been tough. I am more relationship-based. People come in to talk with me. I connect with people; he doesn't. You meet people where they are and journey with them. Eventually they journey with you.

Jeanie does not say that sharing faith has no place in her work. She has learned, though, that the sharing of faith can be more effective if it is based on sensitivity to the life experiences and faith perspectives of the other and a willingness to form a relationship that, over time, becomes mutual.

A Challenge in Relating to Clients

These congregational social workers also have found that evangelism is an expectation *clients* bring to the professional relationship, since the service is being provided in a congregational context. Ike is both a pastor and an administrator in his denomination's social service agency, which provides material resources and a homeless shelter. He described how clients sometimes believe that if they show interest in spiritual matters, they can positively—or negatively—influence the services they receive:

> Clients think if they make me happy by coming to Bible study or coming to church, then somehow they will get some additional benefit in our social services. Or sometimes clients think that because they are not participating in church programs, that's why they are being held accountable to certain rules, or they are being asked to leave the shelter when actually that has nothing to do with it.

In addition to figuring out the role of religion and faith in their work with clients, with the congregants they train, and with the congregation they lead or represent through their work, congregational social workers also have to understand and address the expectations of clients, as Ike describes.

How These Social Workers Address the Challenge

Addressing these challenges takes place over time. For Lynne, it has been an ongoing challenge for many years.

> There is conflict between my view of evangelism and that of my pastor, who is an evangelist at heart. It was quite a challenge in the beginning, and still is, to convince him that there are people in this world that can't even begin to comprehend God's love because of life's circumstances. We have to be Jesus to them before they can be able to understand. He uses ministry as a bait to do evangelism, which I absolutely refuse to do. Over time he has come to accept that. He probably would be happier if I were more aggressive and taught my staff and volunteers to be. I'd like to think that he respects me enough to accept my approach. I think I have been able to teach him.
>
> For example, we have a tutoring program for 100 children every year. I could have 50 "conversions" every Wednesday night, and that would make him happy. But it would be the same children every week. We prefer to teach them God's Word through other means, and then when they mature to the point that they can make a decision, it will be a lasting one.

There are people in this world that can't even begin to comprehend God's love because of life's circumstances. We have to be Jesus to them before they can be able to understand.

Lynne sees evangelism as appropriate in their various programs, including those with children. Her approach is what she calls "relationship evangelism," forming relationships with those that she and her staff and volunteers serve, which can be the context for them to make their own decision based on their life experiences, rather than to please the congregational staff. Lynne has modeled this approach in her work with her pastor over the years. She has used her relationship with him, and his respect for her, to teach him that her approach is no less evangelistic, but rather, an approach that is sensitive to the life situation, the developmental maturity, and especially the unequal relationship between the clients they serve and the program staff.

Like work with clients, Lynne's influence in her pastor's understanding has not been a one-time "telling," but a process that has taken years of working collaboratively and with mutual respect. Social workers are unabashedly change agents, but their change attempts honor the self-determination and choice of clients.

Catarina is the Director of Global Ministries for a Hispanic Protestant congregation, a position that is shared with a religiously affiliated child and family service organization that places social workers in congregations. Catarina estimates that 75% of the membership of the Hispanic congregation and the neighborhood with whom the congregation ministers are undocumented immigrants. She has seen her role as helping her congregation learn how to work with these neighbors. She says that her congregation believes that the way to reach persons is to knock on their doors and invite them to attend church so that they can teach them about God. Catarina, though, has learned from families in the community, many of whom have Catholic backgrounds even if they are not currently connected to a Catholic congregation, that this evangelistic approach offends them. Like Lynn, Catarina has taught her congregation a more relational approach. She has said to her congregation:

> Let's build a relationship. Let's start with an exercise class. We can get to know each other. Then they can get to know us. We build trust, and then we can share a Bible verse and have prayer requests. Little by little through the exercise class, or the parenting class, or the nutrition class, some of them start coming to church.

It has taken time, but Catarina's congregation now sees the effectiveness of Catarina's approach.

Brenda, Director of Social Service Ministries for her congregation, has gone even further in defining the role of evangelism in her work as relationship rather than attempting verbal influence. She has helped her congregation recognize that they are called to be "good neighbors," to recognize that their role is to love and to serve, and not to push people to embrace their understanding of Christianity. The shift has involved some struggle, which will continue. She embraces the struggle as her professional work as a congregational leader:

> I think people, including me, have wanted our service to be in "order to win people to Christ." There certainly is a place to communicate the gospel clearly. But it is also important that as disciples we wrestle with the fact that the goal may not be about the other person coming to Christ. It may be about our own inability to love well. I feel good that I've taught my congregation to help without strings attached. I don't talk much about my faith; I live it. That's social work but it's also me.

Like the other social workers, the struggle to define how evangelism should fit with service has been a personal one for Brenda, as well as one she has addressed with her congregation. The issue is about the professional role of a social worker, but it is more than that—it is about the calling of Christians to love and to serve "without strings attached."

Brenda's focus on "loving well" brings to mind Jesus' story of the Samaritan who stopped to aid the wounded traveler (Luke 10:25-37). In the story, the wounded traveler never speaks. We do not know whether he changed in any way as a result of the care he received from the passing Samaritan. Jesus told the story in response to a lawyer's question, designed to test Jesus rather than to learn from him; the lawyer asked Jesus "Who is my neighbor?" The lawyer's focus was on the expectations and boundaries of service, on who is and is not the neighbor we are called to love.

Jesus turned the question around, however, after telling the parable, and said to the lawyer, "Which of these three, do you think, was a neighbor to the man who fell into the hands of robbers?" The lawyer asked "Who is my neighbor?" but Jesus responded, "Who was a neighbor to the one in need?" The question, according to Jesus, is not "who is my neighbor?" but rather "will we be neighbors to anyone who needs us?" "Neighbor" is not a definition of the one in need; it defines the one who sees and responds to need.

"Who was a neighbor to the one in need?"

That is where the biblical story ends. If the Samaritan used his care for the wounded one as an occasion to lecture him on never traveling dangerous roads alone, or as an attempt to win the wounded one to a Samaritan faith, it is not included in the story. The only words spoken in the parable are not between the Samaritan and the traveler, but the instructions of the Samaritan to the innkeeper, "Take care of him; and when I come back, I will repay you whatever more you spend." The care he provided was open-ended and without expectation.

Leading Congregational Missions[44]

In the Service and Faith Project, the research team interviewed 35 leaders of congregations known for their community ministries, 25 congregants who had actively been involved in community ministry for more than one year, and 16 families who had been engaged in community ministry together. We were trying to learn about how these congregations developed a culture of mission engagement. We sought leaders and congregants who represented as much diversity as possible demographically, theologically, and in the types of services in which they were engaged.[45] This earlier study was not with social workers as subjects, but we think it is informative for congregational social work. The following part of this section reflects the findings of the Service and Faith Project.

We learned that new service projects began because of the concerns and calling of the congregation. Unlike social service agencies that ground their work in community needs assessments, these congregations start with their mission, their passion, and resources that they perceive as God's gifts to be used in service to others. As a consequence of their perception of missions as the expression of the congregation's calling, these congregations developed a culture of mission engagement.

Developing a Culture of Mission Engagement

The congregations we studied had an ethos, norms, and values that expect and support members to be involved in missions. For example, a Presbyterian pastor described how missions permeate church life:

> Someone can stand up on Sunday morning and say, "We need a breakfast provided for 50 workers for Habitat for Humanity next Friday. I need people that will help me serve and I need breakfast foods. Please see me." And people do. There is also an understanding within the church that I can call you and say, "Can you contribute two dozen eggs?" In other words, "If I've got the time to fix it, you could swing by the store and pick them up." It's just an acceptance--that is what we do.

A Methodist salesman who leads several ministries says that community service was "built into the DNA" of his congregation. Several pastors indicated that the congregation had a heritage—a historical identity—of having leaders who were spokespersons for social justice and social ministry long before the current leadership arrived on the scene. They noted that people have joined the congregation because they want to be a part of this identity, and they, in turn, perpetuate the missions engagement culture. This culture is expressed in worship and Christian education, with leaders casting a vision of service as integral to the life of the congregation, encouraging persons to find their niche in service. The Presbyterian pastor went on to describe how service is not an "add on" but integral to worship and Christian education:

> Worship is also hearing needs as well as worshiping God. We interpret scripture together when we are in Sunday school classes and in other small groups to find what we have been called to do and where we are to serve.

The leaders described congregational activities designed to help the congregation connect missions with other Christian practices:

> If you just invite people to come to Bible study, but then never ask them for anything, then you're really doing a disservice on both ends. Every ministry, I hope—some a bit more intentionally than others—but each Bible study, each Sunday school class, any time for spiritual growth the question ought to be either blatantly stated or implied "How and where is God leading you based on what you've understood through your own spiritual experiences?" "How and what ministries will you be a part of?"

These leaders emphasized that it was critical that they be involved and champion missions engagement, even if they later delegated the leadership of the mission engagement to others. In fact, that delegation was a part of the work; it was critical that leaders not just do the ministry themselves, but that they bring others into it, too. Leaders sometimes encouraged an individual involvement broadly, through sermons, teaching, or articles in church publications. They also made personal connections between a ministry and particular members of the congregation because they knew members' gifts and needs.

Launching Mission Activities and Programs

We identified five processes that congregations use in developing new mission activities and programs that, ultimately, contribute to this culture of mission engagement: (1) a catalyst proposed that the congregation become involved; (2) the congregation determined fit with the community; (3) the congregation assessed its capacity; (4) the congregation decided whether or not to support the activity; and (5) the congregation launched and sustained the activity.

(1) A Catalyst Proposed Involvement

A catalyst in chemistry is an agent that begins a reaction between two other entities that otherwise do not interact with one another. The "catalyst" for congregational involvement is someone who is either a member or a leader in the congregation and is also in touch with needs in the community. Several leaders we interviewed pointed out that a congregational member was serving on a community board or was involved in other ways in the community, became aware of needs, and then brought those needs to the attention of the congregation. Rusaw and Swanson identify police officers, social workers, and teachers in the congregation who are already at work in the community as catalysts for mission engagement.

It is not just that congregational members tried to engage their congregations in service, but the congregation also saw them as important linkages and sought out their brokering a connection with the community. One congregational leader described how they try to use their connections to the community through members who are social service professionals: "We say to them, 'Teach us; help us; show us; walk with us; bring those people to us.'"

The "catalyst" for congregation involvement is someone who is either a member or a leader in the congregation and also in touch with needs in the community.

The congregational social workers we interviewed are often themselves the catalysts for engagement; the congregation sought their leadership because they could be that connection to the community. We first interviewed Beth in her position as Associate Pastor, and then three years later, after she had become Senior Pastor in another congregation in another state. She has seen herself in both positions as such a catalyst:

> I really see myself as a person whose job it is to connect people in the church with people in the community who were in need. That's what I see my role is. How do I get the church people connected to people in need in ways that can change lives?

Lynne has also been such a catalyst. Through the 25 years she has served the same congregation, she has also been a catalyst for catalysts—she has helped people operationalize their concerns in ministry initiatives. For example, a church member brought the idea to her, feeling "led" to find a way to help the unemployed. Together, the member and Lynne developed an employment readiness program, which at the time we talked, had helped more than 50 persons find employment in the previous 12 months. All the staff members in the program are unpaid congregation members.

A Lutheran pastor explained that his role is not to start with the needs in the community and find persons to address them, but rather to identify the gifts of the congregation and find ways they can use those gifts in the community:

> There is actually a shift away from plugging people, no matter what they are gifted for, like round people into a square hole, and sort of mashing them in, to believing that people are given gifts and that the better model of discipleship is to fan the flames of those gifts. And they may or may not have others who share that enthusiasm, but they would be given permission and support and encouragement and maybe resources to follow their gift. It is a different model of how to help people be disciples.

The role of catalyst this Lutheran pastor describes requires knowing the members and knowing the neighborhoods of the congregation. One of our alumni is now a congregational social worker; when she was first a student doing an internship in a congregation, she observed that a strategy congruent with church culture "is visiting in homes and workplaces, prompting members to share stories about their experiences of faith in action, about their family, and about their community" (MSW student, personal communication, February 12, 2008).

Not a single leader talked about someone outside the congregation being responsible for initiating the congregation's involvement, such as a government official or agency staff person who approached the congregation.

Not a single leader talked about someone outside the congregation being responsible for initiating the congregation's involvement, such as a government official or agency staff person who approached the congregation. There had to be an internal linkage with someone willing to take the initiative. A national study of 111 congregations engaged in social services confirmed this finding. Those who initiated these congregations' involvement were almost always religious leaders (41.43%) or people or groups within the congregation (38.08%) (Cnaan et al., 2003).

(2) The Congregation Determined Fit with the Community

Once a catalyst had proposed a mission engagement initiative, there was some evaluation of how and whether the initiative fit the congregation's identity. This assessment normally took place informally, not through any structure or organizational approval process. Because congregations are communities, the building and strengthening of relationships is an important function of congregational activity. Best fit occurs when the initiative supports congregants forming relationships with one another as well as with those who are recipients of their care. Ministries that build and strengthen bonds between people are a better fit with congregations than those in which those who are serving never really know those that benefit from their care.

Mission activities that provide interpersonal connections for new congregants also fit the culture of congregations well. For example, an Episcopal leader observed that in his large congregation, persons who are not members of the congregation may first serve in one of the congregation's ministry programs as a way of "trying out" the congregation. He explained about people interested in the congregation: "It's hard to know how to get in here because the church is so big, and they might not be ready for the membership class, because they might think that's too big a commitment." They began, then, by serving.

Ministries that build and strengthen bonds between people are a better fit with congregations than those in which those who are serving never really know those that benefit from their care.

Because congregations are cross-generational by nature, many leaders and volunteers described the importance of being able to include children and teens alongside adults. In fact, these leaders sought projects in which children and teens can participate, because service is seen as vital to Christian discipleship. An Assemblies of God pastor said, "It gives our children a chance to see that the church is more than just a service, an event; they're able to see the church in action." A Presbyterian pastor's congregation had created cross-generational activities to accompany the building of a Habitat for Humanity home in their community; children and adults together made doorstops, planters, and bird houses to give as gifts to new home owners.

(3) The Congregation Assessed Its Capacity

Capacity involves having the people resources (i.e., volunteers, leadership), facilities and funding, and necessary community connections. The people resources tended to be assessed informally, whereas the facilities and funding involved more formalized processes.

People Resources

Assessment of the people resources was sometimes as simple as phoning people in the congregation to see if there was interest in being involved. One purpose of this assessment was to avoid competition between ministries. As a pastor of a Hispanic Christian Reformed congregation explained:

> We can unintentionally end up with factions, with competition. So the tutoring program is going great guns. We've got 42 tutors out there, and tutoring is the hot new ministry. Then we can't find enough youth leaders or Sunday school teachers. Everybody we call is a tutor. So, there have been times when ministry opportunities come along and we say, "That's cool stuff, but, right now, we can't do everything."

An Episcopalian pastor spoke of the need to develop a focus and sees his role as helping the congregation choose that focus rather than being swamped by needs in the community:

> I have tried to give a lens that says, "There are too many needs in the world for us. We've got to choose three things to do well so we don't get blown away and we actually make a difference."

The more relationships between people are called upon and the more they are engaged working alongside one another, the stronger the community's fabric becomes.

If it was determined that the congregation did not have the resources, that did not necessarily stop the mission initiative. Some leaders talked about making it a priority in prayer, believing that God would provide the resources needed. In other words, the fit with the congregation's sense of identity and calling was even more important than whether or not they had the resources available. They recognize that the more relationships between people are called upon and the more they are engaged working alongside one another, the stronger the community's fabric becomes (Halpern, 1999).

Sometimes partnerships with other community organizations and congregations helped these congregations successfully achieve the capacity for the initiative they were considering, such as adding people from other congregations, training for people through other organizations, and providing professional consultation and expertise that the congregation did not have. Again, the connections between the congregation and partners are strengthened through these collaborations for a common purpose.

Finally, it was critical to these leaders that, before they launch a new initiative, they determine that it can be sustained by the congregation and it does not simply become something more for leaders themselves to do.

Facilities

Their buildings were an important resource these congregations offered their communities; many congregations open their building space to groups in their neighborhood. These arrangements were usually formal in that they were arranged with the decision-making groups in the congregation, not just simply as informal relationships between people. Congregations usually did not initiate these agreements; they were simply asked by an outside group, and sponsoring was a fit with the congregation's mission. Even so, the use of the physical facilities was not an insignificant decision for these congregations. For example, a congregation that agreed to house a homeless feeding program in the congregation subsequently remodeled bathroom facilities so guests could shower. Other congregations have bought land around them and expanded their facilities to hold these ministries.

Opening their buildings to the neighborhood and its organization is a key way of connecting and serving for many congregations.

Opening their buildings to the neighborhood and its organizations are key ways of connecting and serving for many congregations. In many communities, congregational buildings may be the primary meeting place in which the community gathers. By making their building available, congregations are "good neighbors" who are generous with their resources and "supportive of the common good" (Cnaan, Boddie, & Yancey, 2005, p. 377). One pastor described using the congregation's facility as a way to "embrace our neighborhood" (Marter, 1998, p. 9). Located in a Hispanic neighborhood, the congregation scheduled cultural celebrations beginning with posada (Hispanic Christmas festival). The congregation provided their building resources and neighborhood cultural groups organized the events.

Financial support

These congregations also determined if and how they would provide financial support as well. Obtaining that support often involves planning a year or more ahead and working with a standing budget committee. Others may take up special offerings of support, or a small congregational group like a Sunday school class may decide to provide regular monetary support. Funding usually comes either from the congregation's mission budget, based on the regular financial support of its members, or from special gifts from within the congregation, although a few of the social workers we interviewed have obtained grants for ministry initiatives.

(4) The Congregation Decided Whether or Not to Support

Congregational commitments to support a ministry initiative varied from very informal to formal. Formalized commitments involve initial sanction by a congregational governing group. Informal commitments emerge over time, with sanction coming after the initiative has developed rather than before. In informal commitments, the initiative is integrated into other programs of the congregation, almost as a side and unintended consequence of that activity rather than as the program's focus. Even formalized initiatives evolved over time, however, as congregations responded to changing need, or their understanding of need, and one program grew from another. An Episcopal teacher who volunteers to prepare and serve a meal for homeless persons explained:

> For a period of time, we served lunch to the senior citizens while they were building the senior citizen center. We had the feeling that we should be serving food to the homeless and so they served it here because we were already doing it for seniors. Then that food program moved but many of the needy had already formed an attachment to our congregation. They would come back here and they were obviously hungry and so one day we just thought maybe we should give them something to eat. It didn't seem that hard to do. So it just kind of grew by their being comfortable here and it just seemed a natural thing to do. Then we moved into an overnight shelter that also began here because it was a really rainy day and we couldn't put them out in the rain, and we stayed overnight.

What began as a "temporary" plan to serve lunch to senior adults while the neighborhood senior center was being built expanded to include persons who are homeless, and then to providing an overnight shelter.

If the decision was made to make an initiative a congregational project, virtually everyone we interviewed said that the pastor's open support was critical: "If the pastor doesn't support something, it's probably not going to go well." But pastors alone were not sufficient sanction in these congregations. There were also decision-making bodies that had responsibility for sanctioning involvement. This sanction was important, particularly when there appeared to be no self-serving purpose for the congregation's involvement. A Methodist volunteer explained how this worked in his congregation:

> We have a very simple mission statement, "Growing closer to Christ through worship, witness, and service." If it [the initiative] fits that, you do it. It's our structure. If someone has a good idea, then they bring it to the administrative council. That is the programmatic group. If it's in somebody's budget, then it doesn't even go to the finance committee; they just appropriate out of their budget. If it's a new thing and needs legs, then it comes to the administrative council. If this is one person trying to do a fairly large program, then it has to have legs.

How projects grow "legs" differs from one congregation to another, but to lead successfully, a congregational social worker has to know the process, whether formal or informal.

(5) The Congregation Launched and Sustained

These leaders and volunteers described a number of factors that they believe contribute to sustained involvement in missions over time: (a) direct involvement of the congregational leader; (b) affirmation of those serving; (c) financial support; (d) social networking; (e) training; (f) opportunities to share stories; (g) an opportunity to reflect on the relationship of service and faith; (h) prayer for the ministry; (i) a welcoming culture; and (j) ongoing planning. Each of these, in turn, contributes to a congregational culture that supports not only a particular mission initiative but also the congregation's continuing and expanding involvement in the community.

a. Direct Involvement of the Congregational Leader(s)

These congregational leaders agreed that it is very important that they be involved, especially in the beginning. They find it personally rewarding; but they also believe that they are setting an example for the congregation. A pastor of a nondenominational church explained:

> Maybe it's that personal modeling. I love going on work camps with high school kids. Both the Sunday morning curriculum and the youth curriculum include service projects. Maybe having kids see one of their pastors with a hammer and saw and just having fun doing that. I hope that's made a difference.

b. Affirmation of Those Serving

Both leaders and congregants described ways that those serving receive affirmation for their work. They are named and recognized in a worship service; pastors ask for permission to use stories about their work in sermons; or a church leader affirms what they are doing in a personal interchange--a casual conversation, a handwritten note, or a phone call.

Those serving also said that they found encouragement in the congregation's worship, even when not overtly addressing the mission initiative. A Baptist bank manager on a home care team for persons with HIV/AIDS describes her experience:

> One Sunday he preached about being a willing worker in the church. That was a point when I was thinking about giving up the Care Team because the others weren't doing what they needed to do, and they weren't coming to the meetings. He brought it home by saying that, "It's not about you; it's about what God wants you to do." He had my number, and there have been many times that he just hit it right on the head. In a sermon, "The Other Side of Through," he said that we'll get our rewards on the other side.

Stories about the ministry in the church bulletin or newsletter, requests for support spoken in the worship service announcements, and bulletin boards not only got the word out about how others could support the ministry but they also recognized those serving as congregational representatives "on mission" in the community.

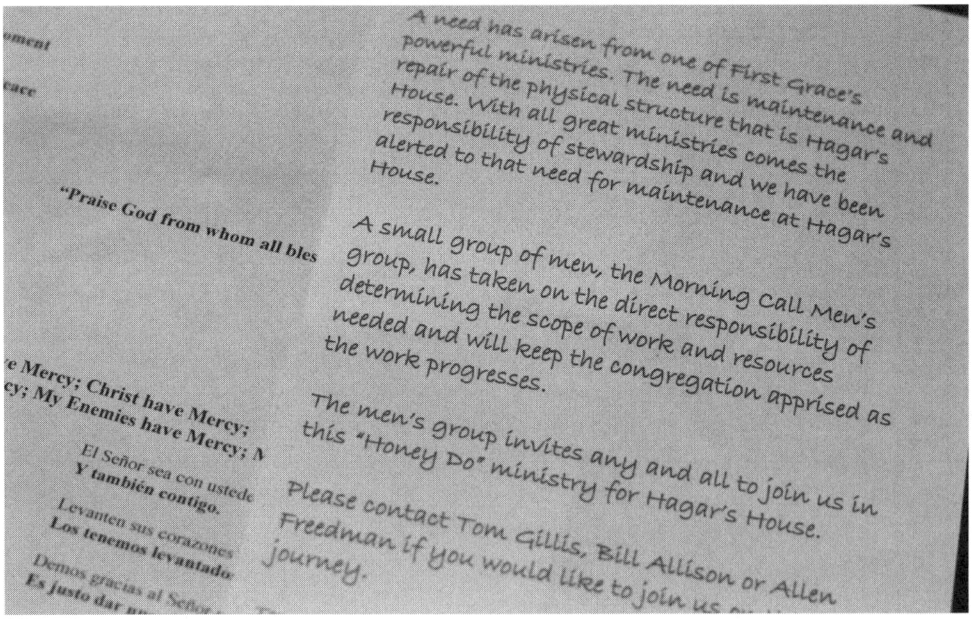

Leaders also recognize those serving explicitly and publicly by projecting their pictures on the screen in a morning worship service, giving plaques, putting a picture of the "servant of the month" on a bulletin board, or hosting a luncheon for those serving. Not only do such celebrations of service affirm those serving, but they also can function as models for others. Nevertheless, several leaders noted that affirmation for service is more complex than in other volunteer settings because of beliefs that good works should not to be touted. Those serving often did not want to call attention to themselves. A Lutheran pastor explained:

Affirmation for service is more complex than in other volunteer settings because of beliefs that good works should not to be touted.

> In the corporate world, people give plaques to put on their walls. But we take seriously what Jesus said in the Sermon on the Mount, "When you give alms, don't let your left hand know what your right is doing." We are very nervous about praising people for service, as if the reason they were doing it would be to receive praise. But then again, we want to give thanks for the spirit that is working within them and that is making a difference in people's lives. So there is this very strange balancing.

In another congregation, the teacher of a Bible class for women who are homeless and mentally ill was reluctant to tell the story of making a small wedding cake. The cake was for a surprise party for a class member who had a wedding anniversary but who had never had a wedding cake. The teacher said in the interview, "If I tell you what I did, then it cancels it out." She explained that being recognized for service negates credit with God, based on the teaching of Jesus that people who publicize their good deeds already have their reward in the recognition they seek.

c. Financial Support

Budget for the programs signifies to those serving the ownership and commitment of the congregation to the ministry. Providing them with a budget underscores their role as representatives of the congregation and communicates that they are worthy of support. One person describes the financial gifts of members as symbolically indicating his congregation was proud of the ministry and, by extension, of what he was doing. Several spoke of the overwhelming response that comes when they ask for donations—more food than they can use, more clothing than they can give away, money pressed into their hands even when they have not asked. The coordinator for a cold weather shelter for persons who are homeless said:

> An elderly woman in our church can't help anymore with the shelter. She is just not physically able to help. She always buys me two big boxes of oatmeal; every year I can expect 2 big boxes of oatmeal from Claire. Oth-

> ers strip their orange trees for me so I can have fresh oranges in the morning. Others volunteer to bring milk or to bring vegetables. I'm not sure I can get through this (emotion choking her voice), but there was a young woman in our church who came to me last week with a bag of quarters, nickels, and dimes. Her three daughters had a lemonade stand a couple of months ago and they decided they wanted the proceeds of the lemonade stand to go to the poor people of the church. And so they gave $22 in nickels, dimes, and quarters for the shelter.

This unpaid coordinator felt strongly supported emotionally and spiritually as well as tangibly by these gestures of tangible support from members of the congregation who participate in what she is doing by bringing the oranges from their yards, groceries they have bought, and the earnings from a lemonade stand.

d. Social Networking

One of the most important supports for those serving is the social network that develops. A married Presbyterian extension agent in her 80s who teaches budgeting and job skills in a homeless shelter described her experience:

> I thought that since I was retired I would lose connection with what is going on in the city. Now that I am involved in the shelter, there are people from all walks of life that volunteer and they all bring their experience to the group. It's almost like a social club now. We're so glad to see each other. It keeps me close to people in the community that I love and respect.

Congregational social workers can facilitate the development of these networks as they structure group training sessions, organize teams, and provide team-based support.

e. Training for Service

A passion to serve without competence in the work of service may lead both to ineffective effort and burnout. Some congregations provided the training themselves; others partnered with an agency in the community to provide whatever training congregants needed to be effective in the work they undertook. Training often includes knowledge about the culture of the neighborhood and the people served. Some also offer ministry-specific training, such as what they need to know to teach English as a second language, manage a benevolence ministry, provide financial counseling, or tutor in a public school. Congregational social workers may train congregants themselves or recruit other professionals from within or beyond the congregation to provide needed training.

Passion to serve without competence in the work of service leads both to ineffective effort and burnout.

f. Opportunities to Share Their Stories

Sometimes, those serving see visible change in people's lives as a consequence of their service, and that change motivates them to continue serving. Some congregations provide opportunity for them to tell about their work. A journalist who teaches budgeting skills in a homeless shelter chuckled as he says about his congregation, "They are pleased with me," because he was given opportunities to talk about the ministry. Notice that the congregation is not just pleased that the ministry is effective, but that they are pleased with the person serving—"pleased with *me*." Moreover, the telling of one's story provides an opportunity for reflection on the connections of experiences to faith and deepening the impact of experience on the teller, as well as the educational impact on those to whom the story is told (Garland, 2002a, 2003b).

g. An Opportunity to Reflect on the Relationship of Service and Faith

Mission initiatives do not always result in changed lives, of course. Leaders support those serving by encouraging them to reflect on why they serve beyond whatever response service recipients make. An Assemblies of God pastor said:

> We do it because we want to honor God's word. For a number of years we did a lot of outreach and we just didn't see the fruit in it. It got really frustrating for some folks. I said, 'We are not doing so that we could see something tangible in our hands, but so that we could be obedient to his word.' Faith is believing in what's not seen. It's part of the process. "I'm going to have faith whether I see it there or not." So during the times when we would do outreach, and we didn't see any good coming from it in our eyes, we had to hold steadfast in that. I think it strengthens faith. When you begin to see the fruit of service, then that's just gravy. I think about Shadrach, Meshach, and Abednego, as they were going into the fiery furnace, they knew God was able to deliver, but they said if they were burned up by the fire, it wouldn't change who God is; God is still God. And that's why, if we did this for 20 years and didn't see any results in our natural eye, that shouldn't change our desire to want to reach out.

A number of leaders talked about facilitating reflection afterwards, connecting the service back to understandings of scripture and of faith. If Christians are serving because they are motivated by their love of God and understanding of the Christian obligation to serve, then this connection of service to calling is vital to sustaining ongoing motivation, even when the impact they had hoped for may be slow in happening.

h. Prayer for the Mission Initiative

Some leaders mentioned that ministry opportunities often begin with prayer for the work and end with reflection and prayer about the experiences. The congregation or groups within the congregation also pray for those serving, as a means of encouraging and supporting them. Congregational social workers may serve as leaders of the prayers of those serving, or of the congregation for the ministry.

i. A Welcoming Culture

Those serving spoke of the importance of the congregation welcoming the recipients of the ministry if they wanted to become a part of the congregation. Alternatively, a rejection of the recipients was a rejection of the ministry itself—and of the ones serving. Several reported that they were dismayed that when they tried to include service recipients in congregational activities, the service recipients were not always welcomed. An Anglo-American teacher, member of a Reformed congregation, served as a tutor in a neighborhood school. She described what happened when the children from that school brought their families to the congregation:

> This is really new for us to have community kids coming in on Wednesday night. We've even had one or two families leave because they're different kids than our regular church kids.

By extension, the teacher felt devalued and angry because of the response of a few in her congregation. Laying the groundwork for the potential success of the ministry in attracting new people to the congregation involves the whole congregation, not just those on the front lines of ministry.

j. Ongoing Planning

Mission initiatives require considerable planning, which a number of those serving described—planning the program for an inner city children's activities program, organizing drivers for a Meals on Wheels program, or planning lessons for an English as a Second Language program. Planning includes evaluating the impact of the program on those serving as well as on the recipients, and sometimes changing direction if the program does not seem to be having the intended effects. Social work as a profession brings particular expertise to the planning process, emphasizing the inclusion of the recipients of service in the planning as well as research-informed knowledge about the social issues and challenges the congregation is seeking to address.

The Impact of Missions on Congregational Life

Both the leaders and the congregants we interviewed described how their mission engagement reinforced a culture of service. Those serving forged stronger relationships with one another. A retired Episcopal widow who led her congregation's ministry advocating for international fair trade and environmentally sustainable practices illustrates:

> Our steering committee was meeting about once a month to do this planning, but now we meet twice a month because the group wanted to become more of a community itself. We spend time now just getting to know each other and supporting one another. It has been a wonderful experience. We're still the steering committee—but we're more than that.

A Christian Reformed pastor describes the influence a ministry with homeless people has had on the congregation:

> This homeless ministry shapes this church community. It brings cohesiveness. It brings trust. And it brings growth. It makes the community love on each other.

Finally, leaders and congregants also identified resulting changes in the congregation's role in the community. They noted that the community became aware of the congregation and its leader and viewed the congregation with greater esteem, leading to more opportunities for engagement. A Baptist pastor explained:

> I think our community ministries, all the things we do, have been able to attract the attention of our community leaders, like supervisors who make decisions about zoning, money, and buildings. Because we have attracted their attention, we have not had a lot of problems getting what we request from the city or the county government.

This strengthening of the congregational community and greater visibility and esteem in the congregation's neighborhood contribute also to the culture of serving of the congregation—laying the foundations for future mission engagement—at least according to those leaders and congregants we interviewed.

We end this summary of the Service and Faith Project, which was based on interviews with leaders and congregants in 35 congregations known for their engagement in the missions in their neighborhood, with a caution about its limitations. We based our findings about the process through which these congregations became engaged in and sustained involvement in specific mission activities on their stories and descriptions of their experiences, not on our own observations of this process. In their own assessment, this is the way it happened, and although outside observers, or even others in the same congregation, may have seen other processes occurring, these experiences were the most significant for the particular individuals participating in this study.

Volunteers—Not.[46]

"Volunteering" is the language of the social sciences to describe doing work without financial reward. People "volunteering" to serve, usually in the time remaining after working a full-time job, perform the bulk of congregation's community service. The terms "volunteer" and "volunteering" are how the congregational social workers we interviewed described the congregants they enlist to serve in congregational ministries.

Nevertheless, throughout this chapter we have tried to avoid using the terms "volunteers" and "volunteering" to describe the engagement of congregational members in Christian service, except as we quoted others. This avoidance represents a shift from our earlier publications, in which we have used the language of volunteering liberally, including articles reporting the findings of the Service and Faith Project. As we have continued to learn and have considered the role of service in the lives of Christians, and taking into account not just the social sciences but also Christian thought, we have come to believe that the term "volunteer" is not only inadequate but also misleading and counterproductive.

The teachings of Jesus use the terms "serve" and "servant" extensively (e.g., Matthew 4:10; 6:24; 20:27; Mark 9:35; 10:43; Luke 1:74; 16:13; John 12:26). Nowhere does Jesus use a term meaning "volunteer." The Apostle Paul alluded to his "labor and toil," working so that he might not financially burden the churches. The churches did not support his leadership financially, evidently, yet who would consider Paul a "volunteer"? His experience of meeting Jesus in the lightning that blinded him while traveling the road to Damascus was hardly a call to "volunteer" if he could find the time (Acts 9:1-6). The decision to become a follower of Jesus demands nothing less than all of life—not just a few hours of time each week, after we manage all the pressing concerns of our lives (e.g., Luke 9:57-62).

Nowhere does Jesus use a term meaning "volunteer."

A volunteer is usually someone who is not paid and who may or may not have professional expertise in the work being done. Christian service may be as a professional—a banker who teaches a budgeting class in a life skills class for homeless families, for example. Christian service may be paid. Almost all of these social workers are paid in a congregational staff position. Their work is their calling (Sherman, 2011). Bob Roberts, a pastor who has engaged his congregation in community development both locally and in Asia, has stated that the calling of religious leaders is to get the people sitting in our pews to use their vocations as their channels of ministry (Roberts, 2007).

Second, to be a volunteer means being free to give service—or not. Volunteer responsibilities are usually considered secondary to vocational choices and other personal responsibilities. More importantly, volunteering is an optional role—something we can choose to do or, if we grow tired of it or are pressed for time, choose not to do. Christian service, however, is not considered "optional" in the life of a Christian (Shelp & Sunderland, 2000). Christians consider themselves called to care for one another, not invited to volunteer only if it is convenient.

Christian service is not voluntary in this sense; it is not an accident or beyond the boundaries. It is the heart of the life of the faith community.

"Voluntary" plants, for example, are those that are considered accidents; they come up from seed scattered accidentally or from roots growing beyond where the gardener planned. Christian service is not voluntary in this sense; it is not an accident or beyond the boundaries. It is the heart of the life of the faith community.

The use of language shapes experience. Christian mission is the congregational function that many of these social workers lead. Christian service is central to a life of faith and to the life of a congregation as expressed through Christian mission. The role of social workers in professional church leadership is crucial to congregants, individually, and the congregation, collectively, in the fulfillment of Christian service to each other and to the utter most parts of the world. Christian missions is contingent on the relationships that congregants have with each other and how they understand their Christian service in the world. A fuller discussion on this topic follows in the paragraphs below.

Figure 6.1. Volunteering vs. Christian Service

Volunteering	Christian Service
Unpaid financially	Both employment and unpaid
Both nonprofessional and professional	Both nonprofessional and professional
Optional	Essential and expected
During "spare" time	Central; throughout all of life activities
Individually meaningful	Individually and corporately meaningful

Evaluating Mission Engagement[47]

The motivation of Christian ministry is to show love of God and neighbor, to do what Jesus taught His followers to do. As recorded in the Gospel of John, Jesus, with the help of the disciples, fed about five thousand people with five barley loaves and two fish that a boy brought as his sack lunch (John 6:9-10). Later in the evening of that same day, when the disciples had gone ahead of Jesus, He caught up with them by walking to them across the water. Their boat was miraculously delivered from the strong wind and rough waters to the distant shore (John 6:16-21). It had been a day chock full of miracles. The next morning, the crowds came looking for Jesus, this worker of miracles. When they found Him, they asked for Him to give them the gift He had displayed. "What must we do to perform the works of God?" they asked.

> Jesus answered them, "This is the work of God, that you believe in him whom he has sent." So they said to him, "What sign are you going to give us then, so that we may see it and believe you? What work are you performing?" (John 6:29-30))

It had been less than 24 hours since the crowd had eaten until they were full at the miraculous wilderness banquet begun by a boy sharing his sack lunch. Perhaps the disciples had talked about Jesus walking on the water and the miraculous deliverance of their boat from a rising storm. Yet they ask for a sign. Had they not seen enough? It is even more telling that they ask Jesus to show them how He did it so they can do miracles too.

When Christians serve out of a motivation to change lives and restore hope in others, they are like the crowd who asked to know how to perform the "works of God." Certainly, Christians want to be the workers of miracles in the lives and communities where they serve. That would confirm for them that their service is really God's work. They want to *see* God at work and they long for concrete signs of eternal significance. Like the crowd, bread for today is not enough. Christians want a hold on that which will last, even which is eternal. They want to *contribute* to it, to be about God's work.

Jesus responds that the work of God is belief in the one God has sent. He goes on to tell us that if we come to Him, we will never be hungry; if we believe in Him, we will never be thirsty (vs. 35). In other words, Jesus' followers cannot put trust in that which they can see, much less in what they can accomplish by their own efforts. To trust Jesus means to live out His command to love and serve neighbors. The energy and motivations for that love and service do not come from the response of those served, as a "sign" that God's work is being done. The compassion and commitment come from the One who sustains, who calls His followers to serve, who meets them and walks with them in the work they do, regardless of the outcome.

Earlier in this chapter, we quoted a pastor who said, "When you begin to see the fruit of service; that's just gravy." He was using a Southern metaphor for something good that comes unexpectedly, as over-the-top, penultimate good is "gravy on the biscuit." In other places it is "icing on the cake." What can be hoped for is the biscuit—or the cake. Anything beyond hope is gravy—or icing. Jesus responds to the crowd's request by saying that He is "the bread of life" (John 6:48). Jesus is the bread—the biscuit, the cake. Living His teachings to love and serve is that which sustains His followers; the service itself is the bread that nourishes. Change in others because of Christian service—that is the gravy or the icing.

When you begin to see the fruit of it, that's just gravy.

Not Motivation—but Outcome

Nevertheless, Christians serve hoping that their service *will* make a difference in people's lives. They want to be used as instruments of healing and hope and opportunity. Those are *outcomes* of service, however, and not the *motivation*. If people's lives do change, the glory goes to God, because outcomes are God's business. If through their faithful service, God uses Christians in the transformation of those they serve, they are to thank God for that blessing—and marvel that God used them, little boys with bread and tuna fish in the face of a multitude. Christians are called simply to give what they have; the miracle of change in others is not theirs to control, only to contribute to through faithful service.

Christian service + **God's intervention +** *Others' response = Outcome*

Ultimately, even God, by giving humankind free will and agency, has chosen not to create change in the lives of individuals and communities without their choice. Even Jesus allowed people to make the choice not to change, not to follow him. Christian service can be blessed by God's intervention, and still the service does not accomplish the hoped-for end. A Christian who provides tutoring and mentoring can be loving and skillful, and God can bless that effort; the teen goes on to become the first to finish high school or attend college. Alternatively, the teen may be influenced by gangs and drugs and spiral downward into drug use and school failure.

Not Just Busy but Effective

A church leader and foster father has committed his congregation to leading other congregations in his state to end the public child welfare waiting list of children needing foster homes. His goal is for every child who needs one to have a foster or adoptive family. In a conversation about his calling, though, he said: "I'm a busy guy; but I don't want to just be busy—I want to be effective."

Service activity can be simply busy-ness if it is uninformed. It may be well-meaning—well-motivated—but still disempowering to those served and even harmful. For example, Carl described the harm he has to try to mitigate when well-meaning mission groups from other states descend on his congregation in order to "do missions"—displacing the leadership he has nurtured, doing for rather than doing with, accentuating that his congregation is "the poor community" rather than seeing the strengths in his congregation from which they can learn. Social workers know well the importance of cultural competence, of identifying strengths and competence in those served as well as needs, of a willingness to learn from as well as to teach, of looking at intervening in systemic as well as individual causes of social problems. That knowledge is what they bring to missions.

Service activity can be simply busy-ness if it is uninformed. It may be well-meaning—well-motivated—but still disempowering to those served and even harmful.

Social workers can help well-meaning and well-motivated Christians see not just the need of people, but also the strengths and gifts of those they serve. They can help them build mutual relationships of friendship, and not just mentoring in which the service recipient is always the needy one. Social workers can conduct program evaluation and research; they can develop mission models that are empowering and lead to social justice.

Thy Kingdom Come

Jesus taught us to pray, "Thy kingdom come, your will be done on earth as it is in heaven" (Matthew 6:10). It is God's kingdom to bring; it is God's will we want done. Yet Jesus went on to teach us not simply to wait passively but to go after it ourselves, to "seek first his kingdom and his righteousness" (Matthew 6:33). We serve as Christians because we love God, and we yearn for God's ways to be our ways. We yearn for God's kingdom on earth as it is in heaven. That yearning motivates us to seek the kingdom by living in our own lives what the kingdom of God looks like.

We look for the kingdom with our actions more than our eyes. Like persons who are blind, we cannot see it, so we reach for it, we feel for it. We feel for it by serving those who need our care, by tackling the social structures that lead to poverty and violence and discouragement in the lives of God's children. Through our actions, we communicate to others that God is committed to justice (Hessel, 1992; Singletary, 2005). Such small projects are actually *seeds* out of which will come God's kingdom (Conn, 1987). With our hands, we push the seeds into the soil of our neighborhoods. Our service plants the germinating seeds of the reign of God on earth; we cannot see the seeds swelling and bursting forth. We sometimes glimpse the first shoots pushing up, but they seem so small. Building houses for people who are economically poor will not eliminate slums. It is a start, however, and we pray that God will receive our work and miraculously expand it, like the loaves and fishes, into the fulfillment of God's will for the world.

We look for the kingdom with our actions more than our eyes. Like blind persons, we cannot see it, so we reach for it, we feel for it.

It is not that our work, however dedicated and skillful and faith-filled it is, can make the Kingdom come. It is not our efforts that control the in-breaking of God's kingdom. The kingdom is God's, not ours, to bring. We reach toward it with our service; and we pray for it.

Chapter 7
From Charity to Justice

The social workers we interviewed identified a wide variety of people their congregations engaged through its mission activities. Looking at a list of the people groups they serve is like looking at the chapters in a social work introduction text. They cross the generations and are dealing with all kinds of life circumstances, problems, and crises. They are people within a stone's throw of the congregation, and they are people on the other side of the world. Figure 7.1 summarizes the diversity of people and their circumstances these social workers and their congregations serve. The groups that these social workers serve most often are children and youths (n=26), families (n=17), persons who are homeless (n=10), and persons living in poverty (n=13).

Figure 7.1. People Groups Served

Ages and stages	Children, adolescents, college students, families, older adults
Life circumstances	Parents, gangs, single adults, married adults, persons with diverse sexual orientations, persons who are differently abled, school children, recent immigrants, pregnant and parenting teens
Physical or emotional challenges	Families coping with various disabilities in a member, mental illness, physical illness, substance abuse, living with HIV/AIDs
Problems or crises	Domestic violence, homelessness, unemployment, food insecurity, imprisoned (or a family member imprisoned), poverty, illiteracy, natural or human-caused disasters
Locations	Local neighborhood and geographic area, other places in the nation, other nations in the world

In addition, some of these social workers also see their role as Christian educators to be helping congregants make *all* of their daily activity a means for Christian mission—in their homes and workplaces as well as through congregational programs.

McNeal calls these life activities "everyday ministry." He quotes one lay leader as saying, "This approach to ministry is so much simpler; I get to minister in the things I am doing already instead of just adding things to my to-do list" (McNeal, 2009, p. 79; see also Roberts, 2010; Sherman, 2011).

The Continuum of Mission Engagement

Mission engagement ranges along a continuum, from addressing immediate needs to seeking to change the systems that create suffering. Many congregations have programs and services that provide individuals and families with what they need for survival or well-being—food, shelter, and clothing. At the other end of the continuum are activities designed to address the factors that create crises for whole populations of people—lack of job opportunities and education, inadequate health care, oppressive social policies, and environmental pollution. In the middle of the continuum are mission activities that are designed to equip people with the skills and resources they need to avoid or overcome crises—job skills training so they can secure a steady income, English classes so that immigrants can manage their daily activities in an American culture, parenting classes so that parents who are vulnerable to being abusive or neglectful can learn effective parenting skills.

Mission engagement ranges along a continuum, from addressing immediate needs to seeking to change the systems that create suffering.

Some of the social workers in our sample spoke of this approach to caring as "empowerment." Congregations engage in missions from one end of this continuum to the other, often simultaneously. The biblical concepts of love and justice—loving their neighbors through service and seeking justice in the face of social injustice—shape their understanding of this continuum as they seek to make current realities a reflection of God's eternal kingdom.

Figure 7.2. The Continuum of Mission Engagement

Responding to Need

The term charity connotes providing material help to others in need. The term originates in Hebrew and means righteousness; in Genesis 18:19, keeping the way of the Lord is defined as "doing righteousness and justice." Charity is the outward demonstration of loving God and neighbor, as in the great commandment, "Love God with all your heart, soul and mind; and love your neighbor as yourself" (Matt. 22:37, 39). Charity is the motivation, the attitude of loving neighbor, and not simply the aid provided.

Jesus taught His followers that responding to the need of others is a demonstration of loving Him, and by extension, loving God—providing food for the hungry, drink for the thirsty, shelter for the stranger, clothing for the naked, care for the sick, and visiting those in prison (Matthew 25:31-46). It matters not who is in need, whether it is someone like us or different, or whether it is someone we know or someone whose path we happen to cross, like the man beaten by robbers and left by the side of the road a Samaritan man happened to be traveling. In that parable, the Samaritan traveler gave charity—physical care, rescue, and money for short-term housing (Luke 10:30-7).

Like the early church's daily food distribution (Acts 6:1), American congregations today frequently minister to others by providing immediate tangible help such as groceries from a stocked food pantry in the church building or a voucher for a nearby store, free meals, used clothing, and emergency financial assistance. Public and private agencies commonly refer individuals and families to congregations for help with utility bills, rent, and other forms of assistance when government programs are unavailable or inadequate. It is not surprising, therefore, to find that when social workers are serving in congregations, they have the responsibility for these kinds of service programs. Some of these services they provide directly; others are programs they administer and congregants themselves are engaged in providing the service—serving food, staffing a food or clothing center.

Congregational social workers often establish policies for when and how much the congregation can help with financial assistance for rent to prevent eviction, utilities to forestall losing heat and cooking capability, prescription medications, bus passes to get to a new job, and books and uniforms for school. Sometimes assistance comes by means of a committee process that is facilitated by the social worker, or the social worker may individually review needs and determine eligibility for financial assistance.

In fact, a national study of congregations found that the most common way congregations involve themselves in social services is meeting emergency needs; almost one third organize food donations, 23 percent distribute clothing, and 8 percent provide services to persons who are homeless (Chaves, 2004). Most (n=31) of the social workers we interviewed lead crisis intervention services, providing direct financial help with unpaid bills, groceries, and/or housing.

The overlap between serving the congregation and serving the community is clear in these ministries. The congregation that Carl pastors is located in a poor inner city neighborhood, across the street from a day treatment facility for persons with chronic mental illness. The congregation began as a mission center. Carl trains the members who run their food pantry, and he says "about 90% of the members who serve in that program receive food from the pantry themselves."

David's congregation prepares food boxes for families whose children are not getting free lunches through the schools during the summer months. Denise has chaired the community outreach committee of her congregation for 10 years. They provide emergency assistance, as well as a "bucket ministry" of basic cleaning supplies for persons who have been homeless as they move into permanent housing.

A number of the congregations provide meals to persons who need it. Some provide this service on their own; Adam, for instance, recruits other congregations and volunteers from the community who help. David describes how they make every effort to feed the dignity as well as the stomachs of those they serve. His congregation invites people who are homeless not only for the meal but also to watch a movie. "We invite them into our 'home,' to get them off their feet, to get cooled off or warmed up. And we waited on them; they just raise their hands and we bring them a drink or more to eat."

Financial assistance can include episodic help as well. Christmas assistance is popular; congregations assist poor families with holiday food and presents. Kelly's work with the Jewish community in her town involved developing a burial service that observed Jewish customs and laws for those who die whose families do not have the financial resources for burial.

Congregations also address health needs. Friar Caleb is a member of a Roman Catholic religious order. At the time of the interview, he was serving a parish in Central America. There he had organized church members to distribute free or low cost medical services, both in the city and in a remote mountain community. Teams of doctors visit the clinics they founded where no medical services had been available otherwise. Some congregations in the United States also provide medical services such as free clinics. Basic hygiene resources may be hard for people who are poor or homeless to obtain. In a very different setting, Adam's congregation provides not only a free breakfast and lunch for people who are homeless, but also showers, toothbrushes, and other hygiene necessities.

Finally, these social workers describe how their congregations are responding to the basic human need for shelter. For example, the community in which David's congregation is located does not have a public shelter for persons who are homeless, so the churches collaborate to provide shelter throughout the winter. When it is his church's turn, David enlists and coordinates the church members to serve. He also works with the coordinating group and enlists the jail to wash the linens every day.

Austin's community does have a public shelter, but it is overcrowded during the hottest and coldest months of the year, so he started a new ministry, Room at the Inn, in which they take in a small group of 15 or so when the shelters are overflowing. Other congregations are involved in building or refurbishing apartments and homes for the poor through local community development organizations and national and international organizations such as Habitat for Humanity.

Congregations are also involved in resettling and meeting the needs of immigrants and refugees. Friar Caleb describes a ministry with undocumented Central American immigrants who have been deported and are simply dropped at the entrance to their home countries; the church provides funds to help them with transportation to their home towns so they do not have to walk across the country on foot.

Congregations are often the first place persons in need seek help and so they serve an "intake" function for the congregation's neighbors. As a consequence, many of these social workers engage in referral to other agencies and services in the community. The crises to which they respond include unmet physical needs but they may include other kinds of crises as well.

Carl began his work, for example, by walking the streets and hanging out in the popular local diner. It was managing a crisis in his "café congregation" that cemented his role as "pastor" in the community. A man known as "Big Ben" lived across the street from the café, where Big Ben ate all his meals. One booth was known as Big Ben's table. He did not show up one day, and so the diner staff called the landlord to check on him. Big Ben had died alone in his room. Carl organized a memorial service for Big Ben in the diner. He used the lunch counter for a pulpit where he spoke a eulogy, and he organized people to collect funds for a plaque, which was mounted in Big Ben's booth. From then on, the people of the neighborhood called Carl "Pastor." People in the neighborhood began coming to him with a myriad of crises, many of them financial. He accepts his role, given the neighborhood's deep poverty and lack of resources, saying, "We hope we can teach and empower to be preventive, but we know that if a church is a hospital, we're a MASH unit," referring to a medical unit that provides immediate medical help on the front lines of a war zone.

Congregations are often on the front lines in response to poverty, providing services like Carl describes even without social workers on the staff. They play an important role in identifying and meeting needs otherwise unaddressed, which can be a first step in societal responses more broadly. In many ways, persons in need utilize congregations as their "first responders" in helping to meet their basic needs. Social workers bring professional knowledge and skill that can help congregations be more effective in response to the complex challenges of poverty and other social problems.

Equipping for Life Tasks and Challenges

These social workers also lead their congregations in ministries that address needs that are more long-term than an immediate crisis. Some congregations provide job skills training, for example, or a job placement service. In the common parable about teaching a man to fish rather than feeding him fish when he is hungry, these are the angler education programs. We call these "equipping" programs.

Counseling, Tutoring, Mentoring

Equipping services may be provided individually, through professional counseling or through volunteer tutoring or mentoring programs. One way to think about counseling and therapy programs is that they are holistically educational—teaching clients to think, feel, and act in new ways and explore the barriers that keep them from making the life changes they desire. Marriage and family counseling, as one example, often teaches new ways of communication, conflict management, and intimacy.

Half of these social workers provide counseling services to congregants or persons and families in the community. Jeffrey is the director of counseling services for a Catholic diocese. He supervises other social workers; they serve 450 clients annually. Clients commonly are women who have experienced violent male partners, and their children who have been witnesses to the family abuse. These social workers also provide marriage preparation courses and counseling.

Social workers in congregations often do short term counseling and then refer to other professionals, recognizing that they cannot carry their other responsibilities and provide all the counseling services that could be offered in a congregation. For others, providing clinical services is their primary responsibility. For example, Inez has the title "church counselor" for her nondenominational Christian congregation. She provides services, without charge, to anyone who asks, whether that person is a member of the church or not. Her work is the congregation's gift to the community; the congregation pays her salary. Another example is Ben, who oversees a no-fee counseling ministry in his congregation for women who have experienced abuse.

Some do charge for counseling services, although using a steeply reduced fee structure from the private rates for clinical services. Inez's congregation, for example, pays her a salary, and congregational members and attendees pay a $10 fee per session, whereas those from the community pay a $20 fee per session, as they are able. The congregation subsidizes the rest of her salary.

Even those whose primary responsibilities are clinical services also have other congregational responsibilities, however. Inez talked about her organization and leadership of Bible studies as one of her professional responsibilities. Glenda provides couples wanting to marry in her congregation with premarital assessments, which she forwards to the parish priest, including any assessment of concern about whether they should marry or not.

Some of the counseling these social workers provide is informal. In his role as youth minister, for example, Gordon talked about his informal conversations with adolescents and his coaching them to "think on their own" rather than giving them advice, as they normally expect from adults.

Many of these social workers also do initial assessments and then refer congregants and community members to other service agencies in the community. Inez provides an example:

> I have a very good relationship with inpatient and outpatient facilities. I work closely with an eating disorders clinic. We didn't want to take the place of other mental health services; we wanted to augment what they do.

Group Educational Services

Equipping services also may be provided in a group setting, taught by the social worker or by other congregational leaders and members. These social workers described the programs that we grouped in the categories of economic and employment issues, mental health, relationships, and physical health (see Figure 7.3).

Figure 7.3. Group Educational Services.

Economic and Employment	Budgeting, English as Second Language, general education (preparation for the GED), home ownership, job readiness, literacy
Mental Health	Grief and mourning, mental illness, self esteem, relationships, divorce recovery
Healthy Relationships	Marriage, parenting, fathering (for men leaving prison), sexual orientation issues, family development
Physical Health	Body image (for pre-adolescent girls), cooking healthily on a limited income, gardening, karate, nutrition, physical exercise, sex education, smoking cessation, weight loss, women's health

Most of these programs target specific groups. For example, Catarina started a program that focuses on nutrition, physical activity, self-esteem, and positive body image for girls ages 9–12. Some programs are designed specifically for congregants, but even these are usually open to people from outside the congregation; other programs specifically target the congregation's neighbors. For example, Ben, pastor of a large church, began a prison ministry both in a local correctional facility, where he leads Bible studies as well as a transitional re-entry father's group.

The list in Figure 7.3 is by no means an exclusive list of the kinds of work social workers do in the congregations where they serve and the neighborhoods of those congregations. Rather, they illustrate that as they work in the community, social workers identify and develop various types of educational programs that address felt needs and, at the same time, have the potential for building community for participants, both those already in the congregation and those who are not. Some of these social workers may refer to this type of work as community development in the broadest sense of the term. Many of these programs overlap with the Christian education function, since they are often grounded in religious teachings and biblical texts.

Social workers also write curriculum for these services. For example, we, and our colleagues, have been directly involved in congregational social work as curriculum writers on topics of parenting, marriage, children in poverty, pornography, and job readiness skills, for example. [48]

The congregational social workers in our research not only offer educational and support services in their own congregations but also they support and collaborate with other service organizations in the community. For example, Jeanie has served as the Mission Outreach Coordinator for her congregation for nine years. She noted " a few" of the partnerships she has led her congregation to develop with organizations such as Head Start and Early Head Start, The National Alliance for Mental Illness, a senior companion program, a foster grandparent program, Parents and Children Together, a stroke support group, and the community mental health center.

Collaboration often means recruiting congregants to serve through such partnerships. Congregations frequently partner with public schools, providing tutoring, as well as collecting and donating school supplies, and upgrading the school's facilities. For example, Beth describes her congregation's five-year partnership with a public elementary school:

> We got the wish list from the teacher. Ninety-five percent of kids are on free lunch, so parents can't afford to stock the teachers' rooms. So we collected and had a blessing of the school supplies. We had big baskets in the church sanctuary, each with a teacher's name attached. The principal came to the worship service when we prayed for the school, and even some of the teachers; they just showed up. We had a child read a blessing over the school supplies, and we prayed for the school, and for the mentors.

As a different model but on the same theme, Jeanie's congregation is an example of one that partners with the local Head Start. They provide child care and a meal for parents so that they can have a "peaceful" dinner. They follow the meal with a parent education session.

Empowerment

Fifteen of these social workers took the focus on equipping one step further, and talked about not just equipping those they serve with knowledge and skills, but also with the power to take greater control of their lives. They used the term "empowerment" to describe their work. For example, Carl is adamant that he does not want his inner city congregation to be "a church in the community where suburbanites come into the community and minister and then leave." His definition of empowerment is equipping the people in the community to minister to one another. He goes on to say that he makes sure that they have roles and responsibilities in the congregation instead of defining them as targets of ministry. "Everybody is expected to give, not just receive," he says. That is empowerment, to have something to give to others.

Carl's focus resonates with a research project conducted with religious leaders in Los Angeles who have formed covenants between suburban and inner city congrega-

> *The challenge for social workers is leading congregations to approach service as mutual collaboration.*

tions. The research team found that, in fact, very few covenants mature to the point the congregations actually regard each other as equal partners, and inner city congregations do not want to be the missionary clients of suburbanites, feeling that their volunteering is humiliating and paternalistic. What is needed are mutual efforts to address challenges both congregations—and their members—face together in order to work. These ministry partnerships must be experienced by participants as joint efforts to find solutions for each other's problems (Orr, Miller, Roof, & Melton, 1994). The challenge for social workers is to lead congregations to approach service as mutual collaboration, including those who receive the congregation's services.

Reciprocity

The concept of reciprocity connotes that both persons are givers and receivers in the helping process. The exchange may not be exactly equal, but both benefit in some way. There is no poverty deeper than having nothing to give to others. Sadly, those who are seen as economically poor or categorized as needy may be seen as powerless and having nothing to give—like the mission groups view the people in Carl's congregation and neighborhood.

Several social workers described the validation that comes when those persons the congregation serves pass on to others the help and care they have received. Though they may not have given back to those who cared for them, they have given forward to others—another form of reciprocity. Beth describes seeing this evidence of effectiveness in the life of a woman they had provided emergency assistance several times during a period of her life in which she was homeless. She has since been able to find employment and permanent housing:

> A couple of weeks ago, she started in a new mentoring program for formerly homeless people—as a mentor! I was so proud of her. It was a privilege to train her.

Megan told a similar story:

> When we give out emergency food, some of those we helped come back and help others in turn. We've had something as small as them dropping off a few food items or they come to help give back. That's a good outcome.

Seeking Justice

If charity is giving a hungry person a fish to eat, and educational programs are angler education, then seeking justice is providing access and even ownership of fishing ponds and a truck to get the catch to market (Rusaw & Swanson, 2004). Entrepreneurs may, rightfully, contend that the old paradigm of teaching a person to fish is not complete unless persons are taught how to not only catch fish to feed themselves, but also given access to the means for improving their overall economic well-being. Seeking justice means creating changes in the systems that perpetuate complex social problems such as school failure, poverty, and family and community violence and replacing them with systems that give all persons access to the resources they need to flourish.

If charity is giving a hungry person a fish to eat, and educational programs are angler education, then seeking justice is providing access and even ownership of fishing ponds and a truck to get the catch to market.

Father Taparelli D'Azaglio first used the term "social justice" in 1840. He was building on Thomas Aquinas' much earlier concept of "general justice," which defines seeking the common good as a Christian virtue (Miller, Allen, & Brumbelow, 2012). D'Azaglio wrote the first curriculum on social justice, responding to the social problems created by industrialization and the growth of cities (Snyder, 2010). Pope Leo XIII was a student of Father D'Azaglio before he was named Pope. He, along with many popes since, has made social justice a part of Catholic thought. Catholic social teaching has continued to build on the principle of social justice, urging Christians to act in collaboration with others to hold public and private social institutions, including governments, accountable to the common good (Berger, 2007).

Catholic social teaching also promotes the principle of "subsidiarity," meaning that people at all levels of society should be included in decisions that affect them. When a congregation, for example, is considering how to respond to the needs and social challenges in a nearby neighborhood or in distant locales, it should consult with and learn from the neighbors who live there and not presume to know what is best for others. The people from the neighborhood become key informants in helping others see the strengths, challenges, and opportunities for change that exist in their neighborhood.

Yet another Catholic principle is "the preferential option for the poor," which calls on Christians to make serving those in poverty and working for economic justice a top priority for individuals and their congregations (Snyder, 2010). Seeking economic justice for persons in poverty is not optional—it is a primary responsibility.

Protestants, too, have emphasized Christian responsibility to seek social justice, not just individual salvation. There is no single authoritative position, however, among Protestants that parallels Roman Catholic thought, given the different polities and organizational frameworks of Protestantism. In our own tradition, there are more than 200 Baptist denominational bodies worldwide, and more than 40 in the United States (McSwain, 2008, p. xi). Each may differ from the others, and within any given denominational body, congregations themselves may differ with one another and with the denomination itself on any issue of biblical interpretation about social justice and social

Our lives are to be lived as a parable about the kingdom, recognizing that it is ultimately God's kingdom to bring to fruition.

action. As McSwain has noted, Martin Luther King, Jr. was a Baptist, and so were those who jailed him, both believing they were seeking social justice (McSwain, 2008).

With that said, there have been strong Protestant voices for social justice. Walter Rauschenbusch was one of the most notable spokespersons for the Social Gospel Movement at the turn of the last century. This movement merged developments in biblical studies with the emerging science of sociology. Those churches who embraced the tenets of the Social Gospel Movement focused on social systemic changes—on social redemption—as well as individual salvation (Dorrien, 2001; Lewis, 2008; Rauschenbusch, 1907).

Martin Luther King, Jr. was deeply influenced by the Social Gospel Movement in his articulation of the Christian responsibility to end racial oppression. King's dream was to build a community that mirrors God's love in, and to, the world. The theological concept of seeking the kingdom of God was the foundational principle of the Civil Rights Movement he led. He believed that our lives are to be lived as a parable about the kingdom, recognizing that it is ultimately God's kingdom to bring to fruition, not something we can achieve on our own. The Christian Community Development Association has built on the theological premises of the Civil Rights Movement (Marsh, 2005).

In another example of Protestant thought about justice, Ron Sider founded Evangelicals for Social Action and published the first edition of the influential *Rich Christians in an Age of Hunger* in 1977. He begins with the premise that "God wants every person and family to have equality of economic opportunity . . . so that by working responsibly they can earn a decent living and participate as dignified members of their community," and that Christians must seek to fulfill this clear biblical demand (Ronald Sider, 2005, p. xiv).

Seeking justice is also familiar language to social workers. Social justice is one of the six core values of the profession, and the NASW Code of Ethics mandates that social workers promote social justice (National Association of Social Workers, 2008). Yet one of the most challenging tasks these social workers say they face is moving their congregations from charity to a focus on social justice, on the forces that create the very problems of those they serve. Their struggle is not surprising; sociologists of religion have noted that few congregations ever make that move from meeting immediate needs to working for social justice (Ammerman, 2000). Of course, this challenge is not unique in social work to congregations as settings for practice.

Brazilian Catholic Archbishop Helder Camara famously said "When I feed the poor, they call me a saint; when I ask why they are poor, they call me a communist" (as quoted in Berger, 2007, p. 37). Because social justice calls for changes in the very social institutions that support those in power, and people in power include Christians, there is pressure to separate seeking justice from giving charity and to stay focused on charity. Charity without social justice, however, can become in-justice. Charity decreases suffering in the moment. When suffering is momentarily reduced, there is less pressure for more systemic change that enables the status quo to continue. Programs of addressing immediate needs also legitimize generosity in the moment as an effective response to ongoing suffering and injustice (Hilfiker, 2000).

Charity without social justice can become in-justice.

After decades of leading her congregation to serve the impoverished children of their city, Lynne ran for the local school board. She had become so frustrated with the state of their local public schools that she had decided it was time to try to bring about systemic change. She lost the election. Her congregation is staunchly Republican and she was running as a Democrat:

> When I ran for the school board, everybody in my campaign was from church. When one lady found out I voted for Obama, she came into my office, turned all of her campaign materials in—her t-shirt, everything—and she said, "I cannot campaign for someone who voted for Obama." I told her how absurd I thought it was to judge me by who I voted for. For a long time she wouldn't speak to me, but she finally got over it.

This woman agreed with Lynne running for office—she was working in her campaign. They agreed on the need for a more just educational system. What they disagreed about—strongly—was the means for achieving that justice politically. Congregants can agree that providing emergency services to families and tutoring for children are good activities to do. When it comes to social policy and politics, however, there can be sharp differences about how to bring needed social change, differences that create conflict so deep that people cannot even bring themselves to talk to one another.

Yet congregations do engage in movements for social justice. Franklin (1994) studied the culture of Black congregations that empowered ordinary people to struggle for social change and justice in the Civil Rights Movement, a movement birthed in church basements and nurtured in Sunday School rooms, and led by pastors. He found that preaching functioned as the chief catalyst for engagement in social action for justice—an avenue denied Lynne as a woman in a congregation where women cannot preach. His finding is further support for the premise that, ultimately, missions—including missions aimed at social justice—cannot be effectively separated from the other functions of congregational life, including its worship life where preaching shapes the congregation's understanding of itself in God's purposes. Keller (2010) suggests that Christian leaders must connect justice to biblical teaching. Trying to develop a heart for social

Preaching functions as the chief catalyst for engagement in social action for justice.

justice based on guilt—we have so much and others have so little—does not work. Rather, social justice must be connected not to guilt but to grace and to the gospel of Good News for all.

One Congregation's Journey from Charity to Justice

North Avenue Presbyterian Church in Atlanta was not one of the congregations represented in our congregational research study, nor was it included in our study of congregations engaged in community ministry. As we were working on this manuscript, though, we stumbled on a story in a religious news publication about North Avenue's engagement in efforts to end human trafficking. So one of us (Diana) conducted phone interviews with a staff member and then visited the congregation to learn from this congregation's experiences.

More than a decade ago, the juvenile courts in Atlanta began to see dozens of young teenage girls, some as young as 9 or 10, coming through their system after being arrested as prostitutes on the streets of the city. Atlanta is the top location in the United States for child prostitution; more than 400 children are bought and sold there each month (McCall, 2013). Some have run away from home and are vulnerable to offers of protection from those who then force them into the sex trade. Others fall into relationships with predators through internet chat rooms. At the time, there were no legal protections for children; in Georgia, buying or selling sex with a minor was only a misdemeanor charge with a fine of $50. And there were no treatment facilities to help children recover their lives (Campbell, 2010).

In 2005, Atlanta Mayor Shirley Franklin became a champion in the fight against sexual exploitation. She commissioned a report that mentioned a few intersections in the city that at the time were hotspots for sex trafficking. One was the very corner where North Avenue Presbyterian Church sits. When Rev. Dr. D. Scott Weimer, senior pastor of North Avenue heard that, he was shocked. He preached about the issue. The congregation responded by offering their own homes as safe shelter. The pastor knew that was a heart-felt and generous offer, but that the congregation needed expertise about this complex social problem, to develop a strategic plan, as well as training the congregation in how to express compassion to this targeted population group. He began meeting with other concerned clergy, and they co-hosted two faith summits on the issue in 2007 and 2008. As a result, eight Atlanta churches formed a new coalition, Galvanize Resources Against Child Exploitation (GRACE), now with the name Street Grace (North Avenue Presbyterian Church, 2013). Gradually, Street Grace broadened its focus from rescuing children to addressing the economic and educational injustices that make some children vulnerable to sexual exploitation. Street Grace is mobilizing community resources with the ambitious goal of ending domestic minor sex trafficking in Atlanta and throughout the United States. More than 30 churches have joined the network (Campbell, 2010).

Early on, Street Grace congregations supported a legislative bill that would send girls under the age of 16 directly to treatment programs rather than arresting and prosecuting them as prostitutes. Several other Christian organizations launched a campaign against the bill, saying that it was an effort to legalize prostitution, and, consequently, the bill did not pass (Campbell, 2010). Undaunted, Street Grace tried again, and since those early beginnings, Street Grace has been successful in supporting legislation that now not only does not prosecute children but also allows their juvenile records to be expunged.

Matt Seadore came to North Avenue Presbyterian Church as Director of Missions and Outreach in 2012 (Matt Seadore, personal communication, June 24, 2013). He was drawn, he says, by the congregation's ethos of mercy and justice, and he is learning about Street Grace by participating in it, along with other leaders and members of North Avenue. Four programs of Street Grace stand out in the life of North Avenue: Lobby Day, Fathers against Child Exploitation, Feeding Vulnerable Children, and the Street Grace Speakers Bureau.

> *Lobby Day*: When Lobby Day was launched in 2009, 25 or so people showed up at the State Capitol to talk with their representatives about the problems of the trafficking of children. Lobby Day has become an annual event. In 2013, 750 people descended on the capitol to hand letters of advocacy for vulnerable children to their representatives. North Avenue leaders and members met at the church and took the mass transit system together to be a part of the day.

Faith Fathers against Children Exploitation: Six men from North Avenue are participating in the program Faith Fathers against Child Exploitation. The goal is to fight the consumer demand for underage sex by encouraging men to abstain from pornography and visiting strip clubs, and to equip them to educate young men and boys about the dignity and value of women.

Feeding Vulnerable Children: Learning that food is a common lure into trafficking for vulnerable children—they are hungry and predators offer them something to eat—North Avenue is participating in Street Grace's Feeding Vulnerable Children. Even the children of North Avenue are helping to make summertime sack lunches for homeless and low-income children who receive free lunches during the school year but are at risk for hunger in the summer months.

Speakers Bureau: North Avenue members have joined the Street Grace Speakers Bureau. Street Grace trains teachers, staff, and parents to know the signs of child vulnerability to human trafficking (Matt Seadore; Street Grace, 2013)

North Avenue Presbyterian Church began its involvement in the social problem of child sex trafficking with the desire to rescue the children on their own street corner—responding to the immediate need. It was a charitable response, to offer to open their

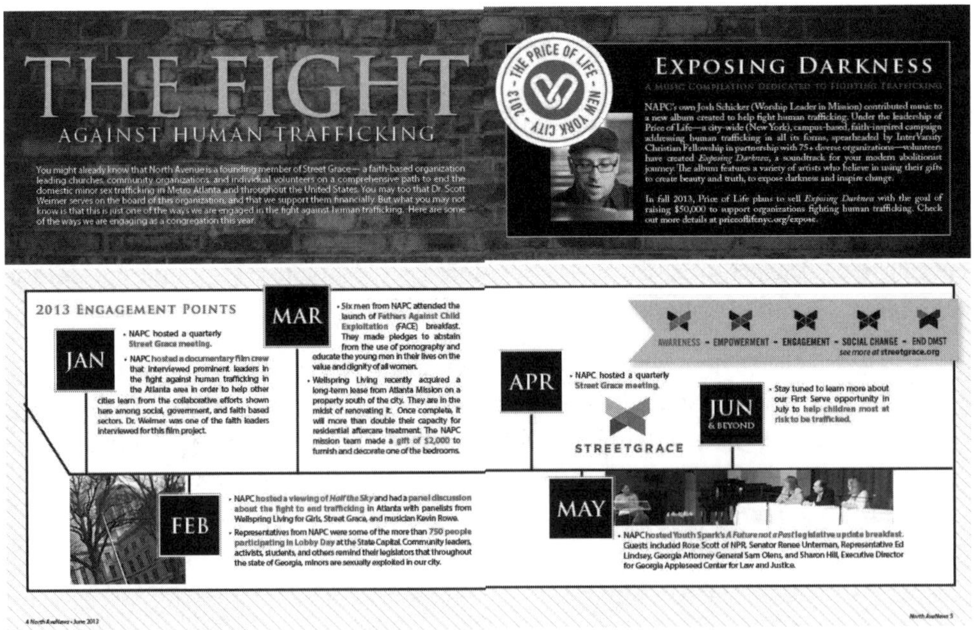
THE FIGHT
AGAINST HUMAN TRAFFICKING

You might already know that North Avenue is a founding member of Street Grace— a faith-based organization leading churches, community organizations, and individual volunteers on a comprehensive path to end the domestic minor sex trafficking in Metro Atlanta and throughout the United States. You may too that Dr. Scott Weimer serves on the board of this organization, and that we support them financially. But what you may not know is that this is just one of the ways we are engaged in the fight against human trafficking. Here are some of the ways we are engaging as a congregation this year.

THE PRICE OF LIFE - NEW YORK CITY - 2013

EXPOSING DARKNESS
A MUSIC COMPILATION DEDICATED TO FIGHTING TRAFFICKING

NAPC's own Josh Schicker (Worship Leader in Mission) contributed music to a new album created to help fight human trafficking. Under the leadership of Price of Life—a city-wide (New York), campus-based, faith-inspired campaign addressing human trafficking in all its forms, spearheaded by InterVarsity Christian Fellowship in partnership with 75+ diverse organizations—volunteers have created *Exposing Darkness*, a soundtrack for your modern abolitionist journey. The album features a variety of artists who believe in using their gifts to create beauty and truth, to expose darkness and inspire change.

In fall 2013, Price of Life plans to sell *Exposing Darkness* with the goal of raising $50,000 to support organizations fighting human trafficking. Check out more details at priceoflifenyc.org/expose.

2013 ENGAGEMENT POINTS

JAN
- NAPC hosted a quarterly Street Grace meeting.
- NAPC hosted a documentary film crew that interviewed prominent leaders in the fight against human trafficking in the Atlanta area in order to help other cities learn from the collaborative efforts shown here among social, government, and faith based sectors. Dr. Weimer was one of the faith leaders interviewed for this film project.

FEB
- NAPC hosted a viewing of *Half the Sky* and had a panel discussion about the fight to end trafficking in Atlanta with panelists from Wellspring Living for Girls, Street Grace, and musician Kevin Rowe.
- Representatives from NAPC were some of the more than 750 people participating in Lobby Day at the State Capital. Community leaders, activists, students, and others remind their legislators that throughout the state of Georgia, minors are sexually exploited in our city.

MAR
- Six men from NAPC attended the launch of Fathers Against Child Exploitation (FACE) breakfast. They made pledges to abstain from the use of pornography and educate the young men in their lives on the value and dignity of all women.
- Wellspring Living recently acquired a long-term lease from Atlanta Mission on a property south of the city. They are in the midst of renovating it. Once complete, it will more than double their capacity for residential aftercare treatment. The NAPC mission team made a gift of $2,000 to furnish and decorate one of the bedrooms.

AWARENESS - EMPOWERMENT - ENGAGEMENT - SOCIAL CHANGE - END DMST
see more at streetgrace.org

APR
- NAPC hosted a quarterly Street Grace meeting.

STREETGRACE

MAY
- NAPC hosted Youth Spark's *A Future not a Past* legislative update breakfast. Guests included Rose Scott of NPR, Senator Renee Unterman, Representative Ed Lindsey, Georgia Attorney General Sam Olens, and Sharon Hill, Executive Director for Georgia Appleseed Center for Law and Justice.

JUN & BEYOND
- Stay tuned to learn more about our First Serve opportunity in July to help children most at risk to be trafficked.

4 North AveNews • June 2013

North AveNews 5

own homes as shelter for children who needed it. Very quickly, however, congregational leaders recognized the need for greater understanding of the challenge before them; they reached out to others who could help them understand how to help. They then used what they had learned to educate others—legislators, teachers, and parents. They also educated themselves as the church newsletter demonstrates. Leaders were also looking for ways to be tangibly involved with the children they sought to protect; they are making sandwiches for children who otherwise might be hungry and vulnerable.

North Avenue's journey toward justice for children began with a passionate pastor's sermon and has continued with strong pastoral leadership. Even so, Seadore says it has not been easy because working for justice is not as appealing as rescuing vulnerable children. Working for justice means trying to do that which is "really good for another" in the long term. At the same time, Seadore says, "Regular people are more powerful than we think; when we come together for the good of others, we can make a difference."

Congregational Social Workers' Experiences in Justice Seeking

At first blush, it appears that "responding to need," "equipping for life tasks and challenges," and "seeking justice" are different activities, and that congregations do—or do not—move up and down the continuum of response to human need. In fact, the social workers we interviewed taught us that blending of the three in a single activity is more common than an activity being discreetly one or the other, like North Avenue's members making sandwiches for hungry children as well as seeking to change state laws.

Joy, one of the congregational social workers we interviewed, developed a program in which she equips teenagers to provide tutoring and mentoring for children at risk of school failure. Her program responds to the immediate needs of children and teenagers to have safe and nurturing activities in the after-school hours. The program is equipping children with skills and the added encouragement they need from a caring teenager to be successful in school. Additionally, Joy is subtly addressing the social injustice of defining teenagers as a problem, the target of ministry, as is sometimes common in congregations' youth ministry programs. Instead, her program defines teenagers as partners in ministry; the teens have a sense of purpose and calling and with resources they want to use for the sake of others.

Carl's approach to the mission groups that visit his small inner-city congregation to "help" in the summertime also is multi-purposed. The groups from congregations in other states come to address immediate needs in the neighborhoods around Carl's congregation, such as providing constructive activities and educational programs for children in the summer months when they are otherwise unsupervised while school is not in session. Carl works with his congregation to make these visits educational for the visitors, as they learn to see his community as one with resources and strengths, not just needs, and to see that the visitors also have needs as well as resources. The result is greater reciprocity, and the people of his congregation, who initially look to the visitors to be "the homeless," "the poor," and "the mentally ill" are redefined as educators and congregational leaders.

Along with nurturing a hunger for social justice in the congregants, congregational social workers can create an environment of empowerment for both the givers and receivers as they seek justice together. The "helpers" assist the "receivers" to make decisions for themselves, instead of one group making decisions for the other. In turn, the "helpers" learn how empowering it is to promote the self-determination of others, rather than to presume to know what is best for another. The "receivers" gain confidence and greater control over their own lives. Carl explains it in this way:

> We have people from the suburbs who come to minister, and I want to help them see that they need to be fixed too, that they need ministry too. I want to get that somebody who is dressed to the nines to see that a homeless person has something to contribute too.

Proclaiming Jubilee

Leading a congregation to seek justice begins with defining social justice as a fundamental theme of Christian scriptures. Walter Brueggemann has pointed out that the most basic laws of Judaism and Christianity, the Ten Commandments (Exodus 20), are not just rules of individual morality but, rather, prescriptions for organizing power and social life for the good of the community. "You shall not covet" (vs. 17) is not just about trying to avoid wishing for what others have, but, more centrally, about people with power and ambition taking from those who are vulnerable to abuse. "In a rapacious economic system, nobody's house and nobody's field and nobody's wife and nobody's oil are safe from a stronger force" (W. Brueggemann, 2010, p. 25).

The Ten Commandments are prescriptions for organizing power and social life for the good of the community.

Keeping Sabbath is not so much about attending church but it is about withdrawing from work and from defining life by economic production and consumption. "Sabbath is an occasion for community enhancement, for eating together and remembering and hoping and singing and dancing and telling stories—all exercises that have no productive value" (W. Brueggemann, 2010, p. 27).

Deuteronomy is arguably the first attempt to provide a social safety net for those vulnerable to oppression, poverty, and hunger. Deuteronomy 24:19-22 names the money crops of grain, olives, and grapes, which were key market commodities. Brueggemann suggests that the story of the Exodus and the giving of laws on Mount

Leviticus 25:1-12

The Lord spoke to Moses on Mount Sinai, saying: Speak to the people of Israel and say to them: When you enter the land that I am giving you, the land shall observe a Sabbath for the Lord. Six years you shall sow your field, and six years you shall prune your vineyard, and gather in their yield; but in the seventh year there shall be a Sabbath of complete rest for the land, a Sabbath for the Lord: You shall not sow your field or prune your vineyard. You shall not reap the aftergrowth of your harvest or gather the grapes of your unpruned vine: it shall be a year of complete rest for the land. You may eat what the land yields during its Sabbath—you, your male and female slaves, your hired and your bound laborers who live with you; for your livestock also, and for the wild animals in your land all its yield shall be for food.

You shall count off seven weeks of years, seven times seven years, so that the period of seven weeks of years gives forty- nine years. Then you shall have the trumpet sounded loud; on the tenth day of the seventh month—on the Day of Atonement—you shall have the trumpet sounded throughout all your land. And you shall hallow the fiftieth year and you shall proclaim liberty throughout the land to all its inhabitants. It shall be a jubilee for you: you shall return, every one of you, to your property and every one of you to your family. That fiftieth year shall be a jubilee for you: you shall not sow, or reap the aftergrowth, or harvest the unpruned vines. For it is a jubilee; it shall be holy to you: you shall eat only what the field itself produces.

Sinai juxtapose on this triad a second triad, that of the immigrant, the orphan, and the widow. These three groups of people are those with no access to valuable commodities. Care for them is to be the mark of God's people. The economic system spelled out in God's law is the operationalization of the concepts of justice and Sabbath, a system for managing wealth and poverty, for caring for the earth and neighbor, and for setting limits on power and powerlessness.

Leviticus 25 spells out God's economic system. Every seventh day was to be a Sabbath, a day of rest, putting limits on work and production. Work may be important, but it is not most important—and Sabbath puts work in its place. Similarly, every seventh year was to be a Sabbath year. Not only is it a year for people to rest from their labor, but the land, too, is to be allowed to rest. For this to be possible, Yahweh promised that there would be a bumper crop in the sixth year so that there would be plenty to eat for two years.

Every seventh Sabbath year—seven times the seven years, or 49 years—the people were to proclaim the Year of Jubilee. It was a year of rest and, in addition, the land and its wealth were to be redistributed. In a rural economy, those who had fallen into debt had lost their land to pay the debt, and sometimes their own freedom, as they had to indenture themselves and their children. In the Year of Jubilee, every 49 years, the

If God's people kept God's laws, there would be no permanent, multigenerational poverty.

land was to be returned to those who had lost it. Those enslaved and in debt were to be set free. Jubilee meant that the economic troubles of one generation would not condemn their children and their children's children to poverty. Every 50 years, a new generation got a fresh start, a newly leveled playing field. God's commandments and laws, if practiced, would have "virtually eliminated any permanent underclass" (T. Keller, 2010, p. 27). Through catastrophe or failing, people will fall into poverty, but if God's people kept God's laws, there would be no permanent, multigenerational poverty.

There is no indication that Jubilee was ever implemented. The rich simply got richer, and the poor poorer. When Jesus launched his ministry, his first sermon proclaimed "the year of the Lord's favor"—Jubilee (Luke 4:16-21). Jesus brought good news for those in poverty. He came to "release the captives" and to "let the oppressed go free" (vs.18)—to free people from indentured servitude. Consequently, he upset the rulers of society. The Good News Jesus brought was less about individual salvation in the next life but more about the in-breaking of God's kingdom—God's order—in this life. It is the vision of Isaiah fulfilled:

> Every valley shall be lifted up, and every hill be made low; the uneven ground shall become level, and the rough places a plain. Then the glory of the Lord shall be revealed, and all people shall see it together, for the mouth of the Lord has spoken (40: 4-15).

The call to Jubilee, to justice, means that Christians are called not just to minister to the poor but also to address the systems that create poverty and oppression—the valleys and hills and "rough" places of our social and economic world. Christian salvation includes not only deliverance from individual sin but also it is the assurance of economic and social well-being for those who are poor and oppressed (Campolo, 1990).

Christians are called not just to minister to the poor but to address the systems that create poverty and oppression—the valleys and hills and "rough" places of our social and economic world.

Christians are located in the valleys of poverty and on the mountaintops of economic wellbeing. In our culture where the assumption is that nobody would be poor if they work hard enough, it is easy to assume that material well-being is a sign of God's blessing and poverty is a result of personal failing. Those assumptions are left unchecked in a society segregated by social-economic class, where the wealthy and middle class do not know people who are poor, nor their stories. That sorting by class, inadvertently, characterizes many congregations. Christians who are middle class may have no personal relationships and so no opportunity to know people who are poor—and the opposite also may be true. Middle class people, for example, may prefer to go to middle class congregations, even if the congregation has chosen to stay in an urban center. People in the congregation do not necessarily "look like" the people in the surrounding neighborhoods. Economic class groupings tend to stay together; this is true of congregations, too.

It takes intentional neighboring—developing relationships with those who are different from themselves—to begin to challenge assumptions about what it means to be poor, and about what it means to have wealth. As congregational leaders engage congregants in ministry alongside those who are different, relationships challenge preconceptions. Knowing the stories and experiences of those who have had different life experiences from oneself expands and deepens understanding and lays the groundwork for mutuality rather than one group ministering to the other. That mutuality is what Carl seeks for those visitors from out of state and the people of his congregation. The hills need flattening just as much as the valleys need filling in; both sides of the equation change in the process.

Congregational social workers understand the fundamental value of social justice in their profession. Their task is to nurture a hunger for social justice through Christian education about the themes, narratives, and teachings of the Bible, through worship of a God who calls us to proclaim Jubilee, through developing a community that is a holy alternative to a society where the rich are ever richer and the poor ever poorer—and through missions and ministry that seek justice for neighbors close by and far away.

Local and Global Missions

"Missions" involves a multitude of activities. Congregants engage in some of these activities alone, with family members, or with specific groups, such as a Bible study group. Others are offered through the organized outreach programs of the church. Still others are conducted through other organizations, some with Christian affiliation and others who are not. Sometimes the congregation blesses people to serve as their representatives; at other times, the congregation may not even know about the activities in which their members are engaged (Garland, 2003a, 2003b). These congregational mission activities may include stocking an emergency food bank's shelves, building a house, rocking babies in a neonatal hospital unit, teaching budgeting skills, mentoring a child, leading a scout troop, driving someone to the doctor, writing letters to deployed military personnel, sitting with an ill neighbor while a caregiver goes to the store, or developing a business plan for a new business in an impoverished community. Congregants often engage in these activities without financial payment, outside their employment careers.

The kinds of mission activities a congregation's people take on reflect their personal resources, abilities, and concerns. The geographical location of a congregation also affects its mission activities. In fact, location is more significant than theological brand or denominational identity in determining the extent to which a congregation is engaged in ministry activities locally; congregations in central and inner cities are more engaged in local ministries than those in the suburbs and rural areas, even though they may have fewer resources (Cavendish, 2000; Cavendish, Welch, & Leege, 1998; Mock, 1992).

Congregations also care for neighbors beyond their own locale and culture, venturing into another "neighborhood" in their city, such as an apartment complex housing refugees from another country, or a government housing complex for low-income families on the other side of town. They may go by plane or church bus to another city or country.

In addition to involving themselves in mission activities, being involved in "missions" means collecting and sending financial contributions to agencies and organizations that are addressing spiritual and human need locally and globally—denominational missions organizations; local food banks and mission centers; and international evangelical, social service, and social development organizations. Congregations also provide financial and prayer support for representatives from their midst who go as their "missionaries"—those who relocate nationally or internationally for a short or a long period of time to work full-time among neighbors in those localities. Nearly three quarters (74%) of Americans say their congregations are financially supporting missionaries working in other countries (Wuthnow, 2009, p. 148). Spending by American congregations in international missions now exceeds $4 billion annually, an increase of almost 50% after inflation, in a single decade; and the number of full-time missionaries serving internationally is at an all-time high (Wuthnow, 2009, p. 1).

This exponential growth can be attributed in large part to the development and democratization of international travel. It was not until the 1800s that global travel was possible enough to allow missions to develop. In the 19th Century, when international travel meant weeks at sea, not hours by plane, "missions" was a lifetime commitment. Sometimes it was more than a lifetime commitment as generations in some families committed themselves to missions. I (Diana) am the daughter-in-law of Ruth Garland, who was herself the daughter of missionaries to India. Ruth grew up in India, and then married another child of missionaries, my father-in-law, and they lived there most of their lives, coming home only to raise more money to support their work.

Some of the early social work training schools prepared women for social work—and missions. Missionaries founded schools and hospitals, believing that one has to address the physical and social needs of people in order to gain trust so that those with whom they ministered could hear the Gospel, or because they had a holistic understanding that the Gospel is not just good news for our souls but it is also about our whole lives—our bodies and health, our relationships, and our well-being.

Historically, congregations have looked to their denominations to link them to the world beyond their geographical neighborhood, to be pipelines from downtown USA to global people groups. One of the reasons congregations have affiliated with, and maintained ties with, a denomination is the sense of being able to support denominational mission and relief agencies to "do good work" on their behalf (Ammerman, 2000, p. 306).

A dramatic shift has taken place in the past 50 years, from missionaries being sent by denominations to congregations now sending their own missionaries. By the 1970s, many of the mainline Protestant denominations were no longer sending missionaries, and most that continued international work were doing so by supporting national and local leaders rather than sending Americans. For example, in 1935, Presbyterians had 2,100 American overseas missionaries; by 1999, they had 772. Similarly during that same 64-year period, Methodist numbers dropped from 1,400 to 413. One outlier is Southern Baptists; in that same period Southern Baptist missionaries increased from 230 to 1,543. More significantly, however, hundreds of new independent mission-sending agencies established themselves and were supporting personnel in numbers that exceeded the total of missionaries supported by all American denominations combined (Ammerman, 2000, p. 193).

Congregations are involved directly—by sending their own members—in providing medical and dental clinics, micro-business leadership programs, orphanages and foster care programs, water purification systems, and sustainable agriculture. During the latter part of the twentieth century, the number of U.S. Christians participating in international short-term mission (STM) work, trips generally lasting less than one year, grew exponentially, from 540 in 1965 to an estimated 450,000 in 1998. By conservative estimates, over the next 10 years, this number grew to more than 1.5 million U.S. Christians who annually participate in short-term international mission work at an average cost of about $1,400 per person (Horton, Rozzi, Aufhammer, Berry, & Camp, 2011). Almost half (44%) of congregants say that their congregations sent a group on an international short-term mission trip during the past year (Wuthnow, 2009, p. 168, 170).[49]

The potential positive impact of short-term missions lies in three areas: (1) impact on the mission team participants; (2) contribution to the ministry and work among those in the host community; and (3) impact on the mission-sending entities. The primary purpose of these trips may be evangelism (such as sharing the Christian message of salvation through preaching, teaching, Vacation Bible Schools, plays, etc.); teaching English as a second language; or providing medical aid, construction, technology transfer, and agricultural or business development. The mission team participants may gain a greater understanding of other cultures, become less materialistic, and increase their long-term involvement in mission work (Horton, Rozzi, Aufhammer, Berry, & Camp, 2011).

Some concerns have arisen, however, about the unintended consequences of short-term missions. Perhaps the money spent on participant travel expenses would have greater impact if it were given directly to those they are attempting to serve. For example, one study found that 10 times as many houses could have been built if local Christian leaders in Honduras had simply been given the money that mission team participants spent on trip expenses. Moreover, local workers needing employment could have done much of the work performed by team members. Some long-term missionaries have noted that culturally uninformed mission teams have actually done more harm than good, damaging relationships that had taken months and sometimes years to build. Because two-thirds of these trips last two weeks or less and the volunteers are not always adequately trained, a number of missiologists have begun to question the wisdom of investing so much money in short-term missions—an estimated $2 billion per year (Horton et al., 2011).

Well-meaning mission groups may actually be creating or deepening social problems, such as the institutional rather than community-based care of children. That is, by building and staffing orphanages in impoverished communities that can provide education, nutrition, and clothing for children, these missions are inadvertently encouraging families and communities to relinquish their children to institutions, believing that they will have greater opportunity for surviving and thriving growing up in orphanages. Imagine how different the outcome for children might be if those same resources were invested in the economic development of these communities, so that they can provide for their own children in family care. Social workers are bringing attention to the possible effects—intended and unintended—of such approaches to missions (Singletary, 2007).

When leaders can guide development of mission efforts that aim for mutuality and an understanding of the systemic nature of social problems, the potential positive effects on team members may offer significant justification for continuing to encourage mission trips—or perhaps more appropriately named missions *education* trips, even when such trips are costly. Anecdotal evidence indicates that those who participate in such work are more likely to be supportive of local and long-term global missions. Mission team members also may become less ethnocentric and less materialistic. Moreover, they may benefit by simply having personal involvement in missions and thereby gain a greater understanding of global Christianity. In other words, the significant positive impact is actually experienced by the mission team itself, with appropriately modest goals of doing no harm and beginning friendships with host communities.

Due to the concerns about the challenges of short term missions and the potential for negative impact on those who are supposedly helped, best practice guidelines

Figure 7.4. Habitat for Humanity[52]

Habitat for Humanity began as a Christian organization and has inspired hundreds of thousands of volunteers, as they help build or repair Habitat houses for more than 600,000 families worldwide, to change how they think, how they act, and how they vote. Habitat for Humanity International is a nonprofit, ecumenical Christian organization … dedicated to eliminating substandard housing and homelessness worldwide and to making adequate, affordable shelter a matter of conscience and action." It bases its work on three theological concepts:

Putting faith in action. To follow the teachings of Jesus Christ we must love and care for one another. Our love must not be words only—it must be true love, which shows itself in action.

The economics of Jesus. When we act in response to human need, giving what we have without seeking profit, we believe God magnifies the effects of our efforts.

The theology of the hammer. Habitat is a partnership founded on common ground—bridging theological differences by putting love into action. Everyone can use the hammer as an instrument to manifest God's love.

have developed for short term missions that encourage pre-trip training in the cultural setting and skills needed, mentoring during the trip, and post-trip integration of the trip experiences with life beyond the trip. When leaders incorporate these practices, current research indicates that the mission team members may have greater potential for lasting transformation in the following areas: (1) greater daily interaction with people of different races, religious beliefs, and socio-economic status; (2) a less materialistic attitude and lifestyle; and, (3) greater commitment to local and global missions (Horton et al., 2011).

How effective am I? Evaluation in a Congregational Setting

Congregational social work provides some interesting challenges for evaluating professional practice, particularly in the area of missions engagement. The ultimate focus of congregational social work is the congregation itself, leading its people to live faithfully in the context of the neighborhood and world that the congregation serves and loves. Neighborhood assessments may be useful foundations for the congregation's ministry and evaluating its impact on neighbors and neighborhoods locally and globally. Those assessments are indirectly reflections of the social worker's practice. But the most direct reflection of the social worker's effectiveness is how congregants are living their lives and serving faithfully and lovingly.

The most direct reflection of the social worker's effectiveness is how congregants are living their lives and serving faithfully and lovingly.

The congregation's service to and love of neighbor is a focus of evaluation for congregational social work. Measuring the impact on the neighborhood/world is difficult at best, however. Positive changes in the neighborhood, the success of a child being mentored by a congregational volunteer, and the graduation from high school of an at-risk teenager engaged in the congregation's afterschool program are certainly to be celebrated, but they are clearly outcomes not only of the congregation's involvement but of many other factors as well—not the least of which is the grace of God. Knowing that the congregation had a hand in the success is joy. The social worker, however, needs to help a congregation temper any conclusion that their involvement has caused whatever happens in the lives of neighbors and neighborhood as a consequence of their involvement.

Just as, or even more, important is the evaluation of the extent to which the congregation's members were present in the life of that child or teenager week after week, loving and caring for them. The congregational social worker's primary evaluation is the extent to which one-time and short-term service results in long-term and lifestyle changes. It is the extent to which the charity of helping a child in trouble becomes a focus on justice, on changing the systems that make children vulnerable to school failure and unable to flourish. Additionally, it is the extent to which understanding and commitment to living as Christians is strengthened. In short, the goal of congregational social work practice is developing a faithful community characterized by the love of neighbor, by seeking justice, and by humbly trying to walk in step with where God is going (Micah 6:8).

The goal of congregational social work practice is developing a faithful community characterized by love of neighbor, by seeking justice, and by humbly trying to walk in step with where God is going (Micah 6:8).

Like the congregations they serve, social workers long to make a desired impact in the world—to see children who might otherwise fail in school succeed because a tutoring program was created, or people who are unemployed find fulfilling jobs through a job readiness program that was developed. They strive for that, long for it, pray for it—but ultimately, the response is determined by not only the social worker's actions but also by the client's self-determination and God's blessing. Social workers are to help the congregation recognize the *contribution* it can make to justice and neighbor love where it is planted.

Focusing on faithfulness rather than measurable impact on issues like poverty and school failure keeps people from being paralyzed by the complexity and enormity of such social problems. Sometimes—perhaps almost always—social justice comes in small increments, and many people have to work toward it, knowing that they may not see the outcome of their work in this life. Building a congregational community that encourages and supports one another in neighboring and justice work enables people to do this long work. "We don't need specific outcome. We need each other" (Wheatley, 2004, p. 350).

Marian Wright Edelman says that the core problem of teen pregnancy and school failure is hopelessness (Edelman, 2004). That is the root problem of our society, not just the world of teens. We look at problems like poverty and hunger and realize that the problems are bigger than our ability to resolve them. We feel hopeless; we cannot change the world, so we might as well just take care of ourselves and those closest to us. The congregational social worker's job is to point our culture to the good news that through us, the Good News, News of Hope, *God* can make a difference. In the process, we can be transformed.

The prophet Micah says to *seek* justice, not necessarily to create it. The people of God are to yearn for justice and work for justice. That yearning and working is "success" for the social worker. Justice is beyond our ability to make happen. When it comes, hallelujah, but it will be because of the many people who sought justice, of which our individual efforts are just one piece. That is humility—walking humbly *with God* (Micah 6:8), recognizing that it is God who blesses our efforts by bringing the justice; justice is not just our doing, or our *not* doing.

Rosalie Bertell shares the story of a young post-World War II bride who noticed an example of American apartheid; Black women who worked cleaning White people's houses stood for an hour or more on the street corner near her home. They were waiting for a bus to take them back to the Black community at the end of their long workdays. The young woman soon learned that they stood there for so long because the busses would not stop if there were only Blacks on the corner. So the young woman went every evening to stand with the Black women who had worked all day, so that the busses would stop. Eventually, the bus drivers understood and began to stop (Bertell, 2004). What would be the measure of her action? That the busses, because of her actions, began to stop for the Black women? That those women were home an hour more each day with their families? Or that she stood there, evening after evening, with her neighbors from across town? Or perhaps that now, decades later, we are telling her story to inspire our generation to seek justice?

Stories like that of Rosalie Bertell bring alive what it means to seek justice and to evaluate faithfulness. Two other stories, one from our own recent past and one from the beginnings of our faith tradition, illustrate the challenges of evaluating the work of growing faithfulness.

An American Example: Rosa Parks

The Rosa Parks story is compelling because she sounds like an "ordinary" person who happened to be in the right place at the right time that bent the course of history toward justice. On December 1, 1955, in Montgomery, Alabama, she refused to give up her seat in the Colored section of a bus when the White section was filled. She was arrested for her defiance, becoming a symbol of the Civil Rights Movement (Williams & Greenhaw, 2005).

In fact, her action was planned and built on her own long preparation and the work of many others who had strategized and prepared the way. More than 50 years earlier, a Montgomery bus boycott had successfully eased some restrictions. Two years earlier, a Baton Rouge boycott had made limited gains for civil rights. Just months before Rosa Parks' actions, a young woman had also refused to move to the back of a Montgomery bus. The NAACP considered making a legal case of her arrest, but when they learned that she was unmarried and pregnant, determined she would not serve well as a symbol for the movement (Loeb, 2004b).

Rosa Parks became involved in the Civil Rights Movement by going to a meeting with some hesitation and uncertainty more than 12 years before that fateful bus ride. She continued going to meetings, working with others to build the community that, in turn, encouraged and supported her. The summer before, she had attended a 10-day training session in civil rights organizing, where she had met an older generation of activists. E. D. Nixon served as a mentor to her. He was head of the Montgomery, Alabama NAACP and had carried people's suitcases on trains as a car porter. JoAnn Robinson taught at a Black college nearby and headed the Women's Political Council that distributed leaflets after Parks was arrested. Without them, Parks would likely never have acted, nor would her actions have had the same impact (Loeb, 2004b).

To know that Rosa Parks did not stand in isolation but rather was supported and strengthened by many others before and after that late afternoon bus ride carries an empowering message. The conventional portrayal suggests that those who work for justice must be ready to take dramatic stands that will instantly change the course of history. It implies that we act with the greatest impact when we act alone, at least initially. The real story is less intimidating and more suggestive that we can all have a role to play. It also suggests that we cannot always evaluate the effectiveness of our actions. Change may not come because of what we do, or even because of those who build on what we have done. It may come long after, and nobody but God may know how what we did contributed to an ultimate bending of the universe toward greater justice (O'Gorman, 1990). It has to be enough that we acted in faithfulness.

A Biblical Story: Moses

Everyone knows Moses' name, but few identify readily the names Shiphrah and Puah. During the time when Moses was born to a slave family in Egypt, Shiphrah and Puah were poor slave midwives, single women in a traditional female occupation—taking care of pregnant women and helping them through childbirth. Like Rosa Parks the housemaid, when one thinks of who bends history, midwives do not come to mind—nor do social workers or store clerks or the other ordinary people who compose most congregations.

Pharaoh had determined to reduce the slave population explosion through genocide and ordered these two midwives to kill the boy babies as they were born. Shiphrah and Puah feared God more than they feared Pharaoh, and so they kept on delivering baby boys—not only delivering in birth but delivering them from the threat of death. When Pharaoh called them to come before him to account for their actions, they simply lied. With all the innocence they could muster, they said, "Hebrew women are not like Egyptian women; they are vigorous and give birth before the midwives arrive" (Ex. 1:19). God is not a God of simple rules: Always tell the truth; be at church whenever the doors are open; give 10 percent of your earnings—then you can expect to be blessed. This God works far more mysteriously. Shiphra and Puah illustrate the greatest commandment, that loving God and loving neighbor is more important than anything else, including reporting facts accurately to someone who will use those facts to harm others. They lied.

Shiphrah and Puah also did not act alone. They had one another. They acted in collusion with the mothers, sisters and a community successfully hiding baby boys from the oppressors.

Shiphrah and Puah's defiance of Pharaoh came years before one of the baby boys they delivered would stand before Pharaoh and declare: "Let my people go" (Exodus 7, 5:1). It was because of their faithfulness that Moses lived long enough to be hidden by his mother, to be watched over by his older sister, to be rescued by the princess, and to become the rescuer of his people—five women courageously raising a boy in defiance of the royal decree. Shiphrah and Puah left the scene long before the parting of the Red Sea. Even Moses did not go into the Promised Land. Moses lived his whole life into the promise God had given him of a promised land for the ragtag homeless band of Israelites he led out of Egypt. He was never able to see the promise fulfilled; he died in the wilderness (Deuteronomy 34:1-8).

Loeb writes that we live in ways we believe are faithful, knowing we will never see the completed structure or can even imagine what it will look like. Shiphrah and Puah probably had no idea where their act of courage would lead, and probably neither did Moses' mother, sister, and adoptive Egyptian mother. In similar ways, we put our feet in front of one another, step by step, carrying the younger ones with us, placing them further down the path that we began, trusting them—or their children—to go where we will not. "Our dreams are often bigger than our lifetimes" (Loeb, 2004a, p. 289).

Faithfulness, not Effectiveness

Evidenced-based practice only goes so far in leading missions and ministry, in working for justice. Given the complexity of systems that create the challenges that congregations face, one cannot predict what will bring about change and what will not.

Bertell tells a story of men who had been taken in a truck to the gas chambers from a World War II German concentration camp. Suddenly, an energetic man grabbed one of the condemned men's hands. Turning it over, he read the man's palm with exuberance, "Oh, he says, I see you have a very long lifeline; and you are going to have three children." Others caught the spirit. First one man, and then another offered up their hands, and the predictions were all for longevity, more children, and abundant joy. Men laughed. The element of surprise planted a shadow of doubt; were they really about to die? The guards were so disoriented by the change of mood among those they were about to kill that they could not continue. Instead, they ordered the men back onto the truck and returned them to the camp (Bertell, 2004).

In fact, the executions continued; later, most of the men died in the camps, but they did not die that day. "If imagination cannot simplistically wish us out of any situation, the flip side is also true; 'realism' can paralyze us into not acting at all" (Bertell, 2004, p. 194).

Moreover, it is not just the evaluation of individual faithfulness, but a community culture of faithfulness that is at the core of the goal of congregational social work practice—and the focus of our evaluation. Jesus does not simply call us to be faithful individuals, but to be His body, His community, promising to be with us when two or more group together in His name (Matthew 18:20).

Evaluating Congregational Social Work

Evaluating congregational leadership in missions and ministry, then, means evaluating how effectively leaders engage the congregation in missions and service as an expression of faith. Reggie McNeal suggests coming up with measures such as time spent mentoring and debriefing people engaged in missions, and planning and facilitating gatherings where congregants share their faith stories and experiences.

> We must change our ideas of what it means to develop a disciple, shifting the emphasis from studying Jesus and all things spiritual in an environment protected from the world to following Jesus into a world to join him in his redemptive mission (McNeal, 2009, p. 10).

We saw evidence that the social workers we interviewed are wrestling with appropriate ways to evaluate their work. We identified three emphases in evaluation related to the missions and ministry of the congregation: (1) congregational faithfulness in service, (2) ministry becoming reciprocal, and (3) their own ability to keep on serving faithfully, even and especially in the face of disappointment.

Congregational Faithfulness in Service

Lynn reports that her congregation is growing "by leaps and bounds." What is significant in evaluating her leadership is not so much the numerical growth in number of congregants, however, but the reasons for the growth—she says that people are joining because they want to be a part of a congregation known for serving and caring about its neighbors. As she says, service has become the culture of the congregation. Ike modestly describes a similar culture in his congregation, "They are even more committed to the ministry and they feel that they can make a significant contribution."

Beth described the impact of her work developing the "adopt-a-school" project:

> I see our church members being relationally engaged with people in need, particularly in our mentoring program. It just makes me want to cry; people who would have never known one another becoming so connected. An 80-year old man has been mentoring the same kid for five years. His kid is now going into middle school. He said "I want this kid to go to college; I have to live until this kid gets to college." The kid's mom is a great mom but is just poor. So he has become a part of their family. He took him to the state university for an open house; he goes to PTA meetings. He's become like a grandparent.

Not only does she describe the culture of service that has developed, but she notes that long-term faithfulness has come to characterize the congregation. She went on to say, as did others, that she believes she has contributed to the shaping of Christian values such as tolerance of human differences:

> It's been slow but there has been progress. Early in my time with the congregation, there was a lady who had tattoos all over her. Somebody asked me to ask her to wear long sleeves. I didn't. I think we've come a long way since then in accepting people where they are. There is a gentleman who is homeless who came here because he needed volunteer hours, so we put him to work in our kitchen. He turned out to be such great help that the church hired him. Seven years ago they wouldn't even have allowed him to volunteer.

David described how he helped his congregation welcome persons with developmental disabilities from a nearby facility into the congregation. One couple began serving by picking up a group home resident and bringing him to church with them, but other group home residents were jealous of the individual attention, so the couple began a Sunday School class for the group home residents and began bringing all the residents with them to the worship service: "The husband was a manager of a Burger King, and he decided to go back to school and got his degree in psychology. That ministry transformed his life."

These congregational social workers were looking for evidence that the congregation was more engaged in missions and ministry that was an expression of their faith because of their leadership; they told these stories as evidence of their impact.

Ministry becoming Reciprocal

Several social workers described the validation that comes when those the congregation serves pass on the care and love that they have received to others. Reciprocity is evidence of empowerment, as we discussed earlier. Beth describes seeing this evidence of effectiveness in the life of a woman to whom they had provided emergency assistance several times during a period of her life in which she was homeless. She has since been able to find employment and permanent housing, and she now is serving as a mentor. Megan described how those they have helped with emergency food have later brought food to be given to others.

Personal Faithfulness

The ultimate bottom line for these social workers is their own faithfulness. Sometimes they see their fingerprints in the lives of others, which is satisfying, whether the others are congregants they are leading and guiding in service, or those they serve directly. Sometimes the satisfaction comes in knowing those they have served have used their service well, as Earl illustrates:

> Just last week, a client told me my work with him saved his life. My prayer and direction with him made it possible to get through this last year. I said 'You're welcome.' And to myself I thanked God that I could walk alongside him. We're on the same journey; we just have different experiences.

Brenda describes the satisfaction that comes in being a presence in the lives of those they serve, saying, "I am grateful for the opportunity to hear someone's story and be present in it." She went on to say that she feels like she has been effective when "people felt seen and heard," when they "were loved well."

Lynne said:

> I've been around long enough that I've seen the children and grandchildren of the first children that I've worked with. I was walking out of the store the other day and my mind was way off as I was thinking and this man said, Hey Ms. Lynne! I looked around and it was one of the kids that had grown up in our tutoring program, and I said, Hi! How are you? I haven't seen you in a long time! And in the conversation I learned that he was in college.

Yet this evidence of success in the life of this young man she had known so long was not the end of the story. This story prompted Lynne to tell the story of one of the children that had grown up in the congregation's tutoring program more than 20 years before, one of the children that she thought "could make it," but who is now in prison for the second time. She was so deeply disappointed. She said, "You can't measure your success the way other people do; it'll kill you if you do." And yet, she continues to serve. That is faithfulness.

Chapter 8
The Path

The two of us have a favorite saying and we cannot remember its source. The saying is "we make the path by walking it." Indeed, we have been making this path called congregational social work by walking it for all of our careers. We have been glad to find one another along the way as walking companions in charting this field of social work practice. We have not been sure where we were going—ever—but just kept following our noses and our Lord into new experiences, new opportunities, and finding along the way surprising old paths others have left before us. Like a walk of established trails in the mountains, sometimes we thought we were following a trail but then we lost it, and so we have hopped from one rock to another, forded a few streams with our boots tied around our necks, and tried to leave some rock

cairns[50] along the way so that others can see where we thought the best path was. We have felt called along this path, but that has not meant that we knew the best route. It has simply been our way.

The task of Moses was to find the path for the Israelites through the wilderness. Moses asked God, "Show me your ways" (Exodus 33:13). God answered by placing Moses in the cleft of a rock and covering him over until God had passed by. Only then could Moses see—not God's face, not God right there with him, but just God's backside. An ancient rabbi commenting on this text says that it means that we can discover God in our lives only as we look where God has been, but we cannot see where God will be in the future, or even where God is right now.

God led Moses and the people with a pillar of cloud they were to follow (Exodus 13:21). When God guides people, God does not hand them a clearly marked road map and instruct them in a GPS-guided voice to turn here, to take this exit, to follow this street. God says, "Follow this cloud." A cloud on the ground is fog. When we follow a cloud, we are walking behind and sometimes, it feels like plodding through a fog. We can see just far enough to know where to put our feet next, but we have no idea where we are going. We walk by faith, not by sight.

That is how this journey has been for us—seeing now as we reflect back how God was shaping our lives and our understanding of our calling to serve. We were oblivious to the fact that we were contributing to the definition of a field of social work practice called congregational social work, nor did we follow what we saw to be a clear path stretching before us. We made our path by walking it. So have these congregational social workers. None of them started out to be congregational social workers. Few of them had even heard of a congregational social worker before they found themselves on this path. They were just following, step by step, a calling to follow the fog. Only in looking back do they see signs of the One who has directed their steps.

Called to Congregational Social Work

Although they may not have charted a career path for themselves called congregational social work, most of these congregational social workers said that they feel "called" to the work that they are doing. "Calling" is the sense that God or some other presence beyond oneself compels one to take a particular direction; the direction is not simply a matter of choosing based on one's own motivations and preferences. Abraham did not spend years planning to emigrate to a new land; he heard God tell him to go, so he went (Genesis 12:1-4). The disciples were not planning to leave their lives of fishing to become itinerant followers of Jesus, the Rabbi; He came and told them to follow Him, so they dropped their nets and followed (Matthew 4:18-22). They did not know where they were going; it was a journey that unfolded, not a destination quickly reached.

These social workers did not play congregational social worker as children, the way some children in pretend play take the role of a teacher with younger siblings, or of a construction worker building roads in a sandbox, or of a doctor or nurse tending to wounded stuffed animals. They had professional and other life experiences that prepared them in various ways, but they did not see that they were preparing themselves for a calling identified as congregational social work. They found, instead, that they understood their calling only by looking back to see how life circumstances aligned to channel their paths and they have "stumbled" along. Some believe that professional doors have opened for them because somehow, God makes it happen. Alice said, "He opened doors for me that I am where I am for a reason." Inez said, "I stumble through life and the right doors open and I stumble through." Becky takes it a step further; she is doing what she was created to do: "I was created to be a social worker; that's me." Helen summed it up for many:

> This is what God has called me to do. This is where God wants me. If I didn't think that, I would not still be doing this.

A Spiritual "Sense" of Calling

Our friend Ellen Netting coined the term "locus of inspiration" when she read our account of these social workers' sense of calling. There is the sense that they were inspired to become social workers from a religious experience or relationship with God, not simply from an internal desire to be professional helpers.

Many of these social workers had a sense of calling like that of Abraham and the fishing disciples, although there was not an audible voice issuing that call directly. The call often came in response to a religious leader's invitation in a worship service to a commitment to vocational ministry. For Austin, it was a Baptist youth camp that set him on a path that would eventually lead him into congregational social work:

> I showed up at the university as a freshman after having had one of those church camp experiences where I went up to the altar at the end of a worship service and said I was called into the ministry. But I didn't know what that meant. Then as a first year student I thought that maybe that meant I should be a doctor, some sort of medical missionary, so I was a pre-med major for a while. But I didn't enjoy biology and calculus and the technical aspects. I was trying to figure out what to do and took a social work class, fell in love with it, and realized that my personality and my natural skills most fit social work as a profession. I never did let go of that sense of calling to working in a congregation but, in all honesty, I didn't have any perspective that I could do social work in a church. I initially had, as a student, assumed that I would be a social worker, but I would also be really involved in my church. That was my thinking and perspective there, but I still never let go of that sense of calling.

"I didn't have any perspective that I could do social work in a church."

Austin did not initially feel called specifically to social work, but more generally to some Christian vocation, which in Protestant tradition meant being a missionary or a pastor. As he explained, his calling into social work evolved as he explored various vocational paths. He had resigned himself to being a social worker by vocation and, being actively engaged in his spare time in church ministry—and then the opportunity to combine vocation and church leadership opened before him.

As Austin indicates, being "called" in Protestant traditions often connotes service as a missionary or pastor, but there is a third path for women in traditions where female leadership is denied, and that is as a pastor's or missionary's wife. Lynne was first a pastor's wife:

> I married a minister and I started to interpret that as my calling. I came into my own and realized my calling was my calling, and my passion was helping people and that's where my gifts were the strongest. So I just decided to go back to school and be able to be better equipped to help people.

Lynne has been leading as a congregational staff member—not the congregation where her husband was pastor—for decades.

Juliet's deceased husband was the senior pastor of their congregation for about 16 years. She is the Pastor of Christian Education and Discipleship, a new title given to her by the present pastor. She says:

> For me personally I think God called me when I was in high school and told me I was going to be a pastor's wife. I didn't want that so I put it in the back of my mind. I think God gives us certain values, traits, certain gifts and desires and it sort of just leads us into that direction.

Many others had similar experiences of feeling called to a Christian vocation, but they had no experience of social work as such a calling. Social work is a path found, sometimes, after initial paths turn out to be dead ends for various reasons, such as Austin's attempt at medical missions. Several women found the social work path after being denied paths into pastoral roles. Pam is one of those, who said:

> When I was 17 years old, I was called into some kind of Christian ministry. I ended up getting a seminary degree but could not be hired as a pastor or a minister. That's when I went into social work.

Abigail describes her calling as a conversation with God that has taken place over time:

> The last semester of my senior year [in high school], I was taking an elective in psychology and an elective in sociology and said, "What is it Lord? Where do I need to go?" He led me toward social work. I said, "Lord, I can't be a social worker; I'm an introvert and I'm a conservative; I'm not that person; I can't be an advocate." He said, "I want you to do this," and He said He would work out the details. He showed me I don't have to be anything political. I don't have to be a great public speaker or anything. He's given me what I need as far as gifting. He's given me an opportunity to use those gifts, but social work is not what I would have chosen for myself. It was all God. It's something I wouldn't change for anything.

Abigail did not mention a calling to a church vocation but rather her wrestling with what she thought social work was, which she did not see as a great fit with her personality and gifts. Nevertheless, this strong sense of calling to prepare herself as a social worker persisted, which she describes as a conversation with God, and so she found her path into social work.

Kathleen's experience was like others, in which social work did not seem to be the vocational ministry she felt called to do, until she found herself doing social work in a congregation and living into the vocational calling she had experienced so many years before:

> When I was 14 years old and got a feeling that God called me to surrender my life to ministry. At that time I didn't really know what that meant. I thought it meant I was going to be a missionary because I was really interested in missions. But when I got into social work at college, I realized that I loved social work and I felt like that was my calling. Eventually through conversations and God really working in my heart, I began to see that those two things could coexist. My calling could be to social work and also to missions.

From a different Christian tradition, Heather, the Director of the Refugee Program for a Catholic archdiocese, talks about "providence," which has a somewhat less personal connotation than "God called me" but recognizes that God is directing the path:

> When I was in high school, I had written a letter about what I wanted to be in ten years. I said I wanted to be working with Tanzanian refugees. I had forgotten all about that letter. I went to my high school reunion, and they gave us those letters. My life truly has not been on that path. It's been working with migrant farm workers, in post-adoption services, and on state policy issues. And now I am finally working with refugees just at the same time I am handed that letter. It's been very providential.

Jeffrey describes an active pursuit of God's will for his life:

> I have tried to attune my mind to be obedient to God's will. So I think I am where God wants me to be. I truly believe that. If I believe anything, I believe that.

Called through Life Experiences

In addition to the spiritual experiences many described, several also talked about how life circumstances contributed to their sense of vocational calling. For example, Kylie grew up in the suburbs attending the church she serves now, which is located in the inner city and where she was exposed to poverty:

I just have a real heart for children in poverty especially. That's kind of where my initial call came from. I grew up in the suburbs, and I also grew up here in this church. I was exposed to issues of poverty. I think God was forming me through being a member here.

Others also attribute their experiences as adolescents in church to their paths into social work, like Austin's experience of youth camp. Others describe mission trips they took to other places in their cities and the world beyond that opened their eyes to social issues that they want to address.

Adding to the influence of their congregations during childhood and adolescence is the influence of family for many of these social workers. Catarina described the impact of watching her parents' ministry in immigrant congregations:

> When people ask me why I got into social work, I say "My parents—growing up watching my mom and my dad doing what they did at the church." God always called my dad as a bi-vocational pastor[51] in small congregations. My dad is still today the kind of pastor that I wish all pastors would be. He takes care of his people, whether he is visiting them at the hospital or taking them to the grocery store. When amnesty happened in 1986, my dad took classes so he could help people fill out the paperwork. He would drive them to the city, and our whole family would go, too.

David attributes his calling to the experience of being on the client end of a helping experience:

> When I went to seminary, I hadn't planned to take social work. I had a family crisis and I reached out to a pastor who gave me advice. I also reached out to a social work student friend, and she was so much more helpful than what I received from my pastor friend. That planted a seed. I took an elective class in social work and fell in love with it. The help that I received from a social worker was so much more substantive and helpful.

Still others have professional experiences that contribute to their sense of calling. A few of these social workers, like Ingrid and Beth, found themselves in a social work school that provided coursework and student internships in congregations, where they found their calling. Beth decided to do her internship in a congregation:

> I just fell in love with the church. It melded my passions for social justice and for the church. I decided I didn't want to work anywhere but the church.

A congregational field internship was one door into congregational social work, but there were other professional experiences that led these social workers into their current work. Ben began by saying "I don't believe in coincidence," and then went on:

> I started out as an engineering major but I did not graduate. . . . I was a clinical supervisor of a residential program for troubled adolescents, and the administration of the agency said, "You've got to get a degree. You can do the work. We're promoting you, but in order for you to keep the position, you have to get a degree." I went back to the university and I walked down the hall looking for a professor, and I ran into the director of the social work program. He asked me what I needed, and I told him. He said, "You don't want to do psychology; you want to do social work." Had I not seen him and gone into his office to get his explanation of what social work is and why should I do it, I never would have been in social work.

Ben was pushed by his employer to complete his college degree, and there the chance meeting with the director of the social work program gave him the path forward.

Calling Confirmed by Evidence

Several of the respondents reported that they understand their calling both from reflection on the path they have taken in the past and also from current professional experiences.

I Am in the Right Place

Some sense a confirmation of their calling in the comfort they feel of being in the "right place." For example, Kameryn is aware of her sense of calling as she works with clients:

"I've been called to this work, and God has chosen me."

> When I'm sitting in the room with a client and we're in session, I'm very aware of the concept of calling. I've been called to this work, and God has chosen me to have this kind of presence and role in people's lives. I find comfort in knowing that as I do the work and, when it's hard, it gives me reassurance and the ability to push through the hard times because I do feel that I'm called to this.

She is "comforted"—she was chosen and called by God to do this work. Megan reports a similar sense of rightness and "fit" she experiences in her work:

> I definitely feel like I was called to be here. Have you heard people say that they told God they'd never do it and then they end up doing that? That was my experience. I really didn't think I'd be in this city. I really didn't think I'd be working with homeless people; I thought I'd be with children's ministry. Then I spent the spring break and the summer here in 2004, and I knew this was home. My feeling is that God really shows you where your

> home is in ministry, and God makes it feel like that, a real home. You're very comfortable with doing it. It may be hard and not always the most comfortable thing to do, but you feel fulfillment from it.

Again the word "comfort" is one that she takes as a sign that she is called, and even when her work is "not always the most comfortable," she feels "fulfilled."

I Have the Right Gifts

As several have already mentioned, the fact that the gifts they perceive God has given them are such a good fit with the profession of social work gives them evidence of their sense of calling. As Austin said above, "my personality and my natural skills most fit social work as a profession." Kelly, who had just retired, said:

> Of all the different careers that I've had, this job is the one in which I felt the most fulfilled. I felt like I could use all part of myself: my analytical tools, my communication tools, my social work tools, my love of people, curiosity about them, and my commitment to the community that I work in and that I'm a part of. I really felt this is what I was meant to do.

Inez said:

> When I was in 10th grade, my mother decided for me to take an interest test. My three occupations were social work, ministry and teaching. And that's been true my whole life. In that way, I feel called, because those are things I'm best equipped to do. It just feels so right.

Becky said simply, "I was created to be a social worker." She went on:

> God equipped me personally. He designed me to be a social worker. He really did. Those skills and tools and everything else were fine tuned and sharpened in social work school.

Finally, Barry said, "This job has allowed me to put all of the things that God has put in my life together to help people."

"This job has allowed me to put all of the things that God has put in my life together to help people."

Other Paths

Only a few of these social workers said they have *not* experienced a sense, spiritual or otherwise, that they are "called" to their work. It seems that the word "calling," which carries connotations for some of altar calls and hearing audible voices, causes them to pause. Barry illustrates:

> I believe that God calls all of us to follow Him, and then he moves us in

> directions to bring us into that situation. I never really sought after any of the positions that I ever had in my life. I always felt that I was called to follow the Lord, but I didn't think I was called to church. When I taught at the Christian college and [was] called to do that, there were opportunities that were put right in front of me that I prayed and thought about and felt that that's where God wanted me to be in that point in time.

Barry says that he does experience God leading him, even though he says that he is "not very strong into callings." Catarina was uncertain:

> I don't know if it was really a calling. I just know I felt the need; I wanted to work at a church. I do know God has me where I am because I need to be here. I'm going to be here until He says it's time for me to not work at a church.

"I don't know if it was really a calling … I do know God has me where I am because I need to be here."

Finally, for Ruby, the term calling refers to all of life, and not just to a profession:

> I wouldn't say my calling is social work; it's just all that I do in relating to people involves my faith. It is sort of like everything in my life is through the lens of my faith.

We can conclude that almost all of the social workers we interviewed feel led by God to the work they are doing, even if the word "calling" and its connotations make its use problematic for some of them.

Unfolding Paths into Congregational Social Work

Since it is virtually unrecognized as a social work specialization both by congregational leaders and by the profession of social work, mapping a path for social workers into congregational leadership is less clear than in other settings, where a professional may contact the agency where she wants to be employed, or screen job listings for settings. Congregations typically do not list "social worker" in employment advertising as the professional they are seeking to hire; most existing positions filled by social workers do not bear this title. Moreover, although one may contact a social service agency to inquire about vacant positions, it would be most unusual in the culture of congregations to volunteer an application unless in response to a job listing. So we explored with these congregational social workers how the vocational path unfolded for them. What was the path they made by walking it?

Social Worker in Other Settings

Some of the interviewees worked in other social work settings before they started working with congregations. Gordon and Pam spent years as child abuse investigators for the state agencies providing child protective services; he is now serving in a congregation as Youth Minister and she is in another congregation as Associate Pastor for Adult Education. Barry was the chair of a social work department in a Bible college before he started working for a congregation as the Pastor of Care Ministries.

Five respondents indicated that they were restless, dissatisfied, or pushed by factors in their previous jobs, which gave an opening for them to find congregational social work. Jeanie says of her previous work setting, "I was beginning to lose my soul; I wasn't making the difference in people's lives that I wanted." For the past nine years, she has served as Mission Outreach Coordinator for her congregation and its mission center.

As these social workers transition from agency settings to congregational leadership, they often begin by defining their work in ways congruent with their previous experiences. For example, Jeanie came from a background in medical social work and now is her congregation's Mission Outreach Coordinator. She began with support groups for those experiencing loss and grief.

Congregations offered these social workers positions because of their previous professional experience and because they had a relationship with them. For example, Lois had been working in a geriatric wellness center when a position opened in her congregation for Director of Senior Adult Ministries, and she took it.

From Congregational Leadership

A number of these social workers came to their current positions as more "traditional" religious leaders—pastor or missionary—even though they also had their social work degrees. They saw their church leadership roles as separate from social work, until they found themselves putting together the two professional identities. For example, Ben was employed as a social work faculty member as well as the pastor of a congregation; it was only as he worked in the community *as a pastor* that he began to see the two identities "really mesh together." Similarly, Daniel had been a pastor, but the poor pay in that position drove him back to school to attain a graduate degree in clinical social work. He was then working as a social worker in the community when his congregation made him an elder. That became the entrée to employment by the congregation:

> I saw how the elders cared for the sheep more than the pastors were. I was working as a social worker at the time, and so they offered me a position at the church to become their pastor of married couples and pastor of counseling.

Others were attending seminary, preparing for religious leadership, and found social work through colleagues in dual degree programs or through the activities of social work programs in their educational institution.

From Congregational Membership

Just as some social workers found a congregational position after already being a leader in the congregation, others, even though they were not in a leadership position, were known by the congregation, whether for their expertise in the community, or as active participants in congregational life. Some had held social work positions in the geographic area. The congregation sought their leadership because it needed their expertise as it sought to live its mission. For example, congregational leaders asked Austin for guidance as they began a ministry with a large homeless population in the congregation's neighborhood:

> At deacons' meetings and such, they were asking questions and wanted to make sure things were being done professionally. That's what I was able to bring.

Even more common, these social workers were already members of the congregation and had earned respect for their gifts and skills, not necessarily because they were professional social workers. They emerged as leaders over time; becoming known in the community and so tapped for their roles. Such emergent leadership seems a natural process for congregations as communities. It is very different than the hiring processes of organizations, which are more likely to begin with a formal job description and a systematic candidate search. Many of these congregational social workers had been members of their congregations since childhood, like Pam, now Associate Pastor and leading her congregation's adult education programs:

> This is my home church. I have been associated with this congregation for almost 19 years. It was difficult because I was one of them and yet the mere fact that they brought me on staff anticipating an ordination said that they recognized gifts and graces in me for ministry.

Others had been in their congregations, although coming as adults, like Daniel, now a Pastor of Care Ministries. He was not yet 30 years old, active in the congregation, and the congregation's leadership wanted more young adults in leadership. First he was a deacon, then an elder, and then they offered him the staff position he now holds.

Like Daniel, others were working as unpaid social workers in their congregation before they were offered paid positions. For example, Brenda is the Director of Social Service Ministries for a nondenominational congregation:

> I attended here about 6 years and in that time got involved in lots of things. I ran a pretty large benevolence ministry as a volunteer and was in a small group with the pastor of our church and his wife. She became a good friend. So when I left [town], I just had a sense that I would be back;

> I didn't sell my house. The pastor said, "I would love sometime for you to be on staff with us if there was ever a fit." At the time they had a staff ministry coordinator who didn't have a social work background. When he left, the church developed this position and said, "We'd love for you to come and help us figure out what we need to do next in social ministry."

Joy oversees a ministry aimed at equipping over 450 teens annually, teaching them to reach out to children who need spiritual and emotional support in experiencing life's issues. She, too, began in an unpaid position before becoming a paid staff member:

> I had attended the church through my childhood. As I finished my social work education, there was a movement within the church to reach people outside of the actual church walls. The youth minister designed a service opportunity for teenagers to reach out to children. They needed somebody to help in developing that program—they called me.

Finally, Abigail relates her experience in this way:

> I was a part of this ministry as a volunteer before I came on staff. I was a school social worker and I was looking for a change. They said, "Have you thought about working at the church?" It ended up working out beautifully. It's been such a blessing for the church and it's been a blessing for me.

Congregational Path to Readiness

In addition to the path the social worker has taken, these congregations, too, had been going in directions that led to their willingness and interest in hiring a social worker. The congregations' paths were as diverse as the paths those social workers took to these congregational roles. Some congregations had experienced neighborhood transitions, with middle class people moving to the suburbs and lower income people moving in. They were casting about for leadership in reaching their new neighbors, and a social worker, often someone they knew or with whom they had connections, seemed to be the right fit—like Abigail and Beth and Lynne.

For some congregations, crises led to their employing social workers. For example, Inez's congregation hired her for a counseling position that was previously filled by a pastor who had used questionable approaches and promoted "a strong anti-psychiatry, anti-mental health perspective." Several outcomes of his work raised concerns, including a young man committing suicide after this pastor encouraged him to discontinue his medication. The congregation subsequently sought someone more professionally qualified for this position—Inez is a licensed clinical social worker.

In a different kind of crisis, the church Jeanie now serves was the recipient of a one-time large charitable gift to do a single project to benefit the community. The money sat for years, unused, as the congregation periodically discussed how to use it. The congregation was decreasing in size; people who died or moved to other communities were not being replaced with new members. Because congregational size is a frequently touted indicator of congregational health and strength, the congregation and its leaders were concerned.

A quick succession of events moved the church into a full-blown crisis. A staff member was sexually assaulted in the church's building by a visitor. Then the pastor left. The next pastor they installed "didn't work out," and they went through a series of interim pastors. The last interim pastor suggested a task force to determine what to do with the funding, and a study group proposed founding a center with programs "for the body, mind, and spirit for the community"—and to give the congregation a path forward out of its struggles—and Jeanie was hired to direct the center.

In every congregation employing a social worker in a role other than senior pastor, the senior pastor was very supportive of having a social worker on the staff. Despite the fact that governance structures vary widely across various church traditions, the pastor usually carries a great deal of power and authority in determining the staff positions and the fit of particular persons in those positions. Several social workers were the first to serve their congregations. They noted that their pastors hired them with lots of hope but little understanding of what they could do. Often, the pastor hired the social worker to respond to a specific need, only to find that the social worker could serve a much broader role in congregational leadership. Abigail's experience illustrates:

Their pastors hired them with lots of hope but little understanding of what they could do.

> I had to teach the pastor what the difference is between a social worker and somebody who just knew about things in the community. When she first hired me on, she said, "You are going to have to create a position for yourself. We are going out on a limb. We've never hired a social worker before. We don't know any churches that have done this. If you can prove that there is a need, then we will keep you on."
>
> Proving the need was easy to do. When the pastor began to see what I could do, she was surprised and said, "Oh my; we really need you more than we realized." That was pivotal.

Pastoral support is pivotal, indeed, when the social worker faces conflict or controversy. Abigail went on to say that her pastor "has my back" when the occasional conflict erupts. Lynne experienced that kind of advocacy in her behalf from her pastor when some people in her congregation objected to her developing a child development center that focused on at-risk children—children coming from backgrounds that made some church members uneasy. She said it was the toughest battle she has had in her work, but her pastor was with her in it saying, "We're going to do this." And they did.

Professional Preparation

We noted earlier that the majority of these social workers received their degrees from public universities; only a minority had attended religiously affiliated schools. Less than half had any formal theological education. So how were these social workers prepared—or not—to serve as congregational leaders?

Preparation in Social Work School

A majority of these social workers did not receive any preparation for congregational social work in the social work schools they attended. Most said that, even though they had no explicit preparation, they have been able to apply and adapt what they learned in school to congregational leadership. Kelly pointed out that much of what she does is generalist social work practice, and so her education gave her the knowledge and skills she needs. Caiden, who is a professor in a state university and serves as the field liaison for the university, supervises students placed in the congregation and believes that a social worker does not need to address religious doctrine and theology to be effective:

> I was able to develop a program using the faith community as central, without confusing it with religious doctrine and theology. Social work taught me how to do that. Church is a culture so you have to know how to work with the community, but you don't necessarily have to deal with dogma or theology.

David, an Associate Pastor, emphasizes the importance of his social work education for his professional responsibilities:

> I think social work education is a hand-in-glove fit with ministry. The knowledge, the skills, the attitudes just fit so well in a church context. In that triumvirate of knowledge, skills, and values is a wonderful preparation for ministry in a community. There are so many good practical things you learn in social work—group dynamics, counseling, interpersonal relationships.

Social work education is a hand-in-glove fit with ministry.

Those who had been prepared educationally to work with congregations disagreed that generalist social work was enough, however. Carl said that his education in a religiously affiliated school included content on congregations as well as generalist social work education, and he says about the importance of all of it: "Because of my education, I understand a congregation."

Others said that they felt prepared because of the holistic nature of social work education and the modeling of the faculty in their Christian universities. It was not just what they taught but their attention to the whole person. This was exemplified in their personal engagement in a community of faith and even in disciplines like regular physical exercise.

Six respondents of the 51 in the sample had the experience of a field internship in a congregational setting as part of their academic preparation. Beth says of her field internship experience: "The field placement was life changing and invaluable; I wouldn't be doing what I'm doing if I hadn't had that field placement."

Ongoing Education

Most of these social workers said that their continuing education has been just as important as their university degree. Austin noted how helpful it is for him to have a religiously affiliated social work school in a university nearby that provides continuing education. What he noted that is even more helpful is to have the opportunity to supervise student internships and to be engaged in the research and service projects of the social work school. He has also been invited to speak about his experiences in classes in the school, and that, too, is learning for him.

Professional reading and attending conferences are also important ways these social workers continue to prepare themselves for the challenges of their work. When we asked about books and articles they had read most recently, they named books in the fields of business or Christian spirituality more often than social work. Alice is a social work professor who also serves in her Assembly of God church. She says reading about spirituality is important: "But spirituality is not integrated enough into social work education." Earl said, "I like the readings of spiritual men and women." Pam, who is the Associate Pastor at a Methodist church, sums it up like this: "I do a lot of reading but it is about religion and congregations; not any of it is social work."

Perhaps the challenge is that there is so little literature written for social work in congregational settings, so these social workers are continuing to integrate faith and practice in what they choose to read. They have the formal social work education and they use continuing education to complement that education with knowledge about their unique practice context.

Mentoring and Consultation

Sixteen interviewees mentioned mentors, supervisors, and colleagues who have helped equip them for their work. Some were teachers in their social work schools with whom they have continued to consult. A few found mentors through the North American Association of Christians in Social Work (NACSW). Catarina described a co-worker's important role as consultant:

> There have been times when things have come up, and I've said to myself, "Really? This is happening at church? This should not be happening at church!" I'll call her to help me calm down and try to see things from a different perspective, and how I should address the situation.

Still others describe their need for mentors and colleagues in order to help them with the sense of isolation that they experience in this context of practice that is not well recognized in the social work profession.

Because so little has been written in about this field of practice, even this research interview gave Austin the opportunity to reflect on his work that he does not normally have: "I know that the purpose of this is to collect information and do research, but for those of us who are participating, it challenges us to think through and describe what we are doing."

Preparation They Did Not Receive

We also asked about preparation they *wish* they had received for the work they are doing. Not surprisingly, many indicated that they had little, if any, preparation for working with congregations. Even though Catarina had grown up the daughter of a pastor, she said,

> Nothing prepared me for congregational social work, not even my undergraduate program in a religiously affiliated university. I wish we had a manual that could help us. I jumped in there, and just learned as I went.

Even though Kathleen graduated from a school that does teach about congregations as contexts for practice, she said, "I wish we had more intentional discussion with other students who were interested in congregations or were doing internships in a church setting, and I wish I'd had more of an opportunity to talk to people who were specifically involved in church work and to have a support network after graduation."

Many said there is much about congregations that they wish they had learned. For example, Becky said, "I don't recall a particular class that sat me down and said, 'If you're going to work in the church, here are some of the boundary issues that you need to be aware of."

Most common, however, was an expressed need for more integration of religion and spirituality in social work education. For example, Jeanie said, "In social work, there is an attitude that talking to someone about their faith life, their spirituality, is off limits."

Although not a common response, a few said they wish they had been more prepared in research and program evaluation. For example, when Ben was asked what preparation he needed that he did not receive in school, he responded:

> Statistics and research! I had to figure it out on my own, and that was frustrating. I knew our fatherhood program makes a difference, but I couldn't prove it, and I didn't know how to set it up to prove that we were doing good work. I just knew that we were. Men were saying, "Your program made the difference." But how do you design something that is credible beyond people saying, "You've got a good program"?

Steven works for a religiously affiliated child welfare agency, where he directs the foster care programs and their work with congregations whose families provide foster care. He said: "I needed training on evaluating outcomes beyond just the anecdotal feel-good stories that we use to raise dollars; at the end of the day, we have to be able to show how we measure impact."

Resources for Congregational Social Work

Every setting for social work practice has its own set of resources and challenges. So, too, does congregational social work. These social workers identified the resources that undergird their work as (1) the congregation's mission of serving; (2) the trust of the congregation; (3) financial support; (4) a network of colleagues in religious leadership; (5) flexibility; and (6) the opportunity to integrate their personal faith with professional practice.

Congregation's Mission of Serving

From the beginning of the Christian church, it has been committed to caring for those in need. The social work profession itself is rooted in the caring responses to human need of religiously affiliated organizations and congregations. It is not surprising, then, that several of our interviewees saw this mission of caring as a resource for their work. That mission is one of the four basic functions of congregational life; it is the reason these congregations have a social worker in leadership.

In fact, these social workers see congregations as a largely unrecognized resource for the larger social work profession. For example, Steven said: "The social work profession can utilize some of those natural helping networks in local congregations to wrap around a family or child that needs lots of help. Rebekah pointed out what she experiences as a growing movement to engage in neighbor care:

> Churches are opening their doors more and more to everybody and not just people who take a wafer in their mouth or people who sing out of the hymnal. Churches are saying that they need to be a haven of hope. That means we are going to love our community and we are going to take care of people. I know there is kind of a growing sentiment to really get outside of the church. Let's do what Christ did and that is to take care of people.

One consequence of caring being a central mission in the church results in a resource many of these social worker named of people who want to be engaged in service—or those many of these social workers identified as "volunteers." This commitment to Christian service provides most of these social workers with ample people resources in their work. Helen, who directs a community service center that is supported by an association of 15 congregations, said that she has more people willing to serve than she can use. Lynne recounts the resource that senior adults are in the ministry programs of the congregation:

> It still requires mature Christians to do the things that we do, and fortunately for us, we have a lot of mature Christians in this church. I refer to them a lot of the times as our "senior saints" because most of our volunteers are senior adults. We have people who look forward to retiring so they can serve in our community ministries. They're mature people that see the value in what we do and they want to be a part of it. I've been around long enough so that I have some concerns that the younger generations may not be that gun-ho as the seniors are.

"We have people who look forward to retiring so they can serve in our community ministries."

Sue, similarly to Steven, uses congregational members from numerous churches to serve in the denominational child and family services agency where she is employed. Their professional and life skills are an important asset for clients: "They are very equipped to help us in what we do in our work, and they bring a lot of skills and abilities that may seem small to them but are significant for our clients and families."

When Pam came to serve as Associate Pastor, she found that the congregation was encouraging service without adequately preparing congregants to serve skillfully and compassionately. Pam says she "put her foot down" and asserted her role as one who could "provide training and knowledge that the church simply does not have":

> Until I came, if Jane Doe wanted to go and do hospital visits, then the message was "Let's cut her loose." I said "Whoa!" I wanted to know that there has been some discussion with Jane Doe about several things. When you go into a patient's room, how long do you stay? It should be very brief. You don't just barge in if there is a nurse or a doctor in the room or even

> a certified nurse's aide in there. I talked with Jane Doe about how to be aware and sensitive.

Pam and others see their responsibility to teach these church members the knowledge and skills they need to go along with their motivation to serve and care.

Trust

These social workers' congregations trust them, seeing them as professionals who share their worldview. That trust is essential for their work. As an attribute and a resource, it needs to be carefully nurtured and protected. Catarina notes that she works in a place that people identify as "a safe place"—"sanctuary" means safety as well as holy for a reason. Catarina noted that because of this trust, the congregation is the first place people call for help: "If I can't help them, they'll go somewhere else, but they'd rather call me first to see what our church can do to help, whatever the concern may be." Pam summed it up:

> The people in this congregation know without a shadow of a doubt that if they have a need, they can to come to me. They want to come to me. They seek me out.

Financial Support

Many of these social workers also enjoy more flexible and available financial support for their work than social workers may in other settings. For example, Kelly's human services committee has an annual budget of $20,000 that she can use for need-based scholarships for children to attend summer camp or for financial assistance to families in crisis in the community or something else that may pop up. She is free to determine with the committee how to use the money. Austin contrasts his experience with finances in the congregational setting with his earlier experience in an agency setting:

> I have the financial resources to do what I feel needs to be done. That wouldn't be the case if I were operating out of what the church puts into the church budget for my ministry. But 90% of what I do is supported by individual gifts from the church members. If somebody gave us a million dollars, we could do lots of new and exciting things. But what we do is completely in scale with what our church should be doing and should be expected to be doing. So I love that I don't beg for money.

Ginger provides clinical services in a pastoral counseling agency supported by the congregations. She appreciates the ability to provide services to clients regardless of their financial resources, also contrasting this setting with her earlier work in a social service agency:

> I feel like we don't have the same types of limits on how we can serve people because, through the congregations and the donations that they provide to the organization, we see people who may not be able to afford counseling, but that doesn't stop us from being able to serve them. Because of that additional supplemental support that we do get, I don't have to say, 'I'm sorry, you haven't paid your bill so I can't serve you.'

Financial support can also bring with it the support of the community in ongoing ways that include not only financial help but social support.

She went on to describe how financial support can also bring with it the support of the community in ongoing ways that include not only financial help but also social support:

> I had a single mom who wasn't able to buy enough food. She had reoccurring cancer and two adolescent children, and she shared with me in one of my sessions that they were struggling. I was aware of a congregation that had a food pantry and also was coordinating a soup kitchen. So I connected her that day, and she was able to pick up boxes of food for her family. She knew some of those people and felt comfortable enough to share her situation with them. They continued to do things for her past that time, to help her through that time in her life. They did a barbeque fundraiser for her, and there were also people from her support group who helped her with that. They were able to help her pay some of her medical bills.

Lynne gives this insight to her congregation's emphasis on giving:

> I learned that being in a wealthy church that a lot of wealthy Christians have been taught to give back to the community and for their church. We had a doctor at our church, a physician, who gave a million dollars to the foundation to help to scholarship children in the children's learning center, and he said, "I don't want one child to go without a diaper." Now to me that's amazing. Even though we actually pay rent to the church from the children's learning center, and I have to break even, we still can scholarship children because of the funding and the gifts of people like that. We have 92 children in that program.

A Network of Colleagues in Religious Leadership

Overall, these social workers participate in networking, especially with other congregations and religiously affiliated organizations. They seek counsel from religious leaders. Moreover, they indicate that they are more likely to seek out other religious leaders and professional religious organizations for support and resources than they are other social work professionals or social work organizations. A social worker in a hospital might consult more with others in medical professions—doctors and nurses—than they would with school social workers or social workers in community development. The same is true for congregational social workers—they need colleagues who understand their context for practice.

They also network with others through collaboration. For example, Joy collaborates with other congregations that provide teenagers to serve in the program for at-risk children she directs. She says: "I'm a part of a network of nonprofits that our church has started; we are working together and developing how we can partner more in adventures." Those "adventures" include divvying up the social services in the neighborhood, so that one congregation provides emergency resources, another congregation provides counseling, her congregation provides children's services, and together they seek funding for their shared work.

Flexibility

These social workers value the flexibility they have in how they use their time that comes with congregational leadership. Austin said, "I do enjoy a very diverse schedule; I wouldn't function well in a position where I did the same thing every day." There are also many meetings during evening and weekend hours, but the flexibility of the setting allows them to come and go and even take care of personal concerns (doctor visits, visits to their children's classrooms) during normal working hours that would be more

difficult in more structured agency settings. They believe that they have more control over their work environment than in some other social work settings. For example, Carl loves the fact that he can take his dogs to work with him.

Prayers of the Community

Some of these social workers noted that they pray with other church leaders over the work that they share together. Rebekah described the prayers with and for her staff:

> I prayed with my staff this morning. We pray for opportunities, for open doors, for wisdom, for guidance. You just can't go wrong when you are praying about what God wants you to do and that you will be led by Him and to have the eyes to see the doors He's opening for you, the boldness to walk through them, and the courage to stand and do what He's asking you to do.

Several noted, too, that they know that people in the congregation pray for them.

Integration of Personal Faith with Professional Practice

We have identified the challenge that comes with being part of a faith community that is also the setting for one's professional work. Boundaries are fuzzy or nonexistent between personal life and professional life. At the same time, these social workers see the integration of their personal faith with their practice as a great resource for them. Their work is an expression of their faith, and in turn, their faith is shaped by the work they do. For example, Ruby noted that she receives "a lot of training within the church." The Bible studies and other opportunities for Christian education are a resource for her professionally as well as personally.

Their work is an expression of their faith, and in turn, their faith is shaped by the work they do.

The Challenges of Congregational Social Work

There are also challenges in this setting for professional social work practice, just as there are in any setting. They include: (1) professional isolation; (2) lack of safety measures; (3) devaluing by the social work professional community; (4) time constraints; (5) managing multiple roles; (6) maintaining confidentiality; (7) disagreement about policies and practices; and (8) deciding when to attempt change. We have discussed several of these more extensively elsewhere in the book, but we wanted to summarize all here, lest we paint congregational social work as the ideal social work practice setting. It is no more ideal—or challenged—than any other setting of social work practice.

Professional Isolation

Since the first study in 1987 (Garland, 1987b), congregational social workers have reported that one of the challenges they face is professional isolation. Very few could name a single other social worker serving on a congregational staff. They feel alone, that there is nobody else doing what they are doing to share the journey. They wished someone would develop a network of congregational social workers. Megan said this:

> The challenge for me is not being surrounded by other social workers on a regular basis. Most of the time, I see other social workers when I go to conventions and meetings where I'm getting continuing education.

Lack of Safety Measures

Congregations have few or none of the safety policies and safeguards found in community agencies, and as a consequence, and depending on the nature of the social worker's responsibilities, they may have the real potential for danger. Some said to us that when they are working with clients or church members who are mentally ill or in a life crisis, they do not have the usual physical precautions found in a social service agency. Or it may be that they are alone in an empty church building, like Catarina, who is the only full-time employee of her congregation.

It is not just clients who create the potential for danger, however. Congregations are vulnerable to exploitation by their members and staff. Five of these respondents had addressed sexual misconduct in a colleague or a lay leader in their congregation; several of the respondents had worked to develop protection policies and put them into place.

Relationships that Oppress Rather Than Empower

We have already described how well intentioned mission activities may, inadvertently, strip a community or neighborhood where they serve of its own resources of leadership and self-direction. Carl describes what happens to the leadership of his congregation when the waves of summer volunteers show up:

> Our own members would fade out in the summertime when the mission teams were here. They didn't feel needed. They were overshadowed.

Fay has addressed her denomination on creating a similar process of disempowering congregations, telling them what their mission is rather than enabling them to define their mission for themselves:

> At the middle level, though, we are still telling congregations what we need from them. So I say, "Please, let congregations have time to dialogue; let them find what is contextually relevant to them."

Devaluing by the Social Work Professional Community

Several of these social workers have experienced a devaluing of their role in the religious community and the larger society by social work faculty where they received their professional education and by other social workers. Often the devaluing is subtle, such as the surprise Chris encountered from others with whom he served on a community task force with the mission of ending homelessness in their city within a decade. They had viewed congregations as contributing to the problem (i.e., "enablers") with ineffective relief efforts rather than as partners in addressing the problem:

> The agencies see the churches as enablers because they hand out coats and sandwiches and bus passes without asking questions. I think it's been interesting for them to see that I'm on the same page with them.

Time Constraints

A challenge expressed by some of these social workers is that there just are not enough hours in the week to meet the demands of their work. As is so true in many professional settings, and not just in congregational social work, the more they do and do effectively, the more responsibilities they are given or the more opportunities they find that they want to explore. Ben is a pastor and he expressed what social workers in a variety of congregational roles experience:

> One of the biggest challenges is how to manage my time. There are only so many hours a day, and I cannot be everything to everybody. I talk to my colleagues all the time, and no one has figured it out. I weigh out the situation by the moment; I make the best decision with what I know at the time.

The more they do and do effectively, the more responsibilities they are given or the more opportunities they find that they want to explore.

Managing Multiple Roles

In Chapter 3, we explored the multiple roles that are so common in congregational social work. These social workers said that, in the absence of preparation professionally for this practice setting and a network of other social workers to help sort it out, managing multiple roles creates significant challenges for them. Inez describes this challenge in her current and former positions, comparing congregational social work to rural social work:

> I don't seem to mind it as much in my current congregation, but in my previous congregation, I was always "on." I knew so much about so many people. I couldn't go to a church picnic without being surrounded by my clients. I used to think at that time, "I wish I worked in a church that wasn't my church." It may be that my tolerance has grown. When you do church social work where you attend, the fact is that there are going to be dual roles. Here everybody knows everybody.

She has managed by maintaining friendships outside the congregation. Those friends are predominantly at the university where she teaches; of course, the friendship network creates yet another set of dual relationships. The big difference is that both friends and colleagues are peers; there is no power differential as there is in the roles of clinician and client.

Maintaining Confidentiality

Maintaining the confidentiality of information was a major challenge for many of these social workers. As Denise said:

> I cannot go anywhere without seeing people who are related to clients, and it is hard to keep from letting something slip. And what do you share with the pastor and what not?

They raised frequently the matter of what to share, or not, with other church staff and how to teach church members who are serving the significance of confidentiality in their work. As Chris said:

> It is a challenge to maintain confidentiality with church volunteers. There is no malicious intent, but just want to help, to be friends, and to do the right thing. It is a constant struggle to make sure that volunteers do not talk and gossip about the clients we serve in the same way that they might about friends. It is not necessarily difficult so much as just needing to be vigilant about it.

Chris' words are significant; *many* of the challenges these social workers face are not that difficult to manage, but they do require foresight, intentionality, education of the community, and "vigilance." Knowing what the potential challenges are in this practice context is an important first step.

The week I was working on this chapter, I (Diana) was in our mountain cabin located in a rural community. I was awakened at 4:30 in the morning by the sounds of emergency vehicles and then a Flight for Life helicopter's landing lights shining in our bedroom window as it sought out a meadow nearby where it could land. One of the neighbors had a medical emergency serious enough to be taken by helicopter to Denver rather than to the small hospital in our town. The next morning, I was in the post office, one of the hubs of the community, and spoke to the postmistress about the drama of the night before. A volunteer fire fighter herself, she said, "I know; I was there." Without thinking what I was asking, I said, "Who was it?" She replied: "I'm sorry; I'm not allowed to share that information." Of course not! I should have known better, but I was concerned about my neighbors and not thinking as a helping professional about client confidentiality. So I did what I should have done in the first place; I went home and started calling my neighbor's homes to see what I could learn.

Congregations are like our rural community. Like our volunteer firefighter/postmistress, congregational social workers have to help congregational members be clear about the role in which they learn information about others, what that dictates about who and what they can share, and how to explain to other concerned community members why they have to withhold information when they do.

Disagreement about Policies and Practices

A congregation's beliefs and values derive from interpretations of sacred texts and historical traditions. Those beliefs and values can be in direct opposition to the beliefs and values of others interpreting the same texts and traditions. Since beliefs and traditions translate into policies and practices, disagreements about how to conduct life together can quickly heat into a clash of theological beliefs. Some examples include the role of women in the congregation's leadership (or not), and the acceptance (or not) of persons who are in various life circumstances (e.g., gay and lesbian, divorced, or cohabiting).

Several of these social workers expressed that they disagree with congregational or denominational policies preventing women from serving in leadership roles. It is not only the women who feel this conflict; Daniel sees his congregation's stand on the role of women and other issues as oppressive. He has managed to place a few lay women in leadership positions in educational and support groups with the following caveat: "I was given autonomy as long as the women who are leading aren't feminists."

For some, this disagreement extends beyond the congregation to the denomination. This disagreement may create for the social worker a situation that requires deciding whether or not to continue working in this setting if no change is going to come in the foreseeable future. David became an Associate Pastor of the congregation where he now serves after many years of employment by a denominational agency that worked with congregations providing social services across the United States. He decided to leave that agency when the policy was enacted that every employee sign the denomination's newly revised creed that dictated positions on several controversial issues, including proscribing women from serving as pastors. David describes his decision using the image of a frog sitting in a kettle of water. The story goes that if a frog is placed in hot water, it will immediately jump out. But if the water is cold and the heat is turned up gradually, a frog does not perceive the change and the consequent danger, and the frog will sit there until it boils.

> I didn't want to be the frog in the kettle. I hopped out, but even so, maybe I stayed too long. Was I compromising too many of my own convictions? But I felt like I was making a contribution, so I stayed on.

The struggle is deciding when to leave versus staying and making compromises on some issues in order to continue to make a contribution, even a contribution toward change in the organizational culture that is so challenging. Undoubtedly, these struggles take place in other social work settings as well. In work in religious organizations and congregations, however, there is the added dimension of religious leadership, which may be experienced as a religious call, as well as the personal faith of the social worker, that creates even more stress and added dimensions to the struggle.

Deciding When to Attempt Change

Some of these social workers described how they had sought to bring about change, and the consequent risk they felt of being personally or professionally rejected. Caiden experienced this when the issue of gay marriage became a "hot issue" in her congregation. She chose to seize the opportunity and did a six week educational program on the topic of sexual orientation. She said that it had been her "toughest issue" so far because, she said, "I wasn't sure how I would be received." Yet she and her congregation weathered it well, in her assessment; she helped them explore their own beliefs and values as well as learn about the continuum of viewpoints of others.

David said he tries "to be wise about how much to reveal my own thoughts and feelings and convictions." He struggles to know when and how to help people "expand their thinking." Like Caiden, the issue he raised seems to be a common struggle for these social workers, which is how to address issues of sexual orientation. David said he is struggling with "how to broach that subject, to help my congregation know that every human being is of worth; helping them realize that their words can be hurtful to gays and lesbians in our congregation, or the parents of gays and lesbians."

On Being a Congregational Social Worker

The fulfillment these social workers experience in their work is much more than balancing out the resources and the challenges of this setting for practice. At the end of the interview with each, we asked them to reflect on the impact working in a congregation has had on them. Congregational social work is demanding work, as is all social work. There was almost no mention of burnout, however; rather, there was talking of the way the position fits their beliefs that God has led them to this work. They told us that being a congregational social worker (1) shapes their own beliefs and values; (2) provides them with community; and (3) gives them fulfillment.

Shapes their Beliefs and Values

In the process of leading the congregation's worship, Christian education, community development, and missions, the social workers find their own beliefs and values shaped by their work. Adam shares the following example:

> There were several transgender folks that would come to the worship service. One guy who dresses like a woman would always sit in the back and I would say, "Come sit up here." He would say "No, no, no, I'm not worthy." I would say, "Sure you are worthy; God loves you just like he loves me. There is no distinction. Show me where in the Bible it says that how a person dresses defines him as unworthy!" It changed me. And it was challenging; how do I explain to my children that he looks like a guy, but he's dressed like a girl? How do I talk about that, especially to our older son who is very inquisitive and very smart? It gives them experiences and understanding that I never had growing up. My wife and I think they will be stronger for it.

Adam was not taught about transgender identity in the Christian education he experienced growing up in the church, nor in seminary. Social work school may have addressed sexual identity from the perspective of human diversity, but not from a Christian worldview. As Adam cares for this group of people in his congregation, he has had to wrestle with what sexual identity means, not only to sort it out for himself, but also to lead his congregation and to teach his own children.

Provides Community

Many of these social workers talked out the sense of belonging they experience both from within and beyond their congregation. Carl describes people calling him by name as he walks down the street, whether members of his congregation or not:

> It's an honor to be pastor of homeless people, people whom others wouldn't choose. When I walk the street, they call me "Pastor Carl." Someone hollers across the street across traffic, "Hey, Pastor Carl!" There won't be a lot of honor in heaven for me, because I get it here.

Adam described how his children have been watched over and cared for by the adolescents in the programs his congregation offers. Brenda says she feels loved by the community.

Gives Fulfillment

We searched for the right word for the sense of "rightness" these social workers feel in what they do and settled on fulfillment, which means feeling content, complete, and satisfied. Brandi, the Congregational Care Minister in her congregation, describes herself as having "the dream job:"

> I get to sit at the feet at really amazing people and listen to stories. Most of the time, it's not so much what I feel like I'm offering, but it is what others are offering me. I get the benefit of everyone's history. Sitting at the feet of some people who have made journeys that I will never make and hearing them. I think to help someone walk through the journey of dying; I think that's holy ground. My personal belief is this life is just a preparation for a better one so if I can help walk alongside someone and extend that hand to them and they extend that hand to me, then we are doing what we are here for. I get to do that every day in my work. That's more than just a vocation. That's more than just a job.

Next Steps

We began this chapter by saying "we make the path by walking it." Writing this book has been a time of reflection on our journey thus far, on what others have written, on research we have done in the past that has taken on new meaning, and on the journeys of these 51 companions who have been making their own paths as we have. We have attempted to share with you what we have learned in our own experiences, and from these 51 colleagues, that describes this field of practice called congregational social work.

When we finished the manuscript for this book, we sent it to all 51 social workers we interviewed initially and gave them a month to read and react to what we had written. We asked them to tell us what we got right, and correct us where we misunderstood. For the most part, they encouraged us to add emphasis in several places, which we have done. Several wanted us to underscore the ways that innovative social work always requires making new paths where there were none. Social work education emphasizes critical thinking, but these social workers also illustrate the importance of *creative* thinking. They suggested emphasizing that congregational social work is often independent practice, with few colleagues close at hand for consultation or supervision; therefore, they suggest that novices may need to practice first in a setting that provides more boundaries, clear policies, and established roles. Alternatively or in addition, social workers need to seek out colleagues and construct the boundaries and policies we need for our work. Finally, social work in any setting has the real potential for challenging one's worldview and faith perspectives, and that is particularly the case in congregational social work. There is wisdom, then, in social workers being sure to construct access to spiritual counsel and direction, to ensure nurture of the soul and spirit as well as obtaining continuing education for professional knowledge and skills.

The Limitations of Our Work

We are deeply steeped in our own faith traditions as Baptists, which perhaps give authenticity if not breadth to our own experiences. We each were trying to figure it out as we walked our own paths before we found one another 15 years ago. By conducting a qualitative research study with social workers from across the Christian traditions, we have attempted to build a broader understanding beyond just our own tradition and experiences. We were limited by the fact that there is no list of social workers on congregational staffs we could use as the basis for a sample, so we drew on our professional connections to find a diverse sample. It appears that the diversity of Christian traditions represented suggests that we have drawn a good sample of congregational social workers, if not a random one.

One glaring limitation to our work is the lack of many congregational social workers representing ethnicities and cultures other than Anglo-European. Future research needs to address this limitation.

We undertook this research to explore and define this field of social work practice from the perspective of the social workers doing the work. Our research has not attempted to evaluate their effectiveness as practitioners. We thought we should try to figure out who they are and what they are doing before we try to evaluate how well they are serving and leading!

We have no doubt that we have made mistakes, overlooked important dimensions of congregational social work, and provided too much emphasis to others. We hope readers will help us in identifying any limitations or distortions in our description. We know that our work is incomplete; as we neared the end of writing, we were comforting ourselves that this is a first, not a last word. Whatever happens next, congregational social workers need to be talking to and learning from one another, and writing about their work so that there will be a trail that others can follow. Enough wilderness wandering! We hope that our work will be a catalyst for those conversations.

Future Research

Every research project worth the trees cut down to make paper to report it ends with pointing to the need for future research. We are not just calling for future research because it is expected that we do so—more research is *really* needed on congregational social work. We hope this book will generate recognition among congregational social workers that they are not alone. We hope that both informal and formal professional networks develop so that this project can be replicated with a much bigger and more diverse sample. We have begun that networking ourselves.

Beyond simply building a better description of congregational social work, we also need to study the congregations that seek social workers to lead them. We know what these social workers said to us, but what would other congregational leaders say is the path that has led them to hire a social worker? What are the descriptors of congregations that employ social workers? Are certain regions of our country, and are certain types of congregations, more heavily represented with congregational social workers than others?

A complicated but important research endeavor will be studying the impact social workers have through their leadership. We assume that social workers have a unique contribution to make; they told us so and we think they do. How do congregations and their people change over time as a consequence of having a social worker in leadership? What is the observable, longitudinal impact of a social worker on the four functions of congregational life? If they do make a unique contribution, what is it, and how can those of us in education prepare congregational social workers to be more effective? Do they bring professional biases that bend congregations in one direction or another over time? Ultimately, the four functions of congregational life—worship, Christian education, being community, and mission engagement—deserve the most effective leadership we can provide.

A Final Word

We hope that we have provided a lens through which you can see congregational social work as a context of social work practice. In the last 40 years, we have wandered about trying to find our way, making mistakes and experiencing some successes as we have tried to figure out this context of practice. We would love for this book to be outdated quickly because others have taken us further on the path. We dream that in 10 years, social workers are as common on church staffs as music or Christian education ministers. We dream that every textbook introducing our profession will include congregational social work as a field of practice, along with medical social work, school social work, and child welfare. We dream that every school or department in social work will see congregations in their communities as contexts of practice for student field internships. We dream that every national social work conference will have a track for congregational social workers. In the meantime, we'll keep following the fog.

Appendix 1
Congregational Social Workers—The Characters

Abigail

Abigail, age 33, is a licensed BSW working as Social Worker (her official title) in a very large Bible church with a staff of 300 persons, where she has been employed since graduating from the state university. She developed an intake process used by every pastor and director of the many ministries of the congregation. Everyone who receives services from the congregation signs an informed consent form that Abigail developed. The form states that the helper may use the Bible and pray with clients as part of the helping process. Those not comfortable with this agreement are referred to other agencies.

Adam

Adam and his wife began as co-directors of a Baptist mission agency for a denomination in 2002. As part of his work for the agency, Adam started the congregation he now pastors. The agency funding has systematically decreased and he has had to build his own financial support. In a predominantly Hispanic city, the population the agency serves is African-American. The work began as a ministry with persons who are homeless. They also began activity programs for the neighborhood children and organizing the community. Adam completed a dual master's degree program—a Master of Divinity (MDiv) and a Master of Social Work (MSW). He sees social work and ministry as "intertwined."

Alice

Alice is a 59-year-old social work professor who volunteers in her Assemblies of God church. She was once a single mom herself, and she now leads a single mom's group in the congregation. She sees herself as a mentor and friend to the women in the group. She is doing research on global human trafficking and had just returned from Eastern Europe when we interviewed her, where she had been doing that research, a trip she paid for on her own. She separates the professions of ministry and social work, and identifies herself as a "Christian social worker."

Austin

Austin is the Director of Community Ministries in a Baptist congregation, a position that is a partnership with a religiously affiliated child and family services organization that places social workers in congregations. As part of his agency responsibilities, Austin supervises several other programs in the larger community that are not part of the congregation, such as an after-school program and an apartment ministry. Both in the congregation and community, Austin has been very active in developing services for persons who are homeless and mentally ill, including an overflow homeless shelter program in their congregation. The congregation also has an extensive emergency services program. The church has a 30-year history of employing social workers to lead their community ministries and has a Center for Community Ministries. Austin successfully advocated for his position to be a member of the ministerial staff rather than an agency social worker located in the congregation.

Barry

Barry is the Pastor of Care Ministries in his urban congregation of more than 3,000 members, where he followed another social worker who had been in this position for many years. The congregation spends over $300,000 a year in helping meet people's needs. Barry leads the visitation ministry with those who are ill or in crisis. He provides counseling for members, and conducts baby baptisms, marriages, and funerals. He was the chair of a social work department in a Christian college prior to joining the congregation's staff.

Becca

Becca is a clinical social worker, identified as a Christian counselor, in a Baptist congregation. She sought this position because she was having difficulty filling her private practice caseload, and the pastoral staff needed help with the burdens of concerns in the congregation, particularly with the care of women in the congregation. She is careful not to imply that she has a pastoral role, and she even uses the word "shepherd" carefully to describe her work with women in this congregation where women evidently do not lead. She organizes and enjoys the work of Christian discipleship groups for youths and women. She has found much of her support and continuing education through the American Association of Christian Counselors, not social work networks or organizations.

Becky

Becky is the director of special ministries in her congregation. Her parents, former missionaries, are deaf, so she was brought up in the hearing and non-hearing world, and she is comfortable in both cultures. Her father believed that there have to be deaf churches because the language is so different. She says "you can't take the Bible and expect a deaf person to understand it in English; they speak another language." The congregation sees her as the "social worker that works with the deaf."

Ben

Ben is a full-time pastor of an ethnically diverse nondenominational Christian congregation, the congregation he grew up in and was pastored by his father. He began serving there while doing Ph.D. studies. He is also the full-time director of a social work program in the nearby university. He is very active in the community in addition to his preaching, Bible study, and counseling ministry in the congregation. He serves on the school board, runs a prison ministry for fathers who are released offenders, a mentoring program for African-American boys, and attends community collaborations. "Pastor" is the identity he thinks about first. He is careful when speaking publicly about identifying the role he is in—social work educator or pastor. He has a Ph.D. in social work and is currently completing a Master of Pastoral Studies degree.

Beth

Beth began in 2003 as a part-time minister with college students at First Baptist Church. She had just completed a dual MSW and MDiv degree program. The senior pastor wanted her on the staff full time, and so the congregation partnered with a denominational agency that engages in community ministry through congregations. Beth became the congregation's Associate Pastor. She had responsibility for the congregation's community ministry, benevolence ministry, and tutoring ministry in a nearby school. Beth loved preaching and someday wanted to be a senior pastor. In 2012, when she was called as pastor to a large downtown Baptist congregation in another state, that dream was fulfilled.

Brandi

Brandi is the Congregational Care Minister in her congregation. When she first started in this role, her primary function was to minister to those who were suffering through grief and loss. Now she is called on to counsel with people who need help in any way. Two sayings guide her ministry: 1) We are all healers who can reach out and offer help and we are all patients in constant need of help"; and 2) "People may not remember what you said and they may not remember what you did, but they will always remember how you made them feel."

Brenda

Brenda is the Director of Social Service Ministries for an urban congregation. Initially, she was responsible for the benevolence ministry (emergency assistance) and a recovery support ministry. She and the church wanted to do less responding to crises and more community development, however, so they have developed a "justice ministry" through which congregational members are learning to be neighbors and form relationships with those who had been coming for emergency assistance. She says that they are "learning to love."

Caiden

Caiden is a social work professor in a state university. In addition to her MSW, completed in 1994, she has a Certificate in Catechetics. She began her work as a Director of Religious Education for a military chapel overseas, where she developed a "faith-based assessment program" for families in which there had been violence or other crises. She was raised Catholic but reached out as a university representative to a United Methodist congregation, where she volunteers to supervise social work interns in the congregation and is now a member. She organized an agency that works through the congregation, using congregational members to work in the community with persons who have difficulty accessing public social services, and with persons who are homeless. She sees herself, and others see her, as a volunteer, not a staff person or religious leader.

Caleb

Friar Caleb is a member of a Roman Catholic religious order. He received his bachelor's degree in computer science and had been working as a computer programmer when he felt a desire to be of more service. After completing his MSW, he spent a year in a South American country where he served as a school counselor and strengthened his Spanish proficiency. At the time of the interview, he had served a parish in Central America for a year. There he organizes volunteers into social action groups to distribute charity, including free or low cost medical services, both in the city and in a remote mountain community. He also provides case management services and lives with two other friars on the grounds of the cathedral. He experiences his work as a combination of clinical, mezzo, and community development.

Carl

Carl began his work in the community as a Baptist inner city missionary in 1990. He started a new congregation in an impoverished neighborhood, which he has continued to pastor for almost 25 years. Carl had previously completed a dual MSW and theology degree program and a Doctor of Ministry. He sees himself as a pastor primarily, although he says that his social work education is invaluable to him. Many of his congregants have chronic mental illness; some are homeless. A day treatment facility for persons with mental illness is located across the street from his church building, and some of the clients have found a home in Carl's congregation. There is great ethnic diversity in the congregation, also reflecting the surrounding community. Carl directs numerous children's programs and other activities that serve the community.

Catarina

Catarina, the daughter of a Baptist pastor, is the Director of Global Ministries for a Hispanic Baptist congregation. The position is a partnership with a religiously affiliated child and family service organization that places social workers in congregations. This congregation is a ministry of a larger Anglo congregation, where it is housed. Catarina estimates that 75% of the membership of the Hispanic congregation and the community members with whom it ministers are undocumented persons. Catarina describes herself as a social worker and a church member but not as a minister. She says that the people of the church do not understand what her job is but they do understand her care. She feels unprepared to do what she is doing despite her BSW and MSW degrees.

Daniel

Daniel, age 36, is Pastor of Care Ministries in a very large Baptist congregation. He began his preparation in Bible college and wanted to do counseling in a congregation, but the pay was too poor, so he pursued his MSW. He was working in a hospital psychiatric clinic when his congregation named him an Elder and then asked him to come on staff to provide counseling and work with married couples, which he did. He then followed his wife's relocation for employment to a new city, where he joined the staff of their current congregation. He has faced significant challenges because the congregation does not value counseling and has a "real anti-social work bias," so he has emphasized his pastoral role. He also faces the challenge of finding himself in a congregation where women are not permitted to have leadership positions. His role includes equipping all congregants to provide spiritual care and mentoring within and beyond the congregation instead of relying on him and his staff for addressing these needs.

David

David recently became an Associate Pastor in a Baptist church after many years of employment by a denominational agency that provided social services across the United States. He is responsible for "the tyranny of minutiae" in the congregation. He supervises staff, enlists church members to help when it his congregation's turn to host the homeless shelter, and manages the congregation's benevolence ministries. He finds himself managing conflict among staff and also members. He perceives that a lot of conflict comes from those "grieving" the changes the congregation is experiencing, such as in its worship style. He sees himself as both a minister and as a social worker. He has helped the congregation welcome persons with developmental disabilities from a nearby facility into the congregation and called it "transformative" when, one Sunday, one of the residents began singing along as one lone voice when the pianist played "Jesus Loves Me."

Denise

Denise earned her BSW degree in 1976 and later her MSW. She is a full-time administrator in a university social work program but also serves as a nonpaid "in-house social worker" in her Methodist congregation, where she has chaired the congregation's community outreach committee for 10 years. The congregation provides emergency assistance, a "bucket ministry" (cleaning supplies in a bucket) to persons who have been homeless as they move into permanent housing, and Christmas assistance. They have also provided a mentoring team for a released prisoner who is a registered sex offender.

Earl

Earl was teaching nearby in the psychology department when he learned 11 years ago that his Church of Christ congregation, where he serves as Elder, wanted to hire a counselor. He talked to the other Elders and they hired him. He provided counseling to those in the congregation, although never to those he also served as Elder. He started sexual addictions support groups. He also led Bible studies that deal holistically with life issues. He was known as a social worker but his title was "counselor minister." He sometimes struggled with serving people in his own faith community and the boundary issues that creates. Earl contacted us a year after the initial interview to say that the congregation terminated him and reallocated the funds to a strengthened senior pastor position, evidently during a time of reallocation of resources to respond to members leaving the congregation.

Elaine

Elaine is director of a BSW program in the university and, although she does not function as a social worker in her nondenominational congregation, she uses her social work skills as an usher and chaplain. She does not see herself as a social worker in the congregation, but as a volunteer.

Fay

Fay serves, sometimes contractually but mostly as a volunteer, at the judicatory level in her Lutheran denomination. She writes curriculum on social justice issues and speaks in congregations. She serves on denominational committees, and she tries to push her own congregation toward a social justice agenda. She would like the recognition that would come if she were paid for her work. She does not want the title of "social worker," however; she went to school to learn social work skills, not to become a professional social worker.

Gina

Gina has both an MDiv and an MSW degree and serves as the national Director of Church and Community Initiatives for a large international child and family service agency. She grew up in an impoverished Hispanic community ("until I was in the ninth grade, I had not seen paved streets"); her father was a pastor of an Hispanic congregation. She is in a collaborative leadership position created by her agency and an Hispanic seminary where she teaches social work and community ministry to Hispanic church leaders. She also supervises community ministers placed by her agency in congregations across the United States.

Ginger

Ginger is field director in a university social work program and works part-time as a "clinical therapist" in a three-person pastoral counseling agency where she is paid a salary. She also does workshops in the community and in congregations.

Glenda

Glenda is a social work professor in a large state university and also has a small private practice. For six years, she has provided volunteer and contractual services in her Catholic parish. Her volunteer work there includes being listed on the parish web site as a professional counselor; she provides crisis counseling and referral. In her contractual role, she provides couples wanting to marry in the parish with premarital assessments, which she shares with the parish priest. She also has been educated as a spiritual director, and she serves members of the congregation in that role as well. She has had to deal with clergy sexual misconduct with adult women in her congregation.

Gordon

Gordon is a youth minister in a Church of Christ congregation, where he has served for three years. Prior to coming to this congregation, he served immediately after graduation with his MSW in child abuse investigations in the city where he completed his MSW in a large public university. He has a BS in Bible from a Christian university. He loves playing a significant role in the lives of children, adolescents and their families, the flexibility of his position, and the fact they are "voluntary" clients.

Haley

Haley has both her MSW and a Master's Degree in Pastoral Ministry. For the past six years, she has served as the Spiritual Director in a Catholic residential treatment center for emotionally disturbed children. Haley serves in the role of pastor for the children, including leading the weekly chapel worship service. For her, as a woman, it is "the next best thing" to being a priest. Sometimes, she works with volunteers from congregations and Catholic schools, but they more often work with the social workers in the agency, and she is clearly in the role and carries the identity of "spiritual director." She writes a curriculum for the children and delivers that curriculum. She engages the children in activities such as singing in a choir and gardening. She also provides spiritual direction for the staff and helps them with the challenges of burnout.

Heather

Heather is the Director of the Refugee Program for a Catholic diocese. She helps resettle nearly 475 refugees a year who are from the Sudan, Ethiopia, Somalia, Congo, Iraq, and Burma. She works with parish churches and particularly with college students in the parishes who work with the refugees to furnish their apartments, find jobs, learn to speak English, settle children into their schools, and generally, help them adjust to their new homes. The words of Jesus guide her work, "I was a stranger in the land and you welcomed me."

Helen

Helen is part-time director for a community service center supported by an association of 15 congregations that provide ample volunteers and financial support. Recently, they have had to cut back her hours because of financial constraints. She has worked for the center for 10 years and is not a member of any of the congregations. She sometimes speaks about missions and provides mission fairs in the congregations. The center provides emergency assistance, referral, and classes in budgeting, cooking, parenting, and healthy relationships. She went to school to prepare for this work and says, "This is my calling."

Howard

Howard was a licensed social worker but relinquished his license and social work identity when he entered seminary. He is now the associate pastor of a large congregation. His responsibilities include pastoral care, preaching, teaching, missions, and evangelism. His social work education gave him a strong foundation for working with people, even though he does not identify himself as a social worker but as a pastor. He works with congregants around issues such as substance abuse, marital conflict, depression, and anxiety.

Ike

Ike grew up the child of missionary parents and now works for the Salvation Army, which is both a social service organization and a church. He has a dual role as a pastor and as an administrator of the social services organization. He says, "I guess the social work part is more the vocation and ministry the calling."

Inez

This is the second nondenominational congregation where Inez has served as a part-time social worker on staff to provide clinical services, at no charge, to persons in the congregation more so than to the larger community. She also is a full-time lecturer in social work, just as she was in her previous position. She had worked in hospice prior to working in congregations. She was a member of the first congregation where she served and went to work in the congregation when she was a doctoral student and needed the flexibility that such a position would provide. She proudly identifies as a social worker and is trying to get her title changed from "church counselor" to "church social worker."

Ingrid

For three years, Ingrid was the social worker for a congregation-based federally funded grant that focused on children of prisoners. Her role was to be a case manager, recruiter, and to develop and train the mentors from the congregation. She found this program to be stressful because of the demands of the grant, and so decide not to pursue a renewal after the initial three years. She had become restless because she had looked forward to working with the children, but instead her time was spent recruiting mentors, not with the families and children. She now works as a food server in the café that is located in the church building.

Jackie

Jackie is the Human Resources and Outreach Coordinator for an international missions organization. She trains and supervises staff members, and she teaches American college students the skills they will need to work in the communities where they will serve. She also trains local pastors and community leaders in two week trainings in African countries, focusing on challenges the pastors face such as AIDS and fetal alcohol syndrome.

Jeanie

When a prominent member of the congregation died, she left a gift to the congregation that was used to start a center to serve the community. Jeanie had been a member of the congregation, and she has served as Mission Outreach Coordinator for the congregation and its center for nine years. Her job was to make the center self-sustaining over time by writing grants and forming partnerships with other congregations. She comes from a background in medical social work, and she began her work in the congregation with support groups for those experiencing grief and loss. Over time, the congregation has increasingly supported the ministry financially and by providing church members as service providers. Jeanie has also been successful in raising funds and connecting with other social services in the community.

Jeffrey

Jeffrey is the director of the counseling services for the Catholic diocese in a large urban area. He supervises the work of other social workers; they manage 450 counseling cases a year. They work with women who have been physically abused by their partners, and with the male abusers and with children who witness abuse. He indicates that this work is twofold: 1) to be sure that the counseling services are delivered to their clients from a Catholic faith base and 2) to provide backup and services to the priests in their dioceses.

Joy

Joy directs a program started in her United Methodist congregation that now is a separate legal entity. The program equips more than 450 teens annually, teaching them to reach out to children who need spiritual and emotional support. Teenagers commit to spending two hours a week for six weeks with the children they are assigned individually. Joy was hired to bring social work expertise to the program, to expand it, and to create measureable outcomes that would appeal to potential funders.

Juliet

Juliet was the pastor's wife in her congregation for 16 years, until the death of her husband. She is employed as a therapist in a mental health center and serves without pay as the Pastor of Christian Education and Discipleship, a new title given to her a year ago by the present pastor. When she was the pastor's wife, her congregational work focused on linking community resources to the church, developing leadership, leading education programs, and developing outreach programs. The new pastor wants her to focus more on the needs of the congregation rather than the neighborhood.

Kameryn

Kameryn is the executive-director of a pastoral counseling agency, closely affiliated with the Baptist churches in two states. Although their specific focus is on the 500 Baptist congregations they serve, the agency provides counseling services to those outside the congregations as well. Congregations contract with the agency for pastoral counseling services. Kameryn started as a counselor in the agency, then became the clinical director, and is now the executive director of the agency. Half of her responsibility is clergy consultation and clergy counseling; the other half is devoted to administering the agency. She said, "Meeting people's needs is a very authentic way for me to live out my faith. I feel like it is a really great opportunity for me to not have two separate lives, but that my spiritual beliefs integrate very closely to who I am as a professional."

Kathleen

Kathleen is the Minister of Benevolence and Missions in her congregation. For several years, the pastor of the church and another pastor in the same town had the vision of collaborating to meet the needs of their small town. After using social work interns over a period of several years, the pastors agreed that one of the churches should hire a social worker to direct this work among the churches; they hired Kathleen. She oversees their benevolence ministries, including a food pantry, a clothes closet, and emergency financial support to pay rent to prevent eviction and to provide other urgently needed assistance. She also involves members of the congregation in missionary activities. She is organizing congregations and social agencies in the town to work collaboratively to address the needs of people.

Kelly

Kelly recently retired as the Executive Director of the Jewish Federation in her town, where she served for 11 years. She had previously engaged in clinical practice in a community mental health center and in a psychiatric hospital. The Federation primarily, but not exclusively, served the Jewish community. She organized activity programs for elders, helped organize other community events, was responsible for a refugee resettlement program and also a burial service that observed Jewish customs and laws. She worked a great deal with volunteers who were particularly active in educating the larger community about Judaism and in addressing anti-Semitism.

Kylie

Kylie is the Director of Community Ministries for a Baptist Church in a changing neighborhood in a large city. She grew up in this church and was a layperson until about six years ago, when she became the children and youth director. She did her

MSW field internship at this church as well. Her current position is a partnership with a religiously affiliated child and family service organization that places social workers in congregations. Nothing that she learned in social work prepared her for congregational social work, she says. She struggles with the fact that some in the church do not share her commitment to social justice.

Lois

Lois is the Director of Senior Adult Ministries for a large Presbyterian church. She is both an LCSW and a certified mediator, mediating between families and older adults who are in transition. She previously worked for a geriatric wellness center. She seeks to empower seniors by providing them with information about resources available to them. She has created a ministry in which senior volunteers serve as "pastor aides." They visit seniors in nursing homes and in their own homes. Lois works with family members, social agencies, hospitals, and the congregation to build relationships of care and community. She has also established an intergenerational day camp at one of the residential care facilities sponsored by the church, where children and seniors can form relationships.

Lynne

Lynne has been Minister of Community Ministries for 25 years in a large Baptist congregation. She had been a pastor's wife for years and wanted to be better equipped to serve, so she went back to school and obtained an MSW degree and seminary education. She was hired into this position after finishing her degrees and has been here ever since. She now oversees 13 programs that range from housing to job readiness and from a day treatment program to family counseling. All of these programs are housed in a building dedicated to community ministries; the building is located on the church property.

Megan

Megan is employed by a ministry center located in a low-income neighborhood and supported by congregations throughout the city. The center serves as a shelter for homeless women and their children. She believes that the churches identify her as a missionary but she is always introduced as the social worker on the center staff so that the churches will view that role as important. She has developed a network of social workers in various social agencies in her city. She believes that ministry goes hand in hand with social work.

Melinda

Melinda is a consulting therapist in private practice. She works through a consortium of professional social workers, therapists, and psychologists and sees 15 clients weekly. She is the Director of Case Management for a ministry program for formerly incarcerated female prisoners re-entering society. She receives a salary from the program, which is supported by several congregations. In this role, she also supervises social work interns from one of the local universities. She meets individually with clients and connects them with community resources, including taking the women to appointments for jobs, housing, and benefits. She has been a social worker for more than 40 years.

Pam

Pam is the Associate Pastor for Adult Education for a Methodist Church. She grew up in a congregation affiliated with the Southern Baptist Convention, but because of limited opportunities for women in leadership, she found a new denominational home with the United Methodist Church. She is currently changing the focus of her leadership from training and educating the laity to creating a program of Christian community care, involving her participation on a number of community boards and developing a ministry with older adults.

Rebekah

Rebekah is the Vice President for a child and family services organization, overseeing the foster care and adoption programs, which have over 800 children in care in 12 offices across the state. Her task has been to expand the reach of the organization from one region to the entire state. She supervises staff members, prepares budgets and administers the programs. She has a major responsibility focused on developing collaborations with congregations.

Ruby

Ruby is the Director of Volunteers for an agency serving older persons. She has been in this position for two decades, first as a volunteer and then as a paid staff person. Her job includes enlisting volunteers to visit and befriend older persons in their homes and assess their needs. She recruits, trains, matches, and provides a personal introduction of the volunteers to the older person. She follows along as the relationship develops, giving support to both the older persons and the volunteers. A congregation provides free office space and some financial support for the agency.

Shirley

Shirley is the Director of Children and Youth on the staff of a Presbyterian Church, where she leads the congregation's efforts to help children and youth in the surrounding impoverished neighborhoods to be successful in school and life. The programs are actually housed in a separate building on the congregation's property and include a Saturday school for elementary students, and enrichment programs for middle and high school students, and a scholarship program for students who have graduated from one of these programs and want to attend college or vocational training.

Steven

Steven works for a large religiously affiliated child welfare agency, where he directs the operations of the foster care program and all its facets—recruiting, screening, and training foster parents, as well as making foster placements of children. His primary calling is to build bridges from congregations to the children and families who need care. He sees the church as his client needing to be empowered, equipped, and tooled so that congregations actually become the providers of ministry.

Sue

Sue is a supervisor for a Presbyterian child and family services program. She oversees the work of 19 social workers; congregations throughout the state provide offices and financial support for the agency. Sue's primary responsibility is administration and supervision of this staff as they provide case management, teach parenting and life skills courses for clients, connect clients to community resources, and provide counseling services. Additionally, Sue builds community service networks with other agencies.

Appendix 2
Glossary

Benevolence:	Giving money, food, and other forms of economic support to persons in poverty.
Catalyst:	A person who is both in the congregation and in touch with needs in the community and so able to ignite a relationship.
Church social work:	Professional social work in an organization, including congregations, whose mission is to put into action the teachings of Jesus; social work in Christian settings.
Church:	The society of all Christians, whatever tradition or time.
Community:	The interpersonal networks through which we attempt to find the meaning in our lives, meet one another's needs, accomplish our personal goals, and feel belonging.
Community ministry:	Programs and services a congregation engages in alone or in partnership with other congregations and agencies to serve individuals and families locally (not in distant places). Those served are usually, but not always, persons who are not currently participants in the congregation, as a means of pursuing the congregation's mission.
Congregation:	The aggregate of people that gather regularly and voluntarily for worship at a particular place.
Congregant:	A person, who, when asked, would say, "This is my congregation," regardless of membership status or frequency of attendance.
Congregational social work:	Professional social work practice that takes place in, or with, a congregation.
Denomination:	A subset of congregations and Christian agencies that share a name (e.g., Presbyterian), culture, and theology that mutually support one another financially and with goods and services, and that collaborate in projects (e.g., missions, schools).

Evangelism: Teaching others about Christianity and attempting to attract them to become Christians and/or members of a congregation.

Faith community: A community created intentionally because people want to be in relationship with one another, often by going out of the way of home and work routines to share common faith commitments, mutual support in living their faith, and shared ideological perspectives.

Faith-based: Organizations that have a religious mission, including both social service organizations and other business organizations and congregations.

Fellowship: The interpersonal relationships of a faith community.

Identity: How individuals describe themselves internally to themselves.

Ministry: Service done in response to the Christian mission to love others as an expression of devotion to Jesus/God.

Missions: All the ways that Christians and their congregations respond to God's call to address human need wherever it exists, whether the focus is individuals, families, neighborhoods, social systems, or society. The focus of missions is on neighbors who are outside the congregation, although the boundary between neighborhood and congregation is a permeable one.

Neighborhood: The geographical location in which people reside and/or work; the place where a person experiences belonging.

Non-sectarian organizations: Organizations that do *not* identify with or discriminate on the basis of religion, including both private and public agencies.

Para-church organizations: Organizations with a Christian mission that operate autonomously from congregational or denominational oversight.

Parish: A district or geographical area assigned to a congregation.

Preferential option for the poor: The principle that serving those in poverty and seeking economic justice is a top priority because poverty is a primary concern of God.

Religiously-affiliated: Social service or business organization that identifies with one or more religious congregations or other religious organizations, often expressed in the organization's name and funding stream.

Role:	The particular set of behaviors enacted in relationship with others; it is who I say I am to others and who others would say that I am in relationship with them.
Service:	Identifying and addressing a human need.
Social ministry:	The social services of a congregation.
Social justice:	Social systems that support the flourishing of all persons.
Subsidiarity:	The principle that people at all levels should be included in decisions that affect them.

Appendix 3
The Research Project

The Louisville Institute provided funding for the project "Social Work with Congregations," which we launched in 2010 and completed in 2012. The project objectives were to:

- Describe social workers as congregational leaders, what they are contributing to the missions and ministry of the congregations where they serve, and the preparation they need for this work.
- Raise awareness among church leaders and the profession of social work of the resource that social workers can be for strengthening the positive impact of congregational ministries.
- Prepare a research-based text for educating social workers for practice in congregations.

This book aims to fulfill these objectives.

Interviewees

We sent information about the research project on the electronic listservs of three organizations: North American Association of Christians in Social Work (NACSW), the National Association of Deans and Directors of Schools of Social Work (NADD), and Baccalaureate Program Directors of Social Work (BPD). The NACSW listserv posting asked for social workers employed full-time or part-time in a congregational setting to volunteer for the study. We asked social work deans and directors to identify any alumni in this practice setting. Based on these three electronic postings, we made contact with 114 self-identified congregational social workers in Christian and Jewish settings.

We interviewed by telephone the first 28 who contacted us as part of the first of two rounds of interviewing. Initially, we interviewed those social workers who identified themselves as social workers in a congregational setting, even though they were volunteering their time to the congregation, i.e., they were not employees. As the project has progressed, however, we limited our subject pool to those who are employed part-time or full-time with one or more congregations. The employer may be the congregation itself (in most cases) or in some cases, an organization that deploys social workers to work in congregations.

After completing the first 28 interviews, we wrote the chapter "Moving Mountains" based on what we had learned (D. R. Garland & Yancey, 2012). We sent that article to all 28 interviewees we could locate and asked for any input they might have. We also presented those findings at professional conferences. We used that feedback to make revisions in our interview protocol for the second phase of the project.

We then contacted and interviewed an additional 23 congregational social workers. We interviewed social workers in the order that they had contacted us, after determining that they met the criteria for the study. We stopped interviewing when we reached the 50 interviewees called for in the initial study proposal, with one additional interviewee for good measure. We were not able to interview all those who contacted us during the study, and we continue to have congregational social workers contact us, interested in our findings.

The Interview

Telephone interviews ranged from 26 to 120 minutes, with an average length (mean) of 67 minutes. The two authors conducted all the interviews. The interview format was semi-structured; we had questions that we included, but we allowed the unfolding conversation to control the order, so long as all questions were addressed sometime during the interview. We used Robert Weiss' approach to qualitative interviewing as explicated in *Learning from Strangers: The Art and Method of Qualitative Interview* as our guide (1994).

Interview questions evolved as we conducted the early interviews and learned what other questions emerged, and how we could ask questions that better elicited the detailed descriptions of social work in congregations we were seeking. We encouraged interviewees to tell stories and elaborate on what they told us. Sample questions include: What programs and areas of responsibility do you have? How does the church see you or identify you? How do other social workers in the community see you? What do you especially enjoy about your work? What do you like least about your work? How does the concept of calling or vocation relate to your work?

At the conclusion of the interview, we asked demographic questions and entered responses into a separate database. Those data included denominational affiliation of the social worker and of the congregation, the official title of the social workers, educational institutions(s), degree(s) and year(s) of graduation, licensure status, gender, ethnicity, age, the number of years in social work practice, the number of years working with congregations, and the number of years in the current position.

We audio recorded and transcribed the telephone interviews. The interviewer assigned each subject, location, and congregation pseudonyms prior to transcription, and those pseudonyms were used in place of actual names during the transcription in order to protect the identity of subjects and their congregations. The tapes were erased after the transcriptions were completed. We placed the transcriptions in an encrypted computer with names and code names in a separate file from the transcripts, to protect the privacy of the interviewees.

Analyzing the Data

We inserted each transcript into the project's database and used the software package, Atlas-ti, to code the data. We used grounded theory as our approach to data analysis (Charmaz, 2006; Glaser & Strauss, 1967; LaRossa, 2005; Strauss & Corbin, 1998). We developed codes that identified the themes in the interviews, developing code families as we worked, returning to old codes and renaming and sorting them as we progressed through the transcripts. The 26 alphabetically-listed code categories we used are listed below, followed by our working definition of the category. We used these categories to organize our codes as they developed, to avoid losing codes in the growing code list.

- Challenge: The professional activities or decisions that created challenges or even dilemmas requiring discernment and/or skill. The focus is professional work as contrasted with personal feelings and experiences.
- Challenges—Personal: Challenges that have a personal impact beyond the workplace. These can be opportunities for personal growth and professional identity.
- Client Population: The persons or groups that the social worker sees as the client.
- Faith and Practice: The description of how faith and practice are related in the context for practice, not the identity of the social worker (coded under "identity"). This category relates to the mission of the program or service more than to the motivation of the social worker.
- Goals: The social worker's goals for the work, as distinguished from personal or professional goals. In many cases (but not all), they are the client system's goals as well.
- Goals—Social Worker: The goals the social worker has for self, as distinguished from goals for clients or congregation.
- Identity: How the social workers integrate faith and social work, and ministry and social work, in their sense of professional self. This is distinct from

the "Faith and practice" code family, which describes how ministry and social work are related in the work that they do.

- Motivation: The internal (to the social worker) factors that brought the social worker into this field or that maintain involvement. Motivations are to be distinguished from "stimulus" codes, or those external factors that pushed or pulled the social worker into the field.
- Organizations: The characteristics of the organizational structure employing the social worker.
- Outcome—Client: What happens in the life of the client as a result of the program or service?
- Outcome—Community: Results of the work for the community and/or congregation.
- Outcome—Social Worker: Rewards, changes or results in the life of the social worker as a consequence of serving in this context.
- Outcome—Servant: Results in the lives of individual servants (i.e., congregants) with whom the social worker works.
- Path—Congregation: The stimuli or processes for the congregation developing the program or approach for which they employed the social worker.
- Path—Professional: The ways social workers come to a position as a congregational social worker.
- Personal Frustrations: The personal feelings of frustrations created by the work. Challenges may create frustrations, and so may consequences and roles, so some quotations may be dually coded.
- Preparation: The academic and other ways a social worker was prepared for the work.
- Program: The program context of the social worker's tasks.
- Preparation—Not: The areas of practices or professional experiences for which the social worker was not prepared.
- Resources: The resources that the social worker has to draw on for the work that perhaps those in other settings may not have access to.
- Roles: The roles the social worker assumes or is given.

- Self-Care: The ways the social worker uses to keep focused, centered, renewed for the work.
- Tasks: The actual work or "tasks" that the social worker does.
- Title: The official title the social worker has, whether self-assigned or given by the organization/congregation.
- Values: The values that the social worker speaks about; they may be Christian values, social work values, or both or neither.
- Vocational calling: A religious/spiritual or pull to this work beyond or outside personal motivation or choice.

Both authors, along with two graduate social work students, coded each of the first 28 transcripts. We independently coded two transcripts and then compared the extent to which we applied the same code to the same interview quotation. Our interrater reliability was established at 85%; that is, we both applied the same code to the same segment of the transcript 85% of the time. We developed 439 codes that we applied to 1,531 interview segments in the first 28 transcripts. By the end of the analysis of all 51 interviews, we had developed 533 codes related to 2,684 interview segments.

After completing the initial coding, the investigator who conducted the interview also wrote a brief case description of the interview subject. We used these descriptions as a reference when studying the data, to put quotations in the larger context of the social workers' stories. These descriptions have been abbreviated to form Appendix 1.

During the axial coding process, we also developed 38 code "families" that related to our growing understanding of what congregational social work involves. The code categories kept us organized by providing groups of codes listed alphabetically, such as "Task: Administration," "Task: Advocacy," and "Task: Assess Community." The code *families* served a different function; they served as a second level of organization around themes that were emerging. For example, the four "functions" of congregations were each a code family: Community, Education, Mission, and Worship. Each of these families included a subset of codes from different code categories. For example, "Education" included 20 codes that came from the two categories of "Programs" and "Tasks"—that is, the programs and tasks that social workers engaged in related to the congregational function of education.

We began our description of congregational social worker by defining these code categories and families, illustrating them with the quotations and narrative to which the codes had been assigned in the database. The result is the description of congregational social work found throughout this book.

Validating Findings with Interviewees

When we began writing this book, we determined that 51 stories were too many for any reader to track in our narrative, so we chose the seven social workers described in Chapter 1 to be the threads we would attempt to weave throughout the book. It had been three years since the initial interviews, so we contacted six of them a second time for a follow-up interview; we were not able to arrange an interview with the seventh. Prior to the follow-up interview with these social workers, we sent a draft of the first three chapters of this book to ask for feedback. We have woven that feedback, as well as the changes and developments that had taken place since the first interview, into the final manuscript.

The final manuscript was also sent to all the interviewees electronically; they were invited to comment and make any corrections prior to our submitting the book for publication. These are their stories; we wanted to tell them accurately.

Appendix 4
Sample Job Descriptions

The three job descriptions below were obtained from congregations that gave us permission to include them here as examples. They have been modified slightly, only to remove identifying information to protect the privacy of these social workers and their congregations.

I. Minister of Missions

Reports to: Associate Pastor

Principal Function:
The minister of missions will lead the congregation to engage in missions locally, nationally and internationally, in collaboration with the Missions Committee, ministry staff and missions partners.

Responsibilities:

I. Lead the church in missions vision.
   A. Foster a missions program with the congregation that is balanced between local, state, national and international mission activities.
   B. Collaborate with the Missions Committee to define the scope and nature of the church's missions program.
   C. In cooperation with the educational ministry staff, develop and maintain missions education programs that reach all age groups within the congregation.
   D. Communicate with the congregation and the community about missions programs.
   E. Demonstrate personal involvement in missions.

II. Lead the church in developing missions partnerships.
   A. Establish and maintain missions-networking relationships with the denomination and local mission/ministry organizations.
   B. Relate constructively to all of the church's local missions partners, assessing needs, connecting volunteers and channeling resources.

C. Coordinate with and support the work of other staff members who need assistance with age-specific missions projects.

III. Provide direct missions ministry where appropriate.
   A. Direct benevolence ministry through direct service or in partnership with other providers.
   B. Develop and supervise any other direct missions ministry in which the church chooses to engage.

IV. Lead in pastoral care to adults and their families.
   A. Provide counseling to adults and their families, as well as others in the community, as needed.
   B. Assist the rest of the pastoral staff in overall pastoral care of the church, including hospital visitation.

V. Participate in Pathways to Ministry leadership.
   A. Collaborate with the Pathways to Ministry program encouraging all Christians to consider the call to vocational Christian ministry and to serve as encouragers and supporters of those called to vocational ministry.
   B. Support the Pathways to Ministry program as requested through residency rotations and coordination.

VI. Participate in overall ministry.
   A. Develop rapport with members of the congregation to encourage their spiritual development and the vitality of the church.
   B. Provide leadership to assigned church committees and ministry groups, especially as liaison to the Missions Committee.
   C. Be actively involved in the community, building relationships with both members and non-members to extend our witness.
   D. Be actively connected to the larger Baptist and Christian world through participation in denominational events, as well as interdenominational and interfaith interactions.

II. Director of Community Ministries

Reports to: National Organization's Director

Principal Function:
The Director of Community Ministries will lead the congregation's community ministry teams by developing, implementing, and integrating a plan to develop community ministries between the local church and the national organization.

Responsibilities:

I. Congregation
   A. Works successfully as part of a team and is responsible for developing and then maintaining strong working relationships with co-workers.
   B. Establishes, supervises, and maintains positive relationships with the congregation's staff and volunteers, organizational leaders and agencies.
   C. Provides leadership and is responsible for designated congregational community ministry teams.
   D. Promotes the development of community ministries in the congregation's geographic community as determined by needs, available resources, and church leadership and volunteers.
   E. Provides intake and referral services for clients served by the local congregation when needed.
   F. Participates in appropriate city meetings and coordinates with the local congregation's city committees, which relate to designated community ministries in order to accomplish the objectives of any collaboration.
   G. Aids in the development of additional resources.
   H. Plans and leads conferences, worship services, workshops, and retreats related to pertinent issues and programs throughout the community.

II. National organization
   A. Provides planning and administrative tasks as required by the local congregation and the national organization.
   B. Assists in the local congregation's development and long range planning for collaboration initiatives.
   C. Manages the appropriate budgets to meet collaboration objectives of the local congregation and the national organization.
   D. Provides input and coordination where designated local congregation and national organization community ministries initiatives interface.
   E. Assists in recruiting, screening, training, matching, and supporting local congregation and national organization volunteers.
   F. Maintains compliance with all agency regulatory guidelines and requirements.

III. Minister of Community Transformation

Reports to: Senior Pastor

Principle Function:
Responsible for directing the church's missional efforts in the city, coordinating with local community partners, other ministry organizations, and those in need, so that the local congregation oversees the provision of compassion, evangelism, and discipleship to targeted communities in expectation that God will use the church to transform lives, give hope, and make disciples of Christ.

Responsibilities:

1. Develop a vision for a coordinated and strategic plan that enhances local missions outreach of the church.
2. Create and develop strategies designed to align with or replace existing strategies with a goal to achieve the church's vision for local missions. Strategies should have measurable outcomes and mirror the local congregation's ministry cycle.
3. Lead local mission outreach, including Jerusalem ministries in the city, Community Ministries (partnerships with organizations in the city), and Benevolence/ Alms and other weekly efforts.
4. Coordinate with other local mission ministers.
5. Educate staff and members on the local congregation's vision for community transformation, strategies, and opportunities.
6. With assistance from the pulpit and Sunday school departments, recruit and equip church members for local missions, with a goal of increasing the local congregation's participation and creating a missional lifestyle in the membership.
7. Utilizing the Communications Team, raise awareness within the congregation of local mission opportunities and the resulting transformation of lives and communities through the congregation's media, including website content and promotional materials for volunteer ministry teams.
8. Engage with local governmental organizations to understand the needs of the community and to identify opportunities for local congregation involvement.
9. Plan entire day of service for the congregation.
10. Coordinate volunteer schedules and opportunities for service day.
11. Develop and use appropriate reporting procedures.
12. Prepare and manage community ministry budget under the supervision and guidance of the Missions Committee and the Minister of Missions.

References

Abbott, A. (1995). Boundaries of social work or social work of boundaries? *Social Service Review, 69*(4), 545-562.

Achtemeier, E. (1987). *Preaching about family relationships.* Philadelphia: Westminster Press.

Allen, C. B. (1987). *A century to celebrate: History of Woman's Missionary Union.* Birmingham, AL: Woman's Missionary Union.

Ammerman, N. T. (1997). *Congregation and community.* New Brunswick, NJ: Rutgers University.

Ammerman, N T. (1999). Engaging faith communities as partners in improving community health: Highlights from a CDC/ATSDR Forum addressing separation of church and state; the science supporting work with faith communities; and exemplary partnerships (pp. 1-17). Atlanta: Centers for Disease Control and Prevention, Public Health Practice Program Office.

Ammerman, N. T. (2000). New life for denominationalism. *Christian Century, 117*/9, (March 15), 302-307.

Ammerman, N. T. (2001). *Doing good in American communities: Congregations and service organizations working together.* Hartford, CT: Hartford Institute for Religious Research.

Ammerman, N. T. (2002). Still gathering after all these years: Congregations in U.S. cities. In A. Walsh (Ed.), *Can charitable choice work?: Covering religion's impact or urban affairs and social services* (pp. 6-22). Hartford: The Leonard E. Greenberg Center for the Study of Religion in Public Life.

Ammerman, N. T. (2005). *Pillars of faith: American congregations and their partners.* Berkeley, CA: University of California Press.

Ammerman, N. T. (2007). Studying everyday religion: Challenges for the future. In N. T. Ammerman (Ed.), *Everyday religion: Observng modern religious lives* (pp. 219-236). New York, NY: Oxford University Press.

Arzola, F. (2011). *Exploring worship : Catholic, Evangelical, and Orthodox perspectives.* Eugene, OR: Wipf and Stock.

Bader-Saye, S. (2004). The emergent matrix: A new kind of church? *Christian Century, 121*(23).

Baker, C. T. (2006). *Welcoming the children: History and programs of Arizona Baptist Children's Services: 1960-2002.* Phoenix: Arizona Baptist Children's Services.

Becker, P. E. (1998). Congregational models and conflict: A study of how instituitons shape organizational process. In N. J. Demerath, P. D. Hall, T. Schmitt, & R. H. Willliams (Eds.), *Sacred companies: Organizational aspects of religion and religious aspects of organizations* (pp. 231-255). New York, NY: Oxford University Press.

Becker, P. E. (1999). *Congregations in conflict: Cultural models of local religious life*. Cambridge: Cambridge University Press.

Bent-Goodley, T. (2001). Ida B. Wells-Barnett: An uncompromising style. In I. C. LaNey (Ed.), *African American leadership: An empowerment tradition in social welfare history* (pp. 87-98). Washington, DC: NASW Press.

Berger, R M. (2007). What the heck is 'social justice'? *Sojourners, 36*(2 February), 37.

Bertell, R. (2004). In what do I place my trust? In P. R. Loeb (Ed.), *The impossible will take a little while* (pp. 191-195). New York: Basic Books, Inc.

Bielefeld, W., & Cleveland, W. S. (2013). Faith-based organizations as service providers and their relationship to government. *Nonprofit and Voluntary Sector Quarterly, 42*(3), 468-494.

Billingsley, A. (1999). *Mighty like a river: The Black church and social reform*. New York, NY: Oxford University Press.

Bird, W. (2007, November 3). *Multi-site church overview: The movement of becoming one church in many locations.* Paper presented at the Religious Research Association Annual Meeting, Tampa, FL.

Bisno, H. (1952). *The philosophy of social work*. Washington, DC: Public Affairs Press.

Blank, S., & Davie, F. (2004). *Faith in their futures: The youth and congregations in partnership program of the Kings County (Brooklyn, NY) District Attorney's Office*. Philadelphia, PA: Public/Private Ventures.

Blinn-Pike, L., Kuschell, D., McDaniel, A., Mingus, S., & Mutti, M. P. (1998). The process of mentoring pregnant adolescents" An exploratory study. *Family Relations, 47*(2), 119-127.

Boddie, S. C. (2002). Fruitful partnerships in a rural African American community. *Journal of Applied Behavioral Science, 38*(3), 317-333.

Boddie, S. C., Cnaan, R. A., & DiIulio, J. J. (2001, January 18-21). *Philadelphia census of congregations and their involvement in social service delivery: Methodological challenges and findings.* Paper presented at the Society for Social Work Research, Atlanta, GA.

Bowlby, J. (1969). *Attachment and loss. Volume I: Attachment*. New York, NY: Basic Books, Inc.

Bowlby, J. (1975). Attachment theory, separation anxiety, and mourning. In D. A. Hamburg & H. K. M. Brodie (Eds.), *American handbook of psychiatry* (Vol. 6). New York: Basic Books.

Bowlby, J. (1988). *A secure base: Parent-child attachment and healthy human development*. New York, NY: Basic Books, Inc.

Branch, A.Y. (2002). *Faith and action: Implementation of the national faith-based initiative for high-risk youth*. Philadelphia, PA: Public/Private Ventures.

Brice, T. S., & Scales, T. L. (2013). The first and the last: A confluence of factors leading to the integration of Carver Schoool of Missions and Social Work, 1955. *Journal of Sociology and Social Welfare, 40*(1).

Brice, T. S. (2012). "Go in peace and sin no more": Christian African American women as social work pioneers. In T. L. Scales & M. S. Kelly (Eds.), *Christianity and social work: Readings on the integration of Christian faith and social work practice* (4th ed., pp. 71-84). Botsford, CT: North American Association of Christians in Social Work.

Brueggemann, W. (2010). *Journey to the common good*. Louisville, KY: Westminster John Knox.

Brueggemann, W. G. (1996). *The practice of macro social work*. Chicago, IL: Nelson-Hall.

Buckner Baptist Benevolences. (2010). Annual report. Retrieved June 16, 2012, from http://www.buckner.org

Bullock, K. O. (1993). *Homeward bound: The heart and heritage of Buckner*. Dallas, TX: Buckner Baptist Benevolences.

Burghardt, W. J. (1997). *Preaching the just word*. New Haven, CT: Yale University Press.

Burkhart, J. E. (1982). *Worship* (1st ed.). Philadelphia, PA: Westminister Press.

Byars, R. P. (2000). *Christian worship: Glorifying and enjoying God* (1st ed.). Louisville, Ky: Geneva Press in conjunction with the Office of Theology and Worship, Presbyterian Church (U.S.A.).

Calhoun, J. A. (2004). *People of faith mentoring children of promise: A model partnership based on service and community*. Washington, DC: National Crime Prevention Council.

Campbell, L.. (2010). Selling our children: Atlanta does battle against the sex trafficking of kids. *Sojourners, 39*(8), 22-26.

Campolo, T. (1990). *The kingdom of God is a party*. Dallas: Word.

Carroll, J. W., Dudley, C. S., & McKinney, W. (Eds.). (1986). *Handbook for congregational studies*. Nashville, TN: Abingdon.

Carroll, J. W., & Roof, W. C.. (2002). *Bridging divided worlds*. San Francisco, CA: Jossey-Bass.

Cavendish, J. C. (2000). Church-based community activism: A comparison of Black and White Catholic congregations. *Journal for the Scientific Study of Religion, 39*(3 (September)), 371-384.

Cavendish, J. C., Welch, M. R., & Leege, D. C. (1998). Social network theory and predictors of religiosity for Black and White Catholics: Evidence of a "Black Sacred Cosmos"? *Journal for the Scientific Study of Religion, 37*(3), 397-410.

Charmaz, K.. (2006). *Constructing grounded theory: A practical guide through qualitative analysis*. London: Sage.

Chaves, M. (1999a). Congregations' social service activities. Retrieved December 8, 2005, from http://www.urban.org/publications/309275.html

Chaves, M. (1999b). The National Congregations Study: Background, methods, and selected results. *Journal for the Scientific Study of Religion, 38*, 458-476.

Chaves, M. (1999c). Religious congregations and welfare reform: Who will take advantage of 'Charitable Choice'? *American Sociological Review, 64*, 836-846.

Chaves, M. (2003). Debunking the assumptions behind charitable choice. *Stanford Social Innovation Review, 1*(2), 28-36.

Chaves, M. (2004). *Congregations in America*. Cambridge: Harvard University Press.

Chaves, M. (2006). All creature great and small: Megachurches in context. 2005 H. Paul Douglas Lecture. *Review of Religious Research, 7*(4), 329-346.

Chaves, M. (2011a). *American religion: Contemporary trends.* Princeton, NJ: Princeton University Press.

Chaves, M. (2011b). Religious trends in America. *Social Work & Christianity, 38*(2), 119-132.

Chaves, M., & Anderson, S. (2008). Continuity and change in American religion, 1972-2006. In P. V. Marsden (Ed.), *Social trends in the United States, 1972-2006: Evidence from the General Social Survey.* Princeton, NJ: Princeton University Press.

Chaves, M., & Garland, D. R. (2009). The prevalence of clergy sexual advances toward adults in their congregations. *Journal for the Scientific Study of Religion, 48*(4), 817-824.

Clerkin, R., & Gronbjerg, K.. (2003, March 6). *The role of congregations in delivering human services.* Paper presented at the Roundtable on Religion and Social Welfare Policy, Washington, D.C.

Cnaan, R. A. (2000). The new Philadelphia story: Preliminary survey results on 401 congregations [Report to the Louisville Institute]. Louisville, KY.

Cnaan, R. A. (2001). Keeping faith in the city: How 401 urban religious congregations serve their neediest neighbors. Philadelphia, PA: Public/Private Ventures.

Cnaan, R. A., Boddie, S. C., & Danzig, R. A. (2005). Teaching about organized religion in social work: Lessons and challenges. In D. B. Lee & R. O'Gorman (Eds.), *Social work and divinity* (pp. 93-110). Binghamton, NY: The Haworth Pastoral Press.

Cnaan, R. A., Boddie, S. C., Handy, F., Yancey, G. I., & Schneider, R. (2002). *The invisible caring hand: American congregations and the provision of welfare.* New York, NY: New York University Press.

Cnaan, R. A., Boddie, S. C., & Yancey, G. I. (2003). Bowling alone but surviving together: The congregational norm of community involvement. In C. Smidt (Ed.), *Religion as social capital: Producing the common good* (pp. 19-31). Waco, TX: Baylor University Press.

Cnaan, R. A., Boddie, S. C., & Yancey, G. I. (2005). Rise up and build the cities: Faith-based community organizing. In M. Weil (Ed.), *The handbook of community practice* (pp. 372-386). Thousand Oaks, CA: Sage.

Cnaan, R. A., Sinha, J. W., & McGrew, C. C. (2004). Congregations as social service providers: Services, capacity, culture, and organizational behavior. *Administration in Social Work, 28*(3/4), 47-48.

Cohen, D., & Parsons, M. (2010). *In praise of worship : An exploration of text and practice.* Eugene, OR: Pickwick Publications.

Congress of the U.S. (1789). *Bill of rights.* Retrieved from http://www.archives.gov/exhibits/charters/bill_of_rights_transcript.html.

Conn, H. (1987). *A clarified vision for urban mission: Dispelling urban stereotypes.* Grand Rapids, MI: Zondervan.

Council on Social Work Education. (2012). Statistics on social work education in the United States. from http://www.cswe.org

Council on Social Work Education. (2014). CSWE: A brief history. Retrieved January 2, 2014, from http://www.cswe.org/About/57763/57765.aspx

Cranfill, J. B., & Walker, J. L. (1915). *R.C. Buckner's life of faith and works* (1996 ed.). Dallas, TX: Buckner Orphans Home.

Creps, E. (2008). *Reverse mentoring*. San Francisco, CA: Jossey-Bass.

CWJC/CMJC: Job Readiness. http://www.wmu.com. Retrieved June 19, 2013, from http://www.wmu.com/index.php?q=ministries/cmjc/cwjccmjc-job-readiness

Davidson, J. D., Johnson, C. L., & Mock, A. K. (1990). *Faith and social ministry: Ten Christian perspectives*. Chicago, IL: Loyola University Press.

Davis, C. A. (1997). *Come go with me: Following Christ's example of ministry and witness*. Birmingham, AL: Woman's Missionary Union.

Doherty, W. J. (2001). *Take back your marriage: Sticking together in a world that pulls us apart*. New York, NY: Guilford.

Dolgoff, R., Loewenberg, F. M., & Harrington, D. (2005). *Ethical decisions for social work practice*. Belmont, CA: Brooks/Cole.

Dorrien, G. (2001). Social salvation: The social gospel as theology and economics. In C. H. Evans (Ed.), *The social gospel today* (pp. 101-113). Louisville, KY: Westminster/John Knox Press.

Dudley, C. S. (1991). *Basic steps toward community ministry*. Washington, D.C.: The Alban Institute.

Dudley, C. S. (1996). *Next steps in community ministry*. Washington, DC: The Alban Institute.

Dudley, C. S., & Roozen, D. A. (March 2001). Faith communities today: A report on religion in the United States today. Retrieved March 1, 2001, from http://www.hirr.hartsem.edu

Dykstra, C. (1986). Family promises: Faith and families in the context of the church. In L. Sawyers (Ed.), *Faith and families* (pp. 137-163). Philadelphia, PA: The Geneva Press.

Dykstra, C. (1991). Reconceiving practice. In B. Wheeler & E. Farley (Eds.), *Shifting Boundaries: Contextual Approaches to the Structure of Theological Education*. Louisville, KY: Westminster/John Knox.

Dykstra, C. (1999). *Growing in the life of faith: Education and Christian practices*. Louisville, KY: Geneva Press.

Edelman, M. W. (2004). Standing up for children. In P. R. Loeb (Ed.), *The impossible will take a little while* (pp. 37-46). New York, NY: Basic Books, Inc.

Elias, J. L. (2012). Adult religious education. In E. P. Isaac (Ed.), *Expanding the boundaries of adult religious education: Strategies, techniques, and partnerships for the new milennium*. San Francisco, CA: Jossey-Bass.

Emerson, M. O., & Kim, K. C. (2003). Multiracial congregations: An analysis of their development and a typology. *Journal for the Scientific Study of Religion, 42*(2), 217-227.

Emerson, M. O., & Smith, C.. (2000). *Divided by faith: Evangelical religion and the problem of race in America*. Oxford: Oxford University Press.

Emerson, M. O., & Woo, R. (2006). *People of the dream: Multiracial congregations in the United States*. Princeton, NJ: Princeton University Press.

Emerson, Michael O., & Yancey, George A. (2011). *Transcending racial barriers: Toward a mutual obligations approach*. Oxford: Oxford University Press.

Encyclopaedia Britannica. (2013). "Lucy Jane Rider Meyer" (American social worker and educator). *Encyclopaedia Britannica. Encyclopaedia Britannica Online Academic Editions.* doi: <http://www.britannica.com/EBchecked/topic/379481/Lucy-Jane-Rider-Meyer>

Evans, C. H. (Ed.). (2001). *The social gospel today.* Louisville, KY: Westminster/John Knox Press.

Farnsely, A. E. II. (2004). What congregations can and can't do: Faith-based politics. *Christian Century, 121*(17), 27-33.

Farris, A., Nathan, R. P., & Wright, D. J. (2004). *The expanding administrative presidency: George W. Bush and the faith-based initiative.* Albany, NY: The Roundtable on Religion and Social Welfare Policy.

Ferguson, J. (1992). Social work practice in the local church. In D. R. Garland (Ed.), *Church social work* (pp. 36-57). St. Davids, PA: The North American Association of Christians in Social Work.

Ferm, M. E. (1962). Parish social work—A pilot project. *Lutheran Social Welfare Quarterly, 2*, 1-8.

Flexner, A. (1915). *Is social work a profession?* Paper presented at the National Conference on Charities and Corrections, Proceeding of the National Conference of Charities and Corrections at the Forty-second annual session, May 12-19, 1915, Baltimore, MD.

Forest, J. (1995). What I learned about justice from Dorothy Day. *Salt of the Earth, 15*(4), 22-26.

Fowler, J. W. (2000). *Becoming adult, becoming Christian.* San Francisco, CA: Jossey-Bass.

Franklin, R. M. (1994). The safest place on earth: The culture of Black congregations. In J. P. Wind & J. W. Lewis (Eds.), *American congregations* (Vol. 2, pp. 257-284). Chicago, IL: The University of Chicago Press.

Freedman, M. (1993). *The kindness of strangers: Adult mentors, urban youth, and the new voluntarism.* San Francisco, CA: Jossey-Bass Publishers.

Freud, S., & Krug, S. (2002). Beyond the Code of Ethics, Part II: Dual relationships revisited. *Families and Society, 83*(5/6), 483-492.

Furman, L. D., & Aker, R.. (2002). To tell the truth. In T. L. Scales, T. A. Wolfer, D. A. Sherwood, D. R. Garland, B. Hugen & S. W. Pittman (Eds.), *Spirituality and religion in social work practice* (pp. 50-52). Alexandria, VA: Council on Social Work Education.

Gamm, G. (2001). The way things used to be in American cities: Jews, Protestants, and the erosion of Catholic exceptionalism, 1950-2000. In A. Walsh (Ed.), *Can charitable choice work?: Covering religion's impact or urban affairs and social services* (pp. 39-55). Hartford, CT: The Leonard E. Greenberg Center for the Study of Religion in Public Life.

Garland, D. E., & Garland, D. R. (2007a). Bathsheba's story: Surviving abuse and loss. *Family and Community Ministries: Empowering Through Faith, 21*(3), 22-33.

Garland, D. E., & Garland, D. R. (2007b). *Flawed families of the Bible: How God works through imperfect relationships.* Grand Rapids, MI: Brazos Press.

Garland, Diana R. (1983a). The social worker and the pastoral counselor: Strangers or collaborators? *Social Work & Christianity*, 22-41.

Garland, D. R. (1983b). *Working with couples for marriage enrichment.* San Francisco, CA: Jossey-Bass.

Garland, D. R. (1986). Christians in social work, Christian social ministry, and church social work: Necessary distinctions. *Social Work & Christianity, 13*, 18-25.

Garland, D. R. (1987a). Myths about marriage enrichment and implications for family ministry. In H. G. Lingren (Ed.), *Family strengths 8-9: Pathways to well-being* (pp. 103-117). Lincoln: Center for Family Strengths, The Department of Human Development and the Family, College of Home Economics, University of Nebraska-Lincoln.

Garland, D. R. (1987b). *Social workers on church staff* Retrieved from http://www.nacsw.org/Publications/GarlandD_SWChurchStaffs1987.pdf

Garland, D. R. (1988). The church as a context for social work practice. *Review and Expositor, 85*, 255-265.

Garland, D. R. (1990a). Creating and nurturing families. *Review & Expositor, 87*, 317-334.

Garland, D. R. (1990b). Developing and empowering parent networks. In D. R. Garland & D. L. Pancoast (Eds.), *The church's ministry with families: A practice guide* (pp. 91-109). Dallas: Word.

Garland, D. R. (1992). *Church social work.* St. Davids, PA: The North American Association of Christians in Social Work.

Garland, D. R. (1994a). *Church agencies: Caring for children and families in crisis.* Washington, DC: Child Welfare League of America.

Garland, D. R. (1994b). Congregational ministries with children. *Review & Expositor, 91*(3), 373-392.

Garland, D. R. (1994c). Family stress: Reflections on personal experience and implications for congregational ministry. *Journal of Family Ministry, 8*(1), 4-19.

Garland, D. R. (1995). The church and divorce. *Review and Expositor, 92*(4), 419-434.

Garland, D. R. (1996a). *Precious in his sight: A guide to child advocacy for the churches* (Revised ed.). Birmingham, AL: New Hope.

Garland, D. R. (1996b). What is family ministry? *Christian Century, 113*(33), 1100-1101.

Garland, D. R. (1998). Church social work. In B. Hugen (Ed.), *Christianity and Social Work: Readings on the integration of Christian faith and social work practice* (pp. 7-25). Botsford, CT: North American Association of Christians in Social Work.

Garland, D. R. (1999a). Community: The goal of family ministry. *Christian Ethics Today, 5*(1), 16-17.

Garland, D. R. (1999b). Making connect-the-dot community work. *Faithworks, 2*(2), 26-17.

Garland, D. R. (1999c). When professional ethics and religious politics conflict: A case study. *Social Work & Christianity, 26*(1), 60-76.

Garland, D. R. (2001a). The faith dimension of family life. *Social Work & Christianity, 28*(1), 6-26.

Garland, D. R. (2001b). Terror in the home. *Faithworks, 4*(6), 21-22.

Garland, D. R. (2002a). Faith narratives of congregants and their families. *Review of Religious Research, 44*(1), 68-91.

Garland, D. R. (2002b). Families and their faith. In B. Hugen & T. L. Scales (Eds.), *Christianity and social work: Readings on the integration of Christian faith and social work practice* (pp. 119-143). Botsford, CT: North American Association of Christians in Social Work.

Garland, D. R. (2002c). Family ministry: Defining perspectives. *Family Ministry: Empowering Through Faith, 16*(2), 18-31.

Garland, D. R. (2002d). "Who is your family?" Membership composition of American Protestant families. *Social Work & Christianity, 29*(3), 183-223.

Garland, D. R. (2003). *Sacred stories of ordinary families: Living the faith everyday*. San Francisco, CA: Jossey-Bass.

Garland, D. R. (2004a). The families in our congregations: Initial research findings. *Family Ministry: Empowering Through Faith, 18*(1), 62-87.

Garland, D. R. (2004b). Family stories: Resources for nurturing family faith in congregational life. *Family Ministry: Empowering Through Faith, 18*(3), 26-44.

Garland, D. R. (2004c). Family stress: Reflections on personal experience and implications for congregational ministry. *Family Ministry: Empowering Through Faith, 18*(1), 7-22.

Garland, D. R. (2004d). Focusing families: Reflections on Genesis 2:7-3:13. *Family Ministry: Empowering Through Faith, 18*(1), 29-35.

Garland, D. R. (2005). The sacred in family stories. *Family Ministry: Empowering Through Faith, 19*(2), 41-60.

Garland, D. R. (2009). Religiously-affiliated agencies and social work. *Oxford Bibliography Online: Social Work*. http://www.oxfordbibliographies.com

Garland, D. R. (2010). *Inside out families: Living faith together*. Waco, TX: Baylor University Press.

Garland, D. R. (2012a). *Family ministry: A comprehensive guide* (revised ed.). Downers Grove, IL: InterVarsity Press.

Garland, D. R. (2012b). Is that church on fire? A unique moment of opportunity for social work leadership. *Social Work & Christianity, 39*(1), 88-99.

Garland, D. R. (2012c). A process model of family formation and development. *Journal of Family Social Work, 15*(3), 235-250.

Garland, D. R. (2013a). Christian families serving together. *Journal of Family and Community Ministries.* http://www.familyandcommunityministries.org/

Garland, D. R. (2013b). Clergy sexual misconduct: Don't call it an affair. *Family and Community Ministries, 26*, 66-97.

Garland, D. R. (2013c). Clergy sexual misconduct: Don't call it an affair. *Family and Community Ministries.*

Garland, D. R. (2013d). Don't call it an affair: Understanding and preventing clergy sexual misconduct with adults. In C. M. Renzetti & S. Yocum (Eds.), *Clergy sexual abuse: Social science perspectives*. Boston: Northeastern University Press.

Garland, D. R., & Argueta, C. (2010). How clergy sexual misconduct happens: A qualitative study of first-hand accounts. *Social Work & Christianity, 37*(1), 1-27.

Garland, D. R., Chapman, G., & Hassler, B. (1992). *Communication & intimacy: Covenant marriage*. Nashville, TN: Baptist Sunday School Board.

Garland, D. R., Chapman, K. C., & Pounds, J. (1991). *Christian self-esteem: Parenting by grace*. Nashville, TN: Sunday School Board of the Southern Baptist Convention.

Garland, D. R., & Edmonds, J. A. (2007). Family life of Baptists. *Family and Community Ministries: Empowering Through Faith, 21*(1), 6-21.

Garland, D. R., & Garland, D. E. (1986). *Beyond companionship: Christians in marriage*. Philadelphia, PA: Westminster Press.

Garland, D. R., & Garland, D. E. (2013). Cracked-pot families and God's grace. *Common-Call, 1*(2), 14-15.

Garland, D. R., & Hassler, B. (1987). *Covenant marriage*. Nashville, TN: Family Ministry Department, The Sunday School Board of the Southern Baptist Convention.

Garland, D. R., Hugen, B., Myers, D., Sheridan, P., Sherwood, D., & Wolfer, T. A. (2002, February). *Effective leadership of faith-motivated volunteers in community service programs*. Paper presented at the Annual Program Meeting of the Council on Social Work Education, Nashville, TN.

Garland, D. R., & Kabat, V. M. (2013). Christians and power: A six session Bible study curriculum (Publication no. July 1, 2011). http://www.baylor.edu/social_work/cfcm/index.php?id=82071

Garland, D. R., Myers, D. M., & Wolfer, T. A. (2008). Social work with religious volunteers: Activating and sustaining community involvement. *Social Work, 53*(3), 255-265.

Garland, D. R., Myers, D. M., & Wolfer, T. A. (2009). Protestant Christian volunteers in community social service programs: What motivates, challenges, and sustains them. *Administration in Social Work, 33*(1), 23-39.

Garland, D. R., Myers, D., & Wolfer, T. A. (2005). The impact of volunteering on Christian faith and congregational life: The Service and Faith Project. from http://www.baylor.edu/~CFCM/

Garland, D. R., O'Connor, M. K., Wolfer, T. A. , & Netting, E. (2006). Team-based research: Notes from the field. *Qualitative Social Work: Research and Practice, 5*(1), 93-109.

Garland, D. R., & Pancoast, D. L. (Eds.). (1990). *The church's ministry with families: A practical guide*. Irving, TX: Word.

Garland, D. R., Ross, R., Rowatt, W., & Chandler, L. (Eds.). (1995). *Life-changing events for youth and families*. Nashville, TN: Convention Press.

Garland, D. R., Sherr, M., & Gardner, L.. (2008). Congregations who care for children. *Family and Community Ministries: Empowering Through Faith, 22*(2), 4-17.

Garland, D. R., & Singletary, J. E. (2008). Congregations as settings for early childhood education. *Early Childhood Services, 2*(2), 111-128.

Garland, D. R., Wolfer, T. A., & Myers, D. M. (2008). How 35 congregations launched and sustained community ministries. *Family and Community Ministries: Empowering Through Faith, 35*(3), 229-257.

Garland, D. R., & Yancey, G. I. (2012). Moving mountains: Congregations as settings for social work practice. In T. L. Scales & M. Kelly (Eds.), *Christianity and social work: Readings in the integration of Christian faith and social work* (4th ed., pp. 311-336). Botsford, CT: North American Association of Christians in Social Work.

Garland, D. R., & Yankeelov, P. (2001). The strengths, stresses and faith practices of congregational families. *Family Ministry: Empowering Through Faith, 15*(3), 28-47.

Garland, D. R., & Yankeelov, P. A. (1998). The Church Census. *Family Ministry: Empowering Through Faith, 12*(3), 11-22.

Garrett-Evangelical Theological Seminary. (2013a). About us. from https://http://www.garrett.edu/160th-anniversary/history-born-of-mergers—born-of-mergers

Garrett-Evangelical Theological Seminary. (2013b). History—Born of mergers. from https://http://www.garrett.edu/160th-anniversary/history-born-of-mergers—born-of-mergers

Glaser, B. G., & Strauss, A. L. (1967). *The discovery of grounded theory*. Chicago, IL: Aldine.

Governor's Advisory Task Force on Faith-Based Community Service Groups. (1996). Faith in action: A new vision for church-state cooperation in Texas. Austin: Governor's Correspondence Office, P. O. Box 12428, Austin, TX 78711.

Grossman, C. L. (2009, December 17). New face of evangelism: 1 church, multiple sites, *USA Today*, pp. 1-2.

Gustafson, J. M. (1982). Professions as "callings". *Social Service Review, 56*(4), 501-515.

Halpern, R. (1999). *Fragile families, fragile solutions*. New York, NY: Columbia University Press.

Harder, J., & Haynie, K.. (2012). Child protection practices in Mennonite Church USA congregations. *Journal of Social Service Research, 38*(2), 248-259.

Harris, H. W., Sherwood, D., & Timmons, E. H. (2002). These things happen: Confronting dual responsbilities. In T. L. Scales, T. A. Wolfer, D. A. Sherwood, D. R. Garland, B. Hugen & S. W. Pittman (Eds.), *Spirituality and religion in social work practice: Decision cases with teaching notes* (pp. 127-130). Alexandria, VA: Council on Social Work Education.

Hart, S. (1996). *What does the Lord require? How American Christians think about economic justice*. New Brunswick, NJ: Rutgers University Press.

Hauerwas, S. (1981). *A community of character: Toward a constructive Christian social ethic*. Notre Dame, IN: University of Notre Dame Press.

Hawn, C. M. (2003). *One bread, one body: Exploring cultural diversity in worship*. Bethesda, MD: Alban Institute.

Hessel, D. T. (1992). *Social ministry* (Revised ed.). Philadelphia, PA: Westminster Press.

Higginbotham, E. B. (1993). *Righteous discontent: The women's movement in the Black Baptist Church 1880-1920*. Cambridge: Harvard University Press.

Hilfiker, D. (2000). The limits of charity. *The Other Side, 36*(5 (September/October)), 10-15.

Hine, D. (Ed.). (1993). *Black women in America: An historical encyclopedia*. New York, NY: Carlson Publishing Inc.

Hoke, L. R. (2009). *A distinctive contribution: Commemorating The Bishop Tuttle Memorial Training School*. Raleigh, NC: Saint Augustine's College.

Holifield, E. B. (1983). *A history of pastoral care in America: From salvation to self-realization*. Nashville, TN: Abingdon Press.

Horton, D., Rozzi, A., Aufhammer, C., Berry, M., & Camp, D. (2011). The effects of short term missions on mission team members. In J. K. Loessin & S. Stripling (Eds.), *2011 Proceedings of the Society for the Scientific Study of Religion--Southwest*. Dallas, TX: Society for the Scientific Study of Religion.

Howe, L. (2000). *A pastor in every pew: Equipping laity for pastoral care*. Valley Forge, PA: Judson Press.

Isaac, E. P. (2012). *Expanding the boundaries of adult religious education: Strategies, techniques, and partnerships for the new millennium*. San Francisco, CA: Jossey-Bass.

Jacobsen, S. (1997). Preaching as if Monday matters. *Congregations, 23*(3 (May/June)), 8-10.

Jeavons, T. H. (2004). Religious and faith-based organizations: Do we know one when we see one? *Nonprofit and Voluntary Sector Quarterly, 33*(1), 140-145.

Johnson, F. E. (1930). *The social work of the churches: A handbook of information*. New York City, NY: Department of Research and Education of the Federal Council of the Churches of Christ in America.

Johnson, T. (2012). The Black Church as a prism for exploring Christian social welfare and social work. In B. Hugen & T. L. Scales (Eds.), *Christianity and social work: Readings on the integration of Christian faith and social work practice* (4th ed., pp. 39-52). Botsford CT: NACSW.

Joseph, M. V. (1975). The parish as a social service and social action center: An ecological systems approach. *Social Casework, 61*, 423-432.

Joseph, M. V., & Conrad, A. P. (1980). A parish neighborhood model for social work practice. *Social Casework: The Journal of Contemporary Social Work, 61*(7), 423-432.

Joseph, M. V., & Conrad, A. P. (2010). The rise of professionalization: Catholic Charities and social work. In J. B. Hehir (Ed.), *Catholic Charities USA* (pp. 47-64). Collegeville, MN: Liturgical Press.

Jucovy, L. (2003). Amachi: Mentoring children of prisoners in Philadelphia (pp. 48). Philadelphia, PA: Public/Private Ventures, Center for Research on Religion and Urban Civil Society.

Justice, J. A., & Garland, D. R. (2010). Dual relationships in congregational practice: Ethical guidelines for congregational social workers and pastors. *Social Work & Christianity, 37*(4), 437-445.

Kayser, J. (2007). The history of the Bishop Tuttle School of Social Work for African American Church Women, 1925-1941. *Arete, 31*(1/2), 150-174.

Keith-Lucas, A. , Kuhlmann, E., & Ressler, L. E. (1994). *Integrating faith and practice: A history of The North American Association of Christians in Social Work, 1950-1993*. St. Davids, PA: The North American Association of Christians in Social Work.

Keller, R. S. (2001). Women creating communities--and community--in the name of the social gospel. In C. H. Evans (Ed.), *The social gospel today* (pp. 67-85). Louisville, KY: Westminster/John Knox Press.

Keller, T. (2010). *Generous justice: How God's grace makes us just*. New York, NY: Dutton.

Kenny, E. (2002). Do we have to go now? Challenges in foster care and adoption. In T. L. Scales, T. A. Wolfer, D. A. Sherwood, D. R. Garland, B. Hugen & S. W. Pittman (Eds.), *Spirituality and religion in social work practice* (pp. 91-95). Alexandria, VA: Council on Social Work Education.

Kierkegaard, S. (1948 (original 1847)). *Purity of heart is to will one thing* (D. V. Steere, Trans.) New York, NY: Harper.

Kysar, R. (1991). *Called to care: Biblical images for social ministry*. Minneapolis, MN: Fortress.

LaRossa, R. (2005). Grounded theory methods and qualitative family research. *Journal of Marriage and Family, 67*(4), 837-857.

Lee, J. M. (1990). Facilitating growth in faith through religious instruction. In J. M. Lee (Ed.), *Handbook of faith* (pp. 264-302). Birmingham, AL: Religious Education Press.

Lewis, P. (2008). Walter Rauschenbusch (1861-1918): Pioneer of Baptist social ethics. In L. McSwain (Ed.), *Twentieth-Century shapers of Baptist social ethics* (pp. 3-22). Macon, GA: Mercer University Press.

Little, E. (2004). The Elizabeth Nesbitt Room: American Sunday School Union Resource. Retrieved March 3, 2013, from http://www.library.pitt.edu/libraries/is/enroom/ASSU/assu.html

Loeb, P. R. (2004a). Introduction. In P. R. Loeb (Ed.), *The impossible will take a little while* (pp. 1-16, 175-182, 221-229, 276-280, 322-327). New York: Basic Books, Inc.

Loeb, P. R. (2004b). The real Rosa Parks. In P. R. Loeb (Ed.), *The impossible will take a little while* (pp. 288-292). New York, NY: Basic Books, Inc.

Marsh, C. (2005). *The beloved community: How faith shapes social justice, from the civil rights movement to today*. New York, NY: Basic Books, Inc.

Marter, J. L. (1998). City lights: Urban ministry pioneers bring new hope to troubled neighborhoods. *Presbyterians Today, 88*(1), 8-11.

Martin, E., & Martin, J. (2002). *Spirituality and the Black helping tradition in social work*. Washington, DC: National Association of Social Workers Press.

Marty, M. E. (1980). Social service: Godly and godless. *Social Service Review*, 463-483.

Maynard-Reid, P. U. (2000). *Diverse worship : African-American, Caribbean & Hispanic perspectives*. Downers Grove, IL: InterVarsity Press.

McCall, A. (2013). Local NGOs working to end child sex trafficking. *Examiner.com*. http://www.examiner.com/article/local-ngos-working-to-end-child-sex-trafficking.

McLaren, B. D. (2004). *A generous orthodoxy*. Grand Rapids, MI: Zondervan.

McNeal, R. (2009). *Missional renaissance: Changing the scorecard for the church*. San Francisco, CA: Jossey-Bass.

McShane, Joseph M. (1992). "To Form an Elite Body of Laymen..." Terence J. Shealy, S. J., and the Laymen's League, 1922. *The Catholic Historical Review, 78*(4), 557-580.

McSwain, L. (Ed.). (2008). *Twentieth-Century shapers of Baptist social ethics*. Macon, GA: Mercer University Press.

Mikulincer, M., & Shaver, P. R. (2005). Attachment theory and emotions in close relationships: Exploring the attachment-related dynamics of emotional reactions to relational events. *Personal Relationships, 12*, 149-168.

Mikulincer, M., & Shaver, P. R. (2007). *Attachment in adulthood: Structure, dynamics, and change*. New York, NY: The Guilford Press.

Miller, D., Allen, S., & Brumbelow, G. (2012). Reflections on social justice. doi:http://www.creativecommons.org/

Miller, D. E. (1998). Postdenominational Christianity in the Twenty-First Century. *Annals of the American Academy of Political and Social Science, 558*(July), 196-210.

Mock, A. K. (1992). Congregational religious styles and orientations to society: Exploring our linear assumptions. *Review of Religious Research, 34*(1), 20-33.

Myers, B. L. (1999). *Walking with the poor: Principles and practices of transformational development*. Maryknoll, NY: Orbis Books.

Myers, L. E. (2006). "You got us all a-pullin' together": Southern Methodist deaconesses in the rural South, 1922-1940. In M. Walker & R. Sharpless (Eds.), *Work, family and faith: Rural southern women in the twentieth century*. New York: Columbia University Press.

NASW News. (2002). Faith-based initiatives discussed. *NASW News, 47*, 1,10.

National Association of Social Workers. (2008). Code of Ethics. from http://www.socialworkers.org/pubs/code/code.asp

Netting, F. E., Kettner, P. M., & McMurtry, S. L. (2012). *Social work macro practice*. New York, NY: Longman.

North Avenue Presbyterian Church. (2013). Retrieved June 25, 2013, from http://www.napc.org/mission

Northern, V. M. (2009). Social workers in congregational contexts. *Social Work & Christianity, 36*(3), 265-285.

O'Gorman, A. (Ed.). (1990). *The universe bends toward justice: A reader on Christian nonviolence in the U.S.* Philadelphia, PA: New Society Publishers.

Oates, M. J. (1995). *The Catholic philanthropic tradition in America*. Bloomington, IN: Indiana University Press.

Oates, W. E. (1970). *New dimensions in pastoral care*. Philadelphia, PA: Fortress.

Oates, W. E. (1985). *People in pain : Guidelines for pastoral care*. Philadelphia, PA: Westminster Press.

Orr, J. B., Miller, D. E., Roof, W. C., & Melton, J. G. (1994). *Politics of the spirit: Religion and multiethnicity in Los Angeles*: Los Angeles, CA: University of California.

Oxford, L. (2012). What healthy churches do to protect vulnerable others and prevent misconduct by church leaders. *Journal of Family and Community Ministries, 25*, 81-106.

Ozment, S. E. (1992). *The Protestants*. New York, NY: Doubleday.

Parent, M. S. (2005). Boundaries and roles in ministry counseling. *Journal of Pastoral Counseling, 8*(2), 1-25.

Peck, R. (2011, May 13). Denomination faces sizable budget cuts. Retrieved from http://www.umc.org/site/apps/nlnet/content3.aspx?c=lwL4KnN1LtH&b=2789393&ct=10037145

Poe, M. A. (2012). Good news for the poor: Christian influences on social welfare. In T. L. Scales & M. S. Kelly (Eds.), *Christianity and social work: Readings on the integration of Christian faith and social work practice* (4th ed., pp. 9-22). Botsford CT: North American Association of Christians in Social Work.

Pohl, C. D. (1999). *Making room: Recovering hospitality as a Christian tradition.* Grand Rapids, MI: Eerdmans.

Polson, C. (2006). *Research report: Taken for granted? Exploring the relationships between social service agencies and religious congregations.* Baylor University, Department of Sociology, Waco, TX.

Popple, P. R., & Leighninger, L. (2008). *Social work, social welfare, and American society.* New York, NY: Pearson.

Popple, P. R., & Leighninger, L. (2011). *Social work, social welfare, and American society* (8th ed.). Boston, MA: Pearson.

Pritchett, M. (2003). *The challenges of intentional neighboring cross-culturally in a low-income neighborhood.* (Research project, MSW program), Baylor University, Waco, TX.

Pryce, J. (2012). Social work for social justice: Strengthening practice with the poor through Catholic social teaching. In T. L. Scales & M. Kelley (Eds.), *Christianity and social work: Readings on the integration of Christian faith and social work practice* (4th ed., pp. 119-128). Botsford CT: North American Association of Christians in Social Work.

Rauschenbusch, W. (1907). *Christianity and the social crisis.* New York, NY: MacMillan.

Roberts, B. (2007). *Glocalization: How followers of Jesus engage a flat world.* Grand Rapids, MI: Zondervan.

Roberts, B. (2010). *Real-time connections: Linking your job with God's global work.* Grand Rapids, MI: Zondervan.

Roberts-Lewis, A., & Armstrong, T. D. (2010). Moving the church to social action. *Social Work & Christianity, 37*(2), 115-127.

Rogers, A., & Baptist Faith and Message Study Committee. (2000). The Baptist Faith and Message. http://www.sbc.net/bfm/default.asp

Rogers, R. K., Yancey, G. I. , & Singletary, J. (2005). Methodological challenges in identifying promising and exemplary practices in urban faith-based social service programs. *Social Work & Christianity, 32*(3), 189-208.

Rusaw, R. (2008, May 6). *Sermon at Externally Focused Church Conference*, Longmont, CO.

Rusaw, R., & Swanson, E. (2004). *The externally focused church.* Loveland, CO: Group.

Saleebey, D. (2004). The Power of place: Another look at the environment. *Families in Society, 85*(1), 7-16.

Scales, T. L. (2000). *"All That Fits a Woman": Training Southern Baptist Women for Charity and Mission, 1907-1926.* Macon, GA: Mercer University Press.

Scales, T. L. (2007). *Jewell Legett and the social curriculum: The education of a Southern Baptist woman missionary at the WMU Training School, 1908-1909.*

Scales, T. Laine. (2008). C. Anne Davis (1938-2006): Shaping an ethic of "Doing the Word". In L. McSwain (Ed.), *Twentieth-Century shapers of Baptist social ethics* (pp. 226-243). Macon, GA: Mercer University Press.

Scales, T. Laine. (2011). "Accepting a trust so responsible": Christians caring for children at Buckner Orphan's Home, Dallas, Texas, 1879-1909. *Social Work & Christianity*, 38(3), 332-355.

Scales, T. L. (2012). "Accepting a trust so responsible": Christians caring for children at Buckner Orphan's Home, Dallas, Texas, 18790=-1909. In T. L. Scales & M. S. Kelley (Eds.), *Christianity and social work: Readings on the integration of Christian faith and social work practice* (4th ed., pp. 53-70). Botsford, CT: North American Association of Christians in Social Work.

Scales, T. L., Harris, H. W., Myers, D., & Singletary, J. E. (2012). Journeys toward integrating faith and practice: Students, practitioners, and faculty share their stories. In T. L. Scales & M. Kelley (Eds.), *Christianity and social work: Readings on the integration of Christian faith and social work practice* (pp. 129-151). Botsford, CT: North American Association of Christians in Social Work.

Scales, T. L., & Kelley, M.. (2012). "To Give Christ to the Neighborhoods:" A corrective look at the Settlement Movement and early Christian social workers. In B. Hugen & T. L. Scales (Eds.), *Christianity and social work: Readings on the integration of Christian faith and social work practice* (4th ed., pp. 23-38). Botsford CT: North American Association of Christians in Social Work.

Scales, T. L., & Kelly, M. S. (Eds.). (2012). *Christianity and social work: Readings on the integration of Christian faith and social work practice* (4th ed.). Botsford, CT: NACSW.

Scales, T. L., Wolfer, T. A., Sherwood, D. A., Garland, D. R., Hugen, B., & Pittman, S. W. (Eds.). (2002). *Spirituality and religion in social work practice: Decision cases with teaching notes.* Alexandria, VA: Council on Social Work Education.

Scarritt-Bennett Center. (2014). Scarritt-Bennett Center: History. Retrieved 2014, January 2, from http://www.scarrittbennett.org/a

Schneider, J. A. (1999). Trusting that of God in everyone: Three examples of Quaker-based social service in disadvantaged communities. *Nonprofit and Voluntary Sector Quarterly, 28*(3), 269-295.

Segal, E. A., Gerdes, K. E., & Steiner, S. (2010). *An introduction to the profession of social work: Becoming a change agent*. Belmont, CA: Brooks/Cole.

Segler, F. M., & Bradley, C. R. (2006). *Christian worship: Its theology and practice* (3rd ed.). Nashville, TN: B & H Publishing Group.

Shelp, E. E., & Sunderland, R. H. (2000). *Sustaining presence: A model of caring by people of faith*. Nashville, TN: Abingdon Press.

Sherman, A. L. (2000). Tracking Charitable Choice: A study of the collaboration between faith-based organizations and the government in providing social services in nine states. *Social Work & Christianity, 27*(2), 113-129.

Sherman, A. L. (2011). *Kingdom calling: Vocational stewardship for the common good.* Downer's Grove, IL: InterVarsity Press.

Sherr, M., Stamey, J., & Garland, D. R. (2009). Empowering faith practices: A validation study of the Christian Faith Practices Scale. *Journal of Family and Community Ministries, 23*(1), 27-36.

Sherwood, D. A. (1999). Integrating Christian faith and social work: Reflections of a social work educator. *Social Work & Christianity, 26*(1), 1-8.

Sherwood, D. A. (2006). Churches as contexts for social work practice: Connecting with the mission and identity of congregations. *Social Work & Christianity, 30*(1), 1-13.

Sherwood, D. A. (2008). Moral, believing social workers: Philosophical and theological foundations of moral obligation in social work ethics. *Social Work & Christianity, 34*(2), 121-144.

Sherwood, D. A. (2012a). Doing the right thing: A Christian perspective on ethical decision-making for Christians in social work practice. In T. L. Scales & M. Kelly (Eds.), *Christianity and social work: Readings on the integration of Christian faith and social work practice* (4th ed., pp. 171-188). Botsford CT: NACSW.

Sherwood, D. A. (2012b). Ethical integration of faith and social work practice: Evangelism. In T. L. Scales & M. Kelly (Eds.), *Christianity and social work* (pp. 301-309). Botsford, CT: North American Association of Christians in Social Work.

Sherwood, D. A. (2012c). The relationship between beliefs and values in social work practice: Worldviews make a difference. In T. L. Scales & M. Kelley (Eds.), *Christianity and social work: Readings on the integration of Christian faith and social work practice* (4th ed., pp. 85-104). Botsford CT: NACSW.

Sider, R., & Unruh, H. (2004). Typology of religious characteristics of social service and educational organizations and programs. *NVSQ, 33*(1), 109-134. doi: 10.1177/0899764003257494

Sider, R. (2005). *Rich Christians in an age of hunger: Moving from affluence to generosity* (5th ed.). Nashville, TN: Thomas Nelson Inc.

Singletary, J. E. (2005). The praxis of social work: A model of how faith informs practice informs faith. *Social Work & Christianity, 32*(1), 56-72.

Singletary, J. E. (2007). Community and family models of care for orphans and vulnerable children in Africa. *Social Work & Christianity, 34*(3), 298-316.

Smedes, L. B. (2001). *Learning to live the love we promise.* Colorado Springs, CO: Waterbrook Press.

Smith, K. E. (2008). Nannie H. B. (1879-1961): A voice for social justice and reform. In L. McSwain (Ed.), *Twentieth-Century shapers of Baptist social ethics* (pp. 40-57). Macon, GA: Mercer University Press.

Smith, K. G. (1984). Developing a Christian counseling ministry located in the local church: A proven model. *Social Work & Christianity, 11*, 29-39.

Smith, K. G. (1988). The local Baptist congregation and the laity. *Review & Expositor, 85*, 645-658.

Snyder, L. (2010). *Think and act anew: How poverty in America affects us all and what we can do about it.* Maryknoll, NY: Orbis Books.

Specht, H., & Courtney, M. E. (1994). *Unfaithful angels: How social work has abandoned its mission*. New York, NY: The Free Press.

Stalwick, H., & Holding Eagle, D. L. (2002). Sugarland's dilemma. In T. L. Scales, T. A. Wolfer, D. A. Sherwood, D. R. Garland, B. Hugen & S. W. Pittman (Eds.), *Spirituality and religion in social work practice* (pp. 173-176). Alexandria, VA: Council on Social Work Education.

Stott, J. (2007). *The living church: Convictions of a lifelong pastor*. Downers Grove, IL: IVP Books.

Stout, H. S., & Cormode, D. S. (1998). Institutions and the story of American religion. In N. J. Demerath, P. D. Hall, T. Schmitt & R. H. Willliams (Eds.), *Sacred companies: Organizational aspects of religion and religious aspects of organizations* (pp. 62-78). New York, NY: Oxford University Press.

Strauss, A., & Corbin, J. (1998). *Basics of qualitative research: Techniques and procedures for developing grounded theory* (2nd ed.). Thousand Oaks, CA: Sage.

Street Grace. (2013). Retrieved June 25, 2013, from http://www.streetgrace.org

Streeter, R. (2000). Recommendation for public officials, religious organizations, and evaluators of faith-based service providers. In R. Streeter (Ed.), *Religion and the public square in the 21st century*. Indianapolis, IN: Hudson Institute.

Sullivan, W. M. (2005). *Work and integrity: The crisis and promise of professionalism in America*. San Francisco, CA: Jossey-Bass.

Taggart, A. D. (1962). The caseworker as parish assistant. *Social Casework, 43*, 75-79.

Talley, T. J. (1990). *Worship: Reforming tradition*. Washington, DC: Pastoral Press.

Texas Adoption Resource Exchange. CHILD: Congregations Helping in Love and Dedication. Retrieved June 19, 2012, from http://www.dfps.state.tx.us/Adoption_and_Foster_Care/CHILD

Texas State Legislature. (2003). *Social Work Practice Act 1999, 76th Leg., ch. 388, Sec. 1, effect. Sept. 1, 1999. amended by Acts 2003, 78th Leg., ch. 892, Sec. 1, eff. Sept. 1, 2003.* Retrieved from http://www.statutes.legis.state.tx.us/Docs/OC/htm/OC.505.htm.

Thumma, S. (2007, November 3). *Growing up and leaving home: Megachurches that depart denomination*. Paper presented at the Religious Research Association Annual Meeting, Tampa, FL.

Trumble, Y. (1999). Mentoring the new workforce. *Report of the Family Resource Coalition of America, 17*(4), 18-19.

Turner, J. (2010). Seeing the poor and moving toward justic: An interactive activity. *Social Work & Christianity, 37*(2), 142-160.

Unruh, H. R., & Sider, R. J. (2005). *Saving souls, serving society.* New York: Oxford University Press.

Unruh, H. R., & Sider, R. J. (2002). Evangelism and social services. In B. Hugen & T. L. Scales (Eds.), *Christianity and social work: Readings on the integration of Christian faith and social work practice* (pp. 305-326). Botsford CT: North American Association of Christians in Social Work.

Van West, C. (2009). Scarrit College for Christian workers. Retrieved from Tennessee Historical Society http://tennesseeencyclopedia.net/entry.php?rec=1177

Warner, L. (2013). "Toward the Light": Lucy Rider Meyer and the Chicago Training School. Retrieved from https://http://www.garrett.edu/160th-anniversary/history-born-of-mergers-chicago-training-school

Warner, R. S. (1994). The place of the congregation in the contemporary American religious configuration. In J. P. Wind & J. W. Lewis (Eds.), *American congregations* (Vol. 2, pp. 54-99). Chicago: The University of Chicago Press.

Warren, R. (1995). *The purpose driven church.* Grand Rapids, MI: Zondervan.

Watkins, D. (1992). Social work consultation and the church. In D. R. Garland (Ed.), *Church social work: Helping the whole person in the context of the church* (pp. 17-35). St. Davids, PA: North American Association of Christians in Social Work.

Weiss, R. S. (1994). *Learning from strangers: The art and method of qualitative interview studies.* New York, NY: Free Press.

Welfel, E. R. (2002). *Ethics in counseling and psychotherapy: Standards, research and emerging issues* (2nd ed.). Pacific Grove, CA: Brooks/Cole.

Westerhoff, C. (2002). *Good fences: The boundaries of hospitality.* Cambridge: Cowley Publications.

Wheatley, M. (2004). From hope to hopelessness. In P. R. Loeb (Ed.), *The impossible will take a little while* (pp. 348-351). New York: Basic Books, Inc.

Whelan, R. W. (1942). *Certain aspects of case work practices in Catholic social work: A series of interviews illustrating case work practices.* Washington, D.C.: National Conference of Catholic Charities.

Whitaker, T., & Arrington, P. (2008). *Social workers at work: NASW Membership Workforce Study.* Washington, DC: National Association of Social Workers.

White, S. J. (2006). *Foundations of Christian worship* (1st U.S., [American]. ed.). Louisville, KY: Westminster John Knox Press.

Williams, D., & Greenhaw, W. (2005). *The thunder of angels: The Montgomery Bus Boycott and the people who broke the back of Jim Crow.* Chicago, IL: Chicago Review Press.

Willimon, W. H. (2004). Living by the Word: Damn preacher. *Christian Century, 121*(3), 18.

Wind, J. P., & Lewis, J. W. (1994). *American congregations* (Vol. 2). Chicago, IL: The University of Chicago Press.

Wineburg, R. J. (2001). *A limited partnership: The politics of religion, welfare, and social service.* New York, NY: Columbia University Press.

Wineburg, R J. (2003). *A public department of social services seeks ways to work with the local faith community.* Paper presented at the Roundtable on Religion and Social Welfare Policy, Washington, D.C.

Wineburg, R. J. (2005, November 18). *Unintelligent design: Federal intervention strategies into local communities.* Paper presented at the 34th Annual Conference, Association for Research on Nonproft organization and Voluntary Action (ARNOVA), Washington, D.C.

Witvliet, J. D. (2003). *Worship seeking understanding: Windows into Christian practice*. Grand Rapids, MI: Baker Academic.

Wolfer, T. A., & Huyser, M. (2008). Radical Christian innovations in social work and social welfare: Introduction to the special issue. *Social Work & Christianity, 35*(4), 363-373.

Wolfer, T. A., & Huyser, M. (2010). *Grappling with faith: Decision cases for Christians in social work*. Botsford, CT: North American Association of Christians in Social Work.

Woods, L. J. (1988). Home-based family therapy. *Social Work, 33*, 211-214.

Wuthnow, R. (2000). How religious groups promote forgiving: A national study. *Journal for the Scientific Study of Religion, 39*(2), 125-139.

Wuthnow, R. (2004). *Saving America?: Faith-based services and the future of civil society*. Princeton, NJ: Princeton University Press.

Wuthnow, R. (2009). *Boundless faith: The global outreach of American churches*. Berkeley, CA: University of California Press.

Yancey, G. I. (1986). *Pornography*. Birmingham, AL: Woman's Missionary Union.

Yancey, G. I., Kilpatrick, B., & Stutts, K.. (2010). Confidentiality in the church. *Journal of Family and Community Ministries, 23*(4), 61-69.

York, T. W. (2003). *America's worship wars*. Peabody, MA: Hendrickson Publishers.

Endnotes

Preface

1 The appendix provides a description of our research methods.

Chapter 1

2 We have provided brief descriptions of each of those we interviewed in an appendix.

3 Throughout the book, we have changed the names and other identifying information of persons and congregations in order to protect their privacy.

4 We have attempted to use "people first" language throughout this book, so instead of using the term "the poor," we use "people who are poor." Social work emphasizes recognizing the dignity and worth of persons regardless of their circumstances. To use the term "the poor" blinds us from seeing that people have other characteristics, including strengths and resources; they are not simply defined by their economic poverty.

Chapter 2

5 Average here refers to the median congregation rather than the mean; half of congregations would fall below this statistic and half above.

6 We have chosen to focus not on the various denominations and congregations and the extent to which they supported the development of social work. For example, the Salvation Army is a Christian denomination that almost from its inception in the mid-19th Century was engaged in social ministries and came to be equated with those ministries by many who do not realize that it is a Christian denomination of congregations. Rather, our review is focused on the institutions and organizations that developed as extensions of and sometimes outside congregations and denominations—educational institutions, African-American institutions, and the professional organization NACSW.

7 This section is based on Diana Garland's personal experiences of serving on the faculty of The Carver School of Church Social Work of The Southern Baptist Theological Seminary from 1979-1996. It is also based on the work of T. Laine Scales, a graduate of the Carver School who has taken on the task of telling this story (Scales, 2000, 2007, 2008).

8 Southwestern Baptist Theological Seminary in Fort Worth, Texas, and New Orleans Baptist Theological Seminary also developed social work education programs in partnership with University of Texas Arlington and Louisiana State University, respectively, but not as accredited programs on their own.

9 The name changed to the National Association of Christian Social Work in 1956 as the first step in that expansion. In 1957 the name changed to the National Association of Christians in Social Work, to emphasize that the organization is not proposing that there is a separate profession called Christian social work, but rather, that the organization provides a home for Christians who are social work professionals. Finally, the name changed to the North American Association of Christians in Social Work in 1983, acknowledging the influential Canadian chapter that had developed within the organization (Keith-Lucas et al., 1994).

10 You will find publications by these authors in the references.

11 Their publications are in the references for this book (Boddie, 2002; Boddie, Cnaan, & DiIulio, 2001; Cnaan, 2000, 2001; Cnaan, Boddie, & Danzig, 2005; Cnaan, Boddie, Handy, Yancey, & Schneider, 2002; Cnaan, Boddie, & Yancey, 2003, 2005; T. Laine Scales, Myers, Harris, & Singletary, 2007; T. Laine Scales & Kelly, 2012; T. Laine Scales et al., 2002; Sherwood, 1999, 2006, 2008, 2012a, 2012b, 2012c; Wineburg, 2001, 2003, 2005; Wolfer & Huyser, 2008, 2010; Woods, 1988)

12 Neither of us was involved in writing this mission statement.

13 Another seven social workers told us that they "speak" in the congregation's worship on occasion.

14 The authors have been in each of these roles, so we speak here from personal experience. There has been no systematic survey of curricula and other church resources to determine how many social workers have been engaged in preparing educational literature for congregations or speaking as experts in congregational gatherings.

Chapter 3

15 To find congregational social workers for this project, we sent information about the research using the electronic listserves of three organizations: the North American Association of Christians in Social Work (NACSW), the National Association of Deans and Directors of Schools of Social Work (NADD), and the Baccalaureate Program Directors of Social Work (BPD). The NACSW listserv posting asked for social workers employed full-time or part-time in a congregational setting to volunteer for the study. Using NADD and BPD listserves, we asked social work deans and directors to identify their alumni who were working with congregations. Based on these three electronic postings, we made contact with 114 self-identified congregational social workers. It was encouraging to us that some of those not included for the study referred us to others who they believed would be more appropriate for the study because they knew their work, first-hand.

16 The highest social work degrees these professionals hold are: the BSW (n=6), MSW (n=40), and PhD (n=5).

17 Those schools represented by more than one graduate were all religiously affiliated. They included Baylor University (n=6), Carver School of Church Social Work (The Southern Baptist Theological Seminary) (n=6), Anderson (n=2), and Boston College (n=2). One respondent each graduated from Abilene Christian, Augsburg, Aurora, Loyola, Northwest Nazarene, and Roberts Wesleyan.

18 Those schools represented by more than one graduate include the University of Texas (Arlington) (n=4), Indiana University (n=3), and the University of Illinois (n=2).

19 The public universities with one graduate each include: Alabama (Tuscaloosa) Arizona State, Aurora, Case Western, Georgia, Houston, Kansas, Kansas State, Maryland, New York, North Carolina (Chapel Hill), Ohio State , Oklahoma, Syracuse, Temple, Texas (Austin), Texas State, Toronto, Washington, Washington (George Warren Brown), Western Michigan, and Wright State.

20 We used the median rather than the mean, since there were a few outliers who had had very long careers that would otherwise skew the data.

21 In a review of state licensure laws, we found that many current laws exempt social workers who are serving as religious leaders, so long as they use a title other than licensed social worker. We found explicit exemptions in the laws of Indiana, New Jersey, Ohio, Tennessee, Texas, and Utah. A number of other state laws simply state that persons cannot represent themselves with the title "social worker" unless they are licensed. Since social workers serving as religious leaders seldom use the actual title "social worker," they normally are exempt from licensure requirements anyway. There are still states that do not provide even this basic level of title protection at the time we are writing, e.g., California. Others protect only the title "clinical social worker"; the title "social worker" is not protected and presumably can be used by anyone.

22 We did not initially ask the question about licensure, and we do not have data for seven of these social workers; the remaining 11 are not licensed.

23 We here transition from what these 51 social workers told us to our own experiences in working with congregations. We want to be clear that this is our voice, and not that of the social workers we interviewed.

24 (X =2.84).

25 In 2013, we compiled this data available from the Council on Social Work Education's listing of accredited programs (http://www.cswe.org/Accreditation/Accredited-Programs.aspx). State universities with dual MSW/MDiv degrees included Boston, Columbia, Monmouth, Rutgers, Chicago, Connecticut, Louisville, North Carolina-Chapel Hill, Pittsburg, Texas-Austin, Virginia Commonwealth, and Washington-St. Louis.

26 For example, using the listing of all accredited programs by CSWE, both private and public, we identified 16 dual degree programs with business administration and 35 dual degree programs with law.

27 Citron is the color symbolizing social work in academic regalia.

28As stated on the website of the Association of Social Work Boards, June 10, 2013: http://www.aswb.org/SWL/statutesregulations.asp

Chapter 4

29 Foot-washing has never received the status of an ordinance in the wider Christian world, however.

30 For more discussion of how to lead congregations in being inclusive of persons with different abilities and of persons of different generations and cultures, see Chapter 13 of *Family Ministry* (Garland, 2012a).

31 We use vocation here inclusively, so that it includes paid employment as well as in non-paid service engagement. James Fowler defines calling simply as "finding a purpose for one's life that is part of the purposes of God" (Fowler, 2000, p. vii).

32 Like Carl, as a denominational missionary working in an inner city, I (Gaynor) led day camps for eight weeks each summer on public school properties and in city parks. Over time, we developed relationships with children's mothers and other family members, who ultimately became a new congregation in the neighborhood.

33 For more than three decades, we have been speaking and writing on topics such as mar-

riage and divorce, parenting, interpersonal power, violence and abuse; child advocacy; and the interrelationship of Christian faith and service (D. E. Garland & D.R. Garland, 2007a, 2007b; Garland, 1983b, 1987a, 1990a, 1990b, 1994b, 1994c, 1995, 1996a, 1996b, 1999a, 1999b, 2001b, 2002c, 2003b, 2004b, 2004c, 2004d, 2005, 2010, 2012a, 2013a, 2013b; Garland, Chapman, & Hassler, 1992; Garland, Chapman, & Pounds, 1991; Garland & Edmonds, 2007; D. R. Garland & D. E. Garland, 1986, 2013; Garland & Hassler, 1987; Garland & Pancoast, 1990; Garland, Ross, Rowatt, & Chandler, 1995; Garland, Sherr, & Gardner, 2008; Garland & Singletary, 2008).

34 For a fuller development of the concept of "befriending," see Garland's *Family Ministry* (2012a).

35 This section is adapted from Justice and Garland (2010).

Chapter 5

36 Garland's *Family ministry: A comprehensive guide* (2012 edition) explores the biblical texts and historical and sociological realities of defining family.

37 The following is adapted from Garland, 2012a.

38 This fishing image is excerpted from Garland, 2012a.

39 When I (Gaynor) became a missionary serving an inner city neighborhood, I had to figure out how I could have balance in my life and not be "on" 24 hours a day, 7 days a week. Neighborhood residents accepted well my decision to live 15 minutes away; I was still available when needed, even when it meant a middle-of-the-night hospital trip. Leaders in some social agencies were critical of my decision to live outside of the neighborhood. In the end, for me, in this setting, the decision about where I live has always been based first of all, as a result of prayer and then on how to have balance in my professional and private life in this context.

Chapter 6

40 Portions of this section have been adapted from (Garland, 2012b).

41 This section is adapted from Garland, Myers, and Wolfer (2009).

42 I (Diana) am grateful to my colleagues in the Service and Faith project: Dennis Myers, Terry Wolfer, Michael Sherr, David Sherwood, Paula Sheridan, Beryl Hugen, Scott Taylor, and Kelly Atkinson. I am also grateful to Lilly Endowment, Inc., for providing funding for the Service and Faith Project.

43 For a description of this research project, see Garland, et al. (2002), Garland, Myers, & Wolfer (2005), Garland, Wolfer, & Myers (2008) and Sherr, Stamey, & Garland (2009). The research team members conducted surveys of congregational attendees, both those who were actively engaged in service and those who were not. The analysis of findings from the 35 congregations is based on the 7,403 responses to a congregational survey and 946 responses to a volunteer survey. Nearly half of the respondents (46.5%, n=3,442) reported personal involvement in community service activities. In addition to the surveys, in all four regions the research team conducted in-depth interviews lasting from one to two hours each with 29 congregational leaders, 25 individuals and an additional 16 families who were actively involved together in community service programs. Congregation leaders identified the families and individuals for interview.

44 This section is adapted from publications from the Service and Faith project described earlier in this chapter (Garland, 2010, 2013a; Garland, Wolfer, & Myers, 2008). For a full description of the project, see those publications.

45 Sixteen of the leaders we interviewed were White, 7 were African-American, and 6 were Latino. They served in the congregation an average 12.2 years with a range from 1 to 35 years. Their congregations were Evangelical Protestant (n =17; e.g., Southern Baptist, Cooperative Baptist Fellowship, Missionary Baptist, Seventh Day Adventist, Christian Reformed, Assemblies of God, "nondenominational") and Mainline Protestant (n =11; e.g., AME, United Methodist, Presbyterian USA, Episcopal). The leaders in turn identified congregants and families who had been actively involved in community ministries. Interviews lasted from one to two hours and were recorded and transcribed. The research team coded the transcripts using a grounded theory approach (Garland, O'Connor, Wolfer, & Netting, 2006).

46 This discussion of Christian service and volunteering is adapted from Garland (2012b).

47 Portions of this section have been adapted from Garland (2010).

Chapter 8

48 More than 25 years ago, I (Diana) was a consultant for the Southern Baptist Convention's Sunday School Board that included writing a series of parenting courses entitled *Parenting by Grace* and marriage education courses entitled *Covenant Marriage* (e.g., D. R. Garland et al., 1991; Garland & Hassler, 1987). The Woman's Missionary Union (WMU), an organization of women auxiliary to the Southern Baptist Convention, also invited me to write a study book used nationally by congregation-based organizations in their annual study of a particular mission concern. That year (1996), the issue was how Christians can be advocates for children living in poverty and otherwise placed at risk (Garland, 1996a). I (Gaynor) wrote materials for WMU to be used in congregations on *Pornography* (Yancey, 1986) as a part of educating congregations about this social issue, which is now seen as strongly connected with sex trafficking. WMU invited C. Anne Davis, also a social worker, to write the book for their 1997 study, focusing on community engagement (Davis, 1997). Davis was also a primary shaper of the design materials for Christian Women's Job Corps, a program of WMU designed to help women—and now men—develop the necessary skills for successful employment. Christian Women's Job Corps and Christian Men's Job Corps are now national program directed by a social worker, with more than 200 registered sites nationally ("CWJC/CMJC: Job Readiness,").

49 Note that saying that half of congregants report that their congregations have done mission trips is not the same as saying half of congregations have done so. Most Americans attend large congregations, and large congregations are more likely to have the resources for such an activity. In order to control for the large numbers of small congregations and the few numbers—but larger attendance—of large congregations, researchers may report statistics about congregations based on a sampling of Americans rather than congregations. Second, it is easier to do a survey of persons than it is of congregations, for which there is no central listing from which to draw a sample.

50 A cairn is a pile of rocks hikers used to mark the path they have taken when it crosses rocky ground and other terrain in which the path would otherwise be difficult to see.

51 A bi-vocational pastor is a pastor in a congregation that cannot afford a full-time salary, so the pastor also works a full-time job elsewhere. Bi-vocational pastors are common in small congregations and congregations in impoverished communities in which the congregation does not have adequate budget for full-time staff.

52 http://www.habitat.org/how/christian.aspx, downloaded November 3, 2013.

Index of Topics

Index of Names

Index of Social Workers Interviewed

Index of Scripture